791

12/5804

CW80919754

DOGS

HOW TO TRAIN AND SHOW THEM

DOGS

HOW TO TRAIN AND SHOW THEM

HILARY HARMAR

David & Charles
Newton Abbot   London   North Pomfret (Vt)

Photographs by Anne Cumbers

British Library Cataloguing in Publication Data
Harmar, Hilary
  Dogs.
  1. Dogs—Training
  I. Title
  636.7'083   SF431

  ISBN 0-7153-8323-X

Phototypeset by ABM Typographics Limited, Hull
and printed in Great Britain
by Butler & Tanner Ltd, Frome
for David & Charles (Publishers) Limited
Brunel House   Newton Abbot   Devon

Published in the United States of America
by David & Charles Inc
North Pomfret   Vermont 05053   USA

Contents

For
My Marvellous Family
and
Barnaby and Sam
the Models

Preface

There have been a great many books written on how to train dogs: there is of course no one method of doing this. All training books show photographs of experts training their dogs, and of dogs behaving faultlessly. It all looks too easy.

I decided to use our daughter as a novice trainer, and we used two dogs which she had hardly seen before: Barnaby the golden retriever and Sam the black labrador. My photographer Anne Cumbers came down to Lake House specially to take the photo graphs . . . on the only cloudy day we had that week!

At a dinner party my suggestion that I was going to use Barnaby as a model for the photographs was met with such comments as: 'Good heavens! He is the most disobedient dog in the county!' I am not too sure that they did not say 'country'. However, after four hours of photography, I feel the results should be most helpful for the novice—old or young—who wishes to train a dog.

Training a dog is not difficult, and it is fun to do. I cannot stress too strongly that all training must be done with kindness, patience, con sistency and understanding. *Never*, never shout at your dog. He has extremely sensitive hearing; he heard you the first time, and if you shout a command your dog will be conditioned to expecting all com mands to be shouted.

I should like to see a law passed, insisting that all dogs should have a fenced-in garden or a long narrow run where they can be kept when not in the house or with their owners. This would save many a dog from a severe beating when he returns home from roaming. He has no idea why he is being beaten and he thinks that he is being punished for coming home. Roaming is a natural instinct, and it does not occur to the dog that he is being beaten for that. Furthermore, if you beat your dog he will immediately lose his trust in you.

I met a dog trainer recently, who told me that his child had been bitten on the face by his dobermann at lunch one day. I asked him what happened to the dog. The Dobermann Club had collected the dog by teatime, which, he said, was lucky for the dog, because he would have beaten him to within an inch of his life when he returned home. But, when I remarked that the dog would not have known why he was being beaten, he replied: 'Yes, I know, but it would have made me feel a great deal better.'

Sadly, there are far too many people who own dogs and profess to love them, but who have no idea how to treat their pets and who do not understand how a dog thinks and reacts. I hope this book will help inexperienced novices, and at the same time guide them to a better understanding of their dogs.

I should like to thank Captain Nigel Bailey for the use of his stately Lake House and his lovely black labrador Sam; the renowned photographer Anne Cumbers; and also Mr John Grotrian for lending me his beautiful but wilful golden retriever Barnaby who, after ten minutes on the leash, gave me a knowing look to tell me that he remembered doing all this eight years before. He is, of course, now known as 'The Wonder-Hound'!

HILARY HARMAR

Part I

TRAINING YOUR DOG

'It is not the size of the dog in the fight that counts but the size of the fight in the dog.' (American proverb)

1

Responsibilities of Owning a Dog

When you own a dog, you are taking on a ten- to fifteen-year project—in fact, what you might almost call a part-time career, as well as a lovely hobby. There are only two animals in the whole animal kingdom who have chosen to enter man's home of their own free will, neither as slaves nor as prisoners. These are, of course, the dog and the cat. The dog is also the only animal that prefers to be with people rather than with his own kind. This explains the very close and special relationship between man and dog, which really is unique. The old adage has always been true, that a dog is man's best friend.

It is sad indeed that many people go through life without experiencing the love and companionship of a dog, but sadder still to realise that there are some people who are totally unfit to own a dog. Such people are selfish, cruel, unthinking and probably incapable of giving love to anything. Perhaps, through no fault of their own, they were brought up without security and love themselves and, never having learnt to love, they go through life without it. Sadly, these are the very people who need the love of a dog. On the other hand, there are many people who have never had the opportunity of owning and loving a dog, but who would be capable of having an excellent relationship with one. If they have never had a dog, they do not know the wonderful companionship that they are missing.

It is very important that children should be brought up with animals, particularly dogs and cats, so that they can be taught to love and care for them, to respect them and to look after them. A love of animals is an important part of every child's education. It teaches the child to form warm and affectionate relationships with people throughout their lives.

I am always unhappy to hear people say that they like only cats, or only dogs. Such people are unbalanced, because everyone should be capable of loving both dogs and cats, and indeed all pets. I also dislike hearing people say: 'I only like large dogs.' It is like saying: 'I only like tall people.' I am frequently asked which breed of dog I like best, and everytime my answer is 'Whichever dog I am with at the moment.'

Understanding Your Dog

Dogs come in every shape, size and colour. Each breed has its own particular basic breed characteristics, and within each breed every dog is endowed with his own character and personality. Just as with people, some dogs are more intelligent than others; some may be stupid, others shy; some may be highly strung, others quiet and good-natured; whilst yet others may be on the sharp side. Some dogs are very strong-charactered, others are adaptable. But on the whole, a dog becomes what his owner makes him.

Dogs have very many endearing characteristics. One of a dog's greatest pleasures is to be with the person he loves. You are his entire world and his universe. You are his god and you can do no wrong. He will do his utmost to please you and all you have to do is to teach him what you want. Your dog will give you unending love, loyalty, devotion and lifelong affection. He will be your most loyal friend and companion, and he will never doubt you or criticise you.

A dog is intensely sensitive to changes in mood in people whom he loves. He is aware of your feelings of happiness and misery, and senses when you are sad. Your dog will show you in every way he can that he really understands. He will work for you, serve you and guard you with his life. He will keep you happy, healthy and amused. He will love his walks with you, keeping you both fit and well, and he will take your mind off your troubles by his charming antics. When you are old and perhaps alone in the world, he will help to keep you sane.

In order to keep your dog happy and healthy you must ensure that he is comfortably housed, with adequate sanitation, correctly fed, and well trained. He must have sufficient outdoor exercise. He must be regularly groomed, and he will need particular attention to his ears, teeth and nails. In addition he must be kept free from both internal and external parasites, and he must be vaccinated against the common dog diseases.

Your dog needs a place of his own with his own toys, and above all you must remember that he is a creature of habit. He has an inbuilt time clock, and he knows to the nearest second when it is time to be let out, time for his walk, time for his dinner, time for play and time for bed.

In order to bring out the very best in your dog, lavish him with love and attention, and above all let him know that he is wanted and appreciated. Talk and talk to your dog. You can never talk too much to him, and he will love every word you say. Your dog's vocabulary will be extraordinarily large, so carry on a good conversation with him. Ask him questions, and use every tone of voice that you can muster. As Samuel Butler once said: 'The great pleasure of a dog is that you may make a fool of yourself with him and, not only will he not scold you, but he will make a fool of himself too!'

Moral Responsibilities

Once you have decided that you really are a suitable person to own a dog, then, and only then, should you have one. Do you fully understand the costs involved? These will include feeding your dog, veterinary expenses for inoculations and any accidents or illnesses that he may suffer during his lifetime, and his stays in kennels during your holidays. There will be extra costs if you intend to exhibit your dog or attend training classes. However, once you own a dog he must be yours for life, not something you discard when he becomes too expensive to keep or when you and your family become tired of him, perhaps in his old age.

No sensible dog owner should ever allow his dog off the lead in any area where there is traffic, or where even one car is likely to come down the road. However well trained your dog may be to heel and to come when called, if a bitch in full season suddenly appears on the other side of the road, no training in the world will overcome instinct. The sex drive is so strong that, regardless of the noise of a 20-tonne lorry, a double-decker bus, a speeding racing car, or your voice, which he is firmly attuned to obeying, nothing will stop him rushing across the road to his death. Remember too that, since the passing of the Animals Act of 1971, should your dog be the cause of a traffic accident, you will be held responsible. So, please take warning: always keep your dog on a leash where there is traffic. There are plenty of glorious places where he can have his freedom without danger.

No dog owner should ever allow his dog to be a nuisance to neighbours. Your dog must be kept within your property, which means that your garden should be fenced securely or your dog should have his own long, fenced run. There can be few things so annoying to neighbours as a dog that yaps and barks incessantly. Equally anti-social is one that is permitted to roam, going into neighbours' gardens and digging up newly planted flowers or making vast holes in their lawns.

For some reason many dogs dislike postmen, dustmen and jobbing gardeners. Although a dog meets these people time after time and knows that they return at regular specified intervals, he will still not tolerate them, regarding them as intruders on his territory. The postman in particular is seen by the dog as someone who knocks on the door but is never invited in like a visitor and, what is more, has the door shut in his face. This treatment is never given to a friend. If the postman is not a friend, the dog reasons, he must be an enemy. If he is an enemy, he must be barked at and, preferably, bitten!

Should your dog bite someone, you can quite rightly be in for serious trouble. If you cannot control your dog or train him not to go for the postman, then you must keep him shut up until temptation is out of his way. You could try inviting the postman into your house and asking him to give your dog a titbit every time he calls. If your dog is considered dangerous, then you may be ordered to have him destroyed.

Vicious behaviour is not confined to dogs. Remember that it is a serious offence to ill-treat an animal. If a person is found to have ill-treated a dog or has been convicted of cruelty, he may be prohibited from owning or keeping a dog for a certain period, depending upon the seriousness of the conviction.

Dog Fights

Dog fights tend to make people very agitated particularly the owners of the dogs, who are well aware of the terrible injuries that dogs can inflict upon each other. If two large aggressive dogs are in combat, common sense tends to be thrown to the wind. People do the most stupid things, which only aggravate the fight. They beat the dogs, twist the skin on their foreheads, squeeze their testicles or kick them, all of which make the fight worse. Each dog, with his adrenalin flowing, fights all the harder, because he feels that all the extra pain he is receiving is caused by his opponent. If the fight is very intense he does not feel any pain at all, so the cruelty is of no avail.

Some people resort to pepper, but this is rarely at hand; likewise buckets of water, which often only refresh the dogs. A strong fire hydrant may work well, but again is rarely available.

People who resort to beating dogs during a fight may very well get bitten by the dogs by mistake. Dog bites can be extremely nasty, both for humans and dogs, especially the deep puncture wounds which nearly always go septic. The dog's saliva is teeming with germs, so that the best precaution to take is to wash the wound in running water, stem the flow of blood, put some antiseptic powder or ointment on the area, cover with a dry dressing and go to a doctor; or, in the case of a bitten dog, to the veterinary surgeon. If you have not had anti-tetanus injections you will require a course, which will remain effective for five years.

What you should do when two dogs start a fight or are locked together in combat is to find something to cover their eyes. Take off your jacket, cardigan or scarf and throw it over the dog's head. No

14

dog will continue fighting if he cannot see. If the owners of the dogs have them on a leash, they must ask an onlooker to throw something over the dogs' faces; then, as soon as the dogs have relinquished their grip on each other, the owners can pull their dogs away. Keep the eyes blindfolded until tempers have simmered down and the dogs are well separated. Better still, ask an onlooker to hold the leash while *you* cover your dog's head with your coat. It will not be damaged once 'the aggressor' is blindfolded (better still, cover the heads of both dogs).

Dogs and the Law

Every dog over the age of six months must be licensed, except for guide dogs for the blind, working sheepdogs and non-working pack hounds. The licence may be obtained from the post office, and more than one dog may be on the licence, provided that you have permission to keep more than one dog.

Every dog is also required to wear a collar when not in the house. The collar must bear the dog's name and his owner's name and telephone number or address. Should the dog stray or become lost, a stranger or the police can then use his name and inform the owner of his whereabouts.

Should you lose your dog you must report the fact to your nearest police station. If you find a dog, then you must take him to the nearest police station and a full report will be made on him. The police will keep the dog overnight and then he will be sent to the nearest pound, where he will be kept for seven days before being destroyed or sent for vivisection. The police will pay the fee for the dog's keep in the pound. Many pet owners find lovely dogs in pounds.

If you own a valuable dog, like all valuable property he should be insured. If you own a large aggressive dog, you would be extremely unwise not to take out a third-party insurance. Farmers who catch a dog worrying sheep or killing livestock have every legal right to shoot your dog.

There are various restrictions concerning dogs, which owners should be aware of. For instance, dogs may not be permitted in certain kinds of property. Where properties are freehold there are no problems in keeping dogs as pets. Leasehold properties often contain clauses prohibiting pets, although permission for pets to be kept may be granted by some animal-loving landlords. Some councils ban the keeping of dogs in council properties, whilst others require written permission to be given.

If travelling with a dog, remember that dogs are only permitted on buses at the discretion of the conductor. They may always travel on the railway or the underground if they are in a container, but if the dog is on a lead, he must be carried on an escalator. He is permitted in a carriage provided that he sits on the floor and not on a seat and that the other passengers do not object. If there are objections, the dog must travel in the guard's van. Some shops permit dogs while others do not. Food shops are usually banned to dogs.

It is an offence for a dog to foul a footpath. An owner walking his dog should always carry a plastic bag and a suitable scoop to remove dog excreta, since it is exceedingly unpleasant for the general public to have to walk on soiled pavements. If your dog has to defaecate he must be made to do so off the pavement (sidewalk).

Breeding and boarding establishments are also controlled by law. The Breeding of Dogs Act of 1973 empowers local authorities to license breeding kennels, to inspect the premises and to prosecute owners for any offences. A breeder is a person who keeps more than two bitches for the purpose of breeding. The kennels must be registered and the breeding establishment approved. Boarding kennels must be registered and inspected by the local authority.

2

Choosing Your Dog

There are so many marvellous breeds of dog to choose from that you must first decide the reasons why you want a dog. Do you want a family dog, one that will be good with tiny children, or one that several teenage boys would have fun with? Do you want a sporting dog or an enchanting toy to cuddle, or do you need a guard dog or a good companion?

Where you live will have an important bearing on your choice. Some breeds are more suitable for a large house in the country with lots of space; others, regardless of their size, are quite happy to live in a small flat in a town. You should also bear in mind the purpose for which a dog has been bred, because obviously he will be happier fulfilling that role. Dogs are adaptable creatures, but they thrive on love and affection, and they are happier when performing tasks for which they have been bred. Clever, intelligent dogs must be kept occupied and, like children, the better trained they are the happier and more secure they feel.

Bearing all the previous observations in mind, you should choose a breed that particularly appeals to you. But there are certain aspects that you should consider most carefully. Firstly, can you afford to keep and exercise this appealing dog? You must make certain that the dog is not too strong physically for you to control with ease—his muscles, pound for pound, are three to four times as strong as those of an average man. Does the dog have a coat that you will find enjoyable to groom, trim or clip? Is the coat one that, although short, belongs to a breed that moults incessantly and has hairs that stick to clothing and are difficult to brush off? Some breeds, such as collies, have coats that moult so profusely that it is like a rug being left behind. It is well to consider the climate, since some breeds are excellent in cold climates while others are better suited to hot climates. Choose a dog that will go with your character, your work and your home, and also with your way of life.

By now you should have been able to eliminate the breeds which are not suitable for you. Next I suggest that you visit a large dog show. Look at the breeds you are interested in and talk to the breeders. Naturally, breeders are biased towards their own particu-

A delightful shih tzu puppy—a breed native to Tibet

lar breed or breeds. Most breeders, however, are only too happy to discuss the merits and problems of their dogs and they really are the best people to advise whether a particular breed would be suitable for your life style and your character.

Remembering that your dog will affect your life for the next ten to fifteen years, make certain that you read a few books on the breed you are favouring: you will find a vast choice of books at any large championship show, or any good bookshop. Try to study a good specimen of the breed. You would be more than wise to buy your dog from a reputable breeder. There are, of course, good pet shops, but any puppy from a pet shop will have had to suffer undue extra stress, will have had more chance of picking up some infection, and will have had a change of diet and water. If the puppy is not sold within a few days, he will probably lack the proper human contact that is so important for his socialising. Remember, a puppy reaches his full potential within 112 days, starting from the twenty-first day of his life.

When you own a dog, you will have to have a veterinary surgeon to look after him from time to time, so you might consider making contact with your nearest veterinary surgeon to ask his advice on your prospective dog.

Having selected your breed, you must now decide whether you want a dog or a bitch. Some people prefer dogs, others bitches. The choice really depends on the breed and for what purpose you want the dog. Male dogs, in general, are more aggressive than females, so they make better watch dogs and guard dogs, though this is not the case with some breeds. They are a little more difficult to house-train, and male dogs are much more inclined to roam unless they are confined. They know, from a distance of three kilometres (two miles), when a bitch is in season, and sex is their strongest instinct.

A bitch, on the other hand, is easier to house-train. She does not cock her leg nor does she need to stake her territorial boundaries. A bitch is better behaved in the house, she is gentler and will not do so much damage as a dog. Females on the whole are more sensitive to children and more loving than males, who may have other thoughts on their minds. The bitch, however, does have one drawback. She will come into season for twenty-one days every six months, and during this time she must be confined. On no account should she be taken on to the road to relieve herself during this period, or you will have every dog in the area waiting patiently outside your door. There are preparations which you can apply to the bitch to counter-act the odour which attracts the opposite sex, and 'Petnix' can be bought to prevent an indoor bitch soiling the house.

Bitches, on the whole, are easier to train, although dogs and bitches are equally intelligent. It is lovely to own a bitch, because it is such fun rearing a fine litter of puppies—although selling the puppies is always a heartbreak.

In the United States more and more dogs are being castrated to stop them roaming, and bitches are spayed to prevent them having puppies. I, personally, prefer to keep my dogs entire as nature intended them and to organise their home life so that they cannot escape.

Puppy Dominance

In order to survive, all creatures must learn their place in the 'pecking order' early in life, whether they are deer, cows, geese or lions, and dogs are no exception. Play and play-fighting are important sequences in the development of all puppies. Puppies in a litter should nearly always be allowed to work out their order of dominance between themselves. It is interesting that the dominant puppy in a mixed litter of males and females will always be the largest male. This puppy will select the teat which provides the most milk, so that he will naturally grow larger and stronger than the others. He will push other puppies off their selected teats and get even more milk for himself. In this way he will reinforce his early dominance. It is fascinating, however, that in an all-female litter the largest puppy will not necessarily be the dominant one—this will be the puppy that 'talks' the most.

When the puppies are four weeks old they will begin to play for fun, and at the same time they will learn their social roles. They will wag their tails and play follow-my-leader, and you will then notice the leader of the pack. As the puppies develop, one may have sharper teeth, another may be stronger, another placid by nature, another lazy, or one may be more aggressive, and so on. Slowly, the fun-play turns to play-fighting, and through this the litter group learn their social relationships to each other: it is most important that each puppy should know whom he dominates and to whom he is subordinate.

No puppy should be separated from his dam and the rest of the litter before the age of seven weeks. If he is removed earlier, he will not learn the essential canine socialisation, and at the same time he will not have had sufficient discipline from his dam. This in turn will probably lead to his picking fights with strange dogs when he becomes an adult.

By the time a puppy is seven weeks old, his brain and nervous system have developed to the capacity of those of an adult dog,

20

though of course he still lacks experience. At this age puppies start to 'gang up' on each other, and a lasting deleterious effect may occur in individual puppies: one may become a vicious bully, whilst another may develop into a cringing underdog. If a puppy leaves the nest at this age, he will avoid such traumatic possibilities. When puppies are left alone with each other for long periods, without sufficient human contact and love, it is as bad for them as being taken away from their dam and brothers and sisters within the litter too early.

Puppies left to themselves will, by the time they are four months old, have established a reasonably stable dominance hierarchy. Each puppy will know his place in the pack order. He will know the pack leader, and serious aggressive fights will no longer take place. In non-aggressive breeds no one gets hurt, but this unfortunately is not so in aggressive breeds. Some terriers are notoriously aggressive. Never more than two should be kept together, and each must be provided with his own sleeping box. If there is only one box, they may well fight to the death over it, but if two boxes are provided, instead of fighting they will quite happily both sleep together in the same box.

It is not always possible to find a puppy of your choice at the age of seven weeks, but there are many advantages in taking such a young puppy into your home, provided that you buy your puppy from a reputable breeder and can devote a considerable amount of time to him during the next few months. It is at seven weeks that the order of dominance is developing. If a puppy can go to his new owner at this stage of his development, he will automatically substitute this person for his dam, and so his new owner becomes very important to him. You are now all he has, and he will trust you and accept you as his new pack leader. By leaving his dam and all his litter mates at seven weeks of age, he is relieved of the more serious play-fights he would have had to endure in order to find his correct place in the pack. Now, however, the pack is simplified to only two. The puppy knows his place and you know your dominant position. He relies on you for absolutely everything—food, love, comfort, warmth, grooming, protection and fun. He must learn discipline and a new language. By taking the puppy at seven weeks of age you will be with him for his important eighth week. You will be able to introduce your puppy slowly to many varying situations before he is sixteen weeks old, ensuring that he becomes a more sociable and trainable dog.

Never take a puppy unless he has been completely weaned for at least one week. Weaning is an extremely stressful period in a puppy's life, and a stressed puppy is most vulnerable and disease-prone. At the same time, a puppy will be particularly under stress

21

when changing homes. The first two weeks are the most likely times when he could catch an infection, since this is the period when his constitution is likely to be weakened.

At eight weeks a puppy is particularly vulnerable, being intensely sensitive to disturbances of any kind at this time. There are therefore advantages, once again, in taking a puppy at seven weeks. If during the eighth week something occurs which terrifies him, you are there to comfort and reassure him immediately. If puppies are not protected at this critical period their character and temperament may be permanently affected.

The disadvantage of taking such a young puppy is that you must spend more time with him. He will not be quite so strong as an older puppy and will naturally take longer to house-train. However, you will certainly become very close to each other.

If you are acquiring an older puppy, provided that you buy from a reputable breeder and not from a pet shop, it will make very little difference whether your puppy is nine or twelve weeks old when you buy him. As long as he has had sufficient human contact and love, and been well reared and cared for, there should be no problems. Obviously, the older a puppy is when you take him from his first home, the stronger and more resilient he will be, and the easier he will be to house-train. If there are obstreperous children at home, I would advise buying a stronger, older puppy. The best time for a dog–man relationship to evolve is twelve weeks. This is really the time when your puppy's simple basic education starts. The thirteenth week is when he will try out his power of dominance, and by the sixteenth week dominance will be established.

Buying an adult dog has certain advantages and disadvantages. The advantages are that he will already have been house-trained and lead-trained, and will have survived all serious puppy problems. He will have had all his inoculations and vaccinations and will also have built up certain immunities. Provided that the adult has had a good home, been loved, well fed, handled correctly and protected all his life, he will settle into a new home within a few days. You will also be able to see whether your dog is sound, of show quality and well trained, and whether he has a good disposition. The main disadvantage of acquiring an adult dog is that you will not have had the fun of bringing him up. It is never too late to train a dog, but it might take a little longer than with a young puppy.

Preparations for Your Puppy

When you make an appointment with a breeder to look at puppies, do make sure that you keep the appointment, or telephone any change of plan. Before leaving home you should have prepared everything you will need for a puppy: a place to sleep, a playpen, toys, collar and lead, food bowls, water bowl, grooming equipment, nail clippers or file, flea powder and a flea comb, bicarbonate of soda for cleaning teeth, friar's balsam for bleeding nails, ear powder, eye drops, a dog thermometer, soft blanket, newspaper, Kaolin preparation against diarrhoea, and of course food. This should consist of Farex or Pablum, fresh or powdered milk, whatever dog meat he has been used to, so as not to change his diet, 'chews' or something similar made of hide for your puppy to chew, and a large bone for him to gnaw, especially when he is cutting his teeth.

If your puppy has not had all his inoculations against distemper and parvo virus or has not been wormed recently, you should make an appointment with your veterinary surgeon immediately. You should also arrange with the breeder for a veterinary surgeon to inspect your puppy and, should there be anything radically wrong, such as being blind in one eye, or deaf or unsound, you should be able to return the puppy within eight hours with an appropriate certificate.

When you collect your puppy, take a box or basket small enough for him to feel comfortable in, lined with strips of newspaper, a soft blanket, a warm hot-water bottle, some chews and a toy. The late owner might let you have an old cardigan or something the puppy knows and likes, just for the journey and perhaps the first night. This transition to a new home is going to be a stressful period for your puppy unless you handle everything quietly and gently. He should be allowed to sleep as much as possible and to have no excitements for the first few days, until he becomes completely settled.

When selecting your puppy, you should certainly see the dam and the sire if possible. This will give you a good indication as to the temperament and soundness of the parents. It is also good experience to see some of the other dogs in the kennels. It is important that the dam's temperament be good, because it is she who has brought up the puppies and disciplined them until now. If her temperament and soundness are above reproach, then you have a good chance of finding a nice puppy. Look for the typical traits in the breed you have chosen, and then cut down your choice to either a dog or a bitch.

At this point here is a word of warning: never touch a strange dog without asking the breeder if you may do so, and most certainly do not touch a sleeping dog, or puppies when they are with their dam. If you want to touch a strange dog or puppy, bend down, close your fingers into a clenched fist and extend the back of your hand for the dog to sniff, talking encouragingly to the dog or puppy as you do so.

Make no sudden movements. The dog will first sniff the back of your hand, and move away. Keep still, and the dog or puppy will return and sniff the back of your hand a second time. If you are accepted, you will probably receive a small lick on the back of your hand. You may now slowly open your clenched fist and pat the dog gently, scratch him behind his ears or rub his chest. You must never force yourself on a dog; allow him to decide when to accept you, especially when you are on his territory.

When you are shown the puppies, move towards them gently and slowly. They will probably come rushing out to greet you. Generally, you will find that there is one puppy in the litter that will appeal to you immediately, but take your time in selecting your puppy. Try to choose a friendly, playful, curious puppy, not necessarily the one that rushes at you wagging his tail, particularly if he belongs to a large breed and seems to be the extrovert and boss of the litter. Enchanting as this may be at this age, when he is older he could be quite difficult to handle and train: you will find that he will try and be one jump ahead of you all the time. If you choose a bossy dog, you will require great strength of character yourself and endless patience.

On the other hand, it is better not to go to the other extreme and choose a very shy retiring puppy, since dogs with this temperament seldom make good pets without a great deal of love and attention and a tremendous amount of patience and understanding. The best pets are probably the medium-sized breeds which are gentle, friendly, playful and curious, with sweet, outgoing characters and lovely temperaments

When choosing your puppy, look out for the following points. The puppy must be sound and healthy, plump but not too fat, and not thin and ribby. The eyes should be bright and clear with no scars on the cornea, the nose should be cold, clean and damp, the ears free of parasites, and there should be no odour. The skin should be pliable and clean, with no rough spots or pink patches surrounded by black. A puppy's coat should be fluffy and glossy, and it should feel slightly oily to the touch, not brittle or dry. There should be no bald patches or fleas—if the puppy has a flea infestation, there will be tiny black eggs sticking to the hairs of the coat. The sharp puppy teeth should be clean and pearly white with nice pink gums. The puppy should feel solid and compact, as should his bones. His nails should be short—a good guide to a puppy's temperament is how he behaves when his nails are cut. His stools should be of a good consistency with no signs of blood or mucus. A 'pot-belly' is a sign of worms.

If you are buying a male dog for exhibition he should be entire, which means he should have two testicles fully descended in the scrotum. However, dogs in many toy breeds do not become entire before they are eleven months old. In some breeds there are particular problems which may only show up much later: for instance, PRA (progressive retinal atrophy), hip dysplasia or slipping stifles. Certain breeds, such as dalmatians, suffer from kidney stones, and in a few breeds which are brown, white or merle (blue-grey flecked with black) dogs may be prone to deafness, eg white bull terriers. It is well worth your while to be aware of any particular breed problems in your choice of dog.

Choosing a show dog is a difficult problem even for the breed specialist. Promising young puppies often fail to come up to their early expectations, and rather ordinary puppies occasionally surpass their owner's early hopes. Obviously, the older the puppy is when you choose him, the more chance you have of selecting an outstanding dog. Smaller breeds mature more rapidly than the large breeds. You should try to choose a dog in a large breed between the ages of a year and eighteen months. However, the price of such a good potential show dog will be considerably higher than for a puppy and, moreover, you will have missed out on the lovely puppy period.

Breeders often become over-stocked, because they 'run on' too many puppies, so that you may well be able to find a breeder who will help you select a good show puppy, provided you make it clear that you are keen to exhibit. And, of course, if the puppy turns out to be a top winning dog, this reflects back on the breeder.

Try to choose an original name for your dog and one that is suitable for the breed. Always avoid any name that rhymes with a command, so that at a later period when he is being trained he will not confuse his name with a command. For example, Ray sounds too like 'Stay', Kit like 'Sit', Rum like 'Come', Fred like 'Bed', Neil like 'Heel', and so on.

To sum up, there is a tremendous variety of breeds which could be named as the most popular type of dog for living in the home as a companion. There is no one breed more intelligent than another. There are outstanding dogs in all breeds, just as there are exceedingly stupid ones. Each breed has been bred for a particular reason, so that dogs of one breed will be better at their special work than dogs which have been bred for a different purpose.

The easiest dog to have in your home is one that is small-to-medium size, and not too strong for you to manage and control. Choose a dog that is easily dominated and managed, that has plenty of character, and choose one that will show you how much he loves

25

you and how much he needs your affection too. You, as the average dog owner, need a dog that possesses a mild degree of territorial defensive behaviour, so that he will bark when necessary. At the same time, you will need one that will not be unduly aggressive to strangers and other dogs once you have let him know that you approve of their intrusion on his territory.

If you decide that you would like to go in for obedience training, then choose one of the many breeds that excel in and enjoy obedience work. Dogs kept as pets make the best obedience dogs. There are many dogs which are unsuited to obedience training and do not enjoy it, but many of these breeds enjoy other forms of training, such as trick training, and they also enjoy being generally useful to their owners, for example by carrying the shopping bag, fetching garments or slippers for their owners, collecting the newspaper, and so on.

NB My book *Showing and Judging Dogs* (1977) contains most of the breed standards, as well as photographs of each breed. If you study these you will be able to see what the desired temperament in each breed should be, the size of the dog and his type of coat.

3

Caring for Your Dog

When you first arrive home with your puppy, try to keep everything as quiet as possible. Talk to him gently and cuddle him, giving him all the confidence and reassurance that you can. Do not allow all your family to crowd round the puppy and talk to him all at the same time.

You must decide, before the puppy arrives, in which room you intend to keep him. Many people find a kitchen is a warm and suitable place, and your puppy will be happier if he is confined in a playpen lined with newspaper. Your puppy's most important and first possession of his very own is his bed. So give him a warm box or basket of a suitable size, lined with a soft blanket. The bed should be small enough for the puppy to be able to curl up and lie down in comfortably, and it should have an easy exit, so that when the puppy wants to relieve himself he can get out and do so without soiling his bed.

Depending on the age of the puppy and on the weather conditions on his arrival in his new home, you may be able to take him outside into the garden to relieve himself. Before you do so, give the puppy a drink of water so that he will soon feel the urge to urinate; then a little later take him to a suitable part of the garden and place him on the ground. Encourage him to do what is required by urging him to 'Hurry up!' When the puppy has sniffed around and finished, praise him quietly and profusely and carry him back to the house. Allow him to explore just one room for the first few days. Never permit your puppy to have the run of the house until he has been house-trained.

Do not give your puppy a large meal on your arrival home: most puppies are greedy and he might over-eat in his excitement. If he is nervous he may refuse to eat, but do not worry about this; just give him a little warm milk and glucose or honey. Always give your puppy his meals in the same bowl and put the bowl in the same place each time. Dogs are great creatures of habit, and they appreciate it and learn more rapidly if there is a time and place for everything—a specified time for play, for eating, for being groomed, for sleeping, and for relieving themselves. Once a good routine is established life becomes easy for all concerned.

During these early days special attention should be paid to the puppy's comfort. He must be kept warm and dry and free from draughts. He should have his own water bowl with fresh water changed several times a day, but he should not be permitted to drink immediately after eating. The puppy's diet should be as near as possible to what he was accustomed in his previous home. The most stressful period for the puppy is the first two weeks in his new home, and this is the most likely period during which he might become ill. All young puppies require constant supervision if they are to be prevented from getting into mischief.

The first few days of owning a new puppy are perhaps the most difficult. Not only is the owner's life disrupted and made more difficult for a short period, but the puppy's entire life has changed. He has lost the comfort and support of his dam and the fun and competition of his siblings. Everything is new, frightening and strange. Nothing smells the same—and what the puppy's nose tells him is far more important than what he sees.

The first few nights are bound to be difficult. If you intend the puppy to sleep downstairs, give him his last meal late at night and then take him out to relieve himself. It is best to take him to the same place as previously and he will quickly learn what to do. Then, when he is inside again, give him a warm hot-water bottle, a loudly ticking clock or perhaps a radio playing soft music. If your puppy is of a loud and noisy breed, you might ask your veterinary surgeon if you could give him part of a baby's aspirin, so that the entire household can have a good night, until he becomes used to his new surroundings. The other alternative is to take the puppy into your bedroom for at least the first few nights. The advantage of this is that the moment you hear him stir you can take him into the garden and so start his house-training programme. However, once you start your puppy sleeping with you the habit could be difficult to break. It is probably better to start off as you intend to continue, though it is perhaps kinder to allow a frightened and lonely little puppy to share your room until he has become accustomed to his new surroundings and recognises his bed as his refuge and something of his very own. He will not object to sleeping alone after the first two or three nights, wherever his bed is placed.

If there are children in the family you must explain carefully that the new puppy is really like a small baby. He must not be frightened by sudden noise or loud voices, and he must be touched very gently, stroking his hair down in the direction in which it grows. Before the puppy is introduced to the whole family, make everyone sit down on chairs or on the floor and tell them to close their hands and to keep very still. Bring the puppy into the room quietly, talking to him and then gently put him on the floor. Let him run around exploring anything he sees and allow *him* to make the first approach to every member of the family. He will doubtless sniff the back of each hand and then go back and give the hand a little lick of acceptance. When the puppy does this, the owner of the hand should talk to the puppy quietly and sweetly, encouraging him. He may open his hand and stroke the puppy. The puppy now, with more confidence, will greet each member of the family and will gradually become accustomed to all the strange things around him. Provided that nothing frightens him, the puppy will settle down quickly.

It is probably now time for his first meal. Follow the breeder's instructions carefully and do not give him too much to eat. Take him to the same place as before to relieve himself, bring him in without any fuss and put him into his bed. If the puppy whimpers, talk to him caressingly and put him back into his bed. By this time he will be very tired and will drop off to sleep.

Puppies that have been brought up with only women around them have difficulty in responding to men, and vice versa. Puppies that have never encountered young children may be worried by the high tones of children's voices and also by their sudden movements, so that great care must be taken during these early days to ensure that the puppy is never frightened.

It is important at this stage to understand that dogs associate ideas with certain acts. A dog does not reason as we do. A frequent mistake made by a new dog owner is to scold his dog at the wrong time, that is to say some while after the misdemeanour has been committed. If a dog has run away and been missing for several hours, it is useless for the owner, who has been understandably worried, to shout at him when he returns. The dog is delighted to see his owner again and rushes up wagging his tail, expecting to be greeted with pleasure. When, instead, he is scolded or even beaten, the dog does not understand the reason for his owner's fury, and associates the anger with his coming home, not with running away, which happened too long ago to be connected.

Unfortunate associations of events can sometimes affect a puppy for life. For instance, somebody nearby might drop a bucket with a loud clatter while a stranger is stroking your puppy. The loud noise terrifies the puppy and, thereafter, he associates strangers with the frightening sound of the crashing bucket. As a result, he might always in future appear afraid of strangers. It is therefore important that great care be taken during the early months to ensure that a puppy does not become nervous by associating unpleasant

29

happenings with certain people. He must make agreeable associations with pleasant acts.

Obviously, some dogs and some breeds are a great deal more sensitive than others, and it is your responsibility to guide your puppy and to teach him all he requires to know in this strange new world of which he is now a part. It is essential that, from as early an age as possible, your puppy should be subjected to as many situations as you can manage: strange places, sights, sounds and people; buses, trains, planes, cars; and so on. Since a dog's nose is so important to him he must learn all about strange smells that he will encounter. But these things are all well ahead. The puppy will have more basic problems to deal with in the immediate future.

Some breeds are by nature 'one-man dogs' but, even if this is one of his traits, a puppy should be able to make friends with strangers. He should be neither shy nor over-friendly. A puppy becomes spoilt if he receives too much attention and love from one person only. He may become particularly attached to this person, to the extent that if a stranger tries to touch the dog or the owner, the puppy may growl and even bite. Any puppy that growls or bites should be reprimanded promptly in no uncertain terms and put on the floor.

Unfortunately, many stupid owners are rather proud of the possessiveness of their pets, and even encourage them to growl. It is sad to encounter such dogs. They grow up introspective and shy, later becoming nervous, and ending up as 'fear-biters'. The fault in these cases is almost certainly not hereditary but caused by the behaviour of the stupid owners and the dogs' environment.

Puppies require to be groomed gently with a soft brush. With toy breeds like pomeranians, brush the puppy lying on your lap. The puppy must learn to lie on his back and on his side and to stand still on the table for his grooming, so this is a good time to start a little early training. When you want your puppy in a certain position say gently but firmly 'Sit', 'Stand', 'Stay', as appropriate. With large breeds, instead of having your puppy on your lap or on a table, place him in a corner of the room. Press his hindquarters down gently and say 'Sit', then immediately brush his neck and shoulders, which he will enjoy. Keep praising him while he is complying. Then go on to brush his chest which he will appreciate even more. If the puppy tries to get up, repeat in a friendly voice 'Sit', and finish that part of the grooming rapidly.

When you brush his back, help your puppy to stand by placing your hand under him, and sweetly say 'Stand!' Before the puppy has time to move start brushing his back, his sides, and down his hindquarters. Should he move, help him to stand again and repeat

30

the word firmly. The moment he is still, just say 'Stay!' Your puppy is going to learn these three most important words, which later become commands, at a very early age almost without knowing it. He is learning by the two tones of your voice, and most of all by the lavish praise which you give him when he is doing what you want, and by the constant repetition. In this way a habit is formed. If he fails to do what you want you must correct him by changing your tone, but without raising your voice. Later, you must speak to him more firmly, implying your authority. You must be swift in showing the puppy the meaning of your words. Remember all the time that he is very young, and that you can only teach him by kindness, firmness and praise to respond to you. Your puppy wants to please you, and by so doing he is satisfying himself.

If there are other animals in your home, or children, you must make certain that no jealousy arises on the arrival of a new puppy. It is most upsetting for an old dog to have his nose put out of joint by a lively young puppy. An old dog may well feel resentful of a puppy having four meals a day to his one. You could perhaps give the old fellow a titbit each time the puppy is fed, or, better still, feed the puppy out of sight of the older dog.

All animals will get on together if given the chance, especially cats and dogs. They should be allowed to accept each other gradually, with no undue fuss being made of one rather than another. Do not allow a young puppy to tease an old dog or to usurp his place or bed. Dogs do not normally ever hurt young puppies seriously, but they may well put the puppy in his place from time to time. Once the puppy understands who is dominant, then that will be the end of the situation.

Feeding

Whatever their age, dogs should be fed separately and each should have his own feeding bowl. Dogs like their meals served punctually and in the same place, and they should be left alone to eat in peace and quiet and at their own pace. If one dog will not eat, try putting another dog at his bowl for competition. Never permit children to go near a dog whilst he is eating or gnawing a bone. It is a dog's natural instinct to guard his food, so that it is most unfair to thwart or tease him at mealtimes. A well-trained dog will always permit his owner to take away a bone, but in this case there is mutual trust and training between dog and owner.

One of the first lessons a puppy can learn at feeding time is his name and to come when called. Each time you take your puppy his food call him by name.

31

One cannot stress too strongly the importance of correct feeding throughout a dog's life. Quality and correct quantity are the best maxims, particularly during a puppy's first five months. This is the period of his most rapid growth, and so he will require a high-protein diet. All puppies require plenty of milk until they are seven months old, and some like milk even when they are nearly a year old. Fresh milk is probably best, though some puppies tolerate powdered milk better, although the shelf-life of the latter is not particularly long.

There are no hard and fast rules about dog feeding. A well fed dog will look healthy, his coat will shine, his eyes will be bright, his teeth clean, his stools of a good consistency and colour, he will have plenty of energy, be alert, and will show in every way that he is a happy, contented and well adjusted dog. Some breeds require more food per kilo of body weight than others: small breeds require more than large breeds. A great deal depends on whether the dog is a working dog, a hunting hound, a gundog or a lap dog. Climate also makes a considerable difference to how much dogs should be fed. Dogs working in arctic conditions require more food than those in the tropics. Old dogs need less than growing puppies. Therefore, it is not possible to say how much food an adult dog should be given, but a rough guide is 30 grams of food per kilo (1oz per 2·2lb) of body weight. The breeder from whom you bought your dog will be able to tell you exactly how much your dog should have from the time you bought him until he is adult.

Over the years, an enormous amount of research has been carried out by the major dog food companies into what constitutes the most nutritious form of feeding, including the correct proportions of vitamins and trace elements. If you feed your dog on commercial foods, either tinned or dried, you will know that your dog is receiving a correctly balanced diet, provided that the ingredients are stated. Beware of food, however, which is no more than finely ground up bones with flavouring matter, which has recently appeared on the market. Always read the labels, and ascertain the protein content of commercial dog foods. Puppies, bitches with puppies, and certain sick dogs require more than 20 per cent protein. The average house dog will do well on 14 per cent protein. Some of the dehydrated foods may be lacking in fat content, so if your dog's coat looks a little dry, add some fat to his diet. A novice dog owner will probably make fewer mistakes if he feeds his dog on commercial dog foods rather than on meat and biscuits, plus the necessary additives. Dogs love treats, so give your pet the occasional cheese, bacon rind and chocolate, and also hard-baked liver. Keep your dog's figure in good shape. If he starts to get too fat, cut down his food intake. If he seems a little on the thin side feed him up. Dogs, like people, become bored with a monotonous diet. Your dog will enjoy his meals more if they are varied with three kinds of tinned food and two kinds of dehydrated food. It takes on average eighteen hours for food to pass through the digestive system of an adult dog, and so feeding once a day is adequate for most dogs.

Most seven-week-old puppies require six meals a day, the midday meal consisting of ground meat or canned meat. Some large breeds may need to start eating meat at three weeks of age. A twelve-week puppy requires five meals a day, two of meat and three of milk and cereal. A sixteen-week puppy requires four meals a day, two of meat and two of milk and cereal, until he is six months old. From six months until one year, a puppy will require two meals a day, the meat being given in the evening. From one year until old age, many dogs are content with one meal a day. However, some old dogs prefer two or even three small meals a day. Small, active dogs, like chihuahuas, do better on dehydrated food in the morning and meat at night. No young puppy can survive without food or water for more than eight hours, so pay particular attention to feeding times.

Clean water is essential. It should be replenished several times a day. Do not allow your puppy to drink water immediately after he has eaten, nor should he be permitted to play strenuously after eating or drinking. In some breeds this may cause bloat, and can even result in death. The water bowl of a dog kept out of doors should be emptied at night to prevent rodents drinking from it. An infected rat can pass on leptospirosis to dogs. Many people prefer earthenware water bowls, since they are easy to clean. This is particularly important if you have a dog that slobbers and leaves his saliva round the bowl.

Exercise and Play
All dogs require some exercise, how much they need depending on the breed and the age of the dog. Do not exercise dogs immediately after a meal. Many dogs get enough exercise in their run, and small dogs get sufficient exercise running around a house. Most dogs love to go for walks, especially where there are interesting scents, and they enjoy being let off their leads to roam around, with their owner in view. A good way to exercise a dog, once he has been taught to retrieve, is to throw a ball. Puppies must never be overtired by being expected to walk too far for their age. All dogs that are happily adjusted prefer to be with their owners rather than to wander off by themselves. After exercise, especially in snow or rain, a dog must be dried thoroughly, especially his tummy and feet. An old towel or

newspaper can be most effective for getting off the worst of the mud.

After his bed, the next most important possessions of your puppy are his toys. He learns to love them and to play with them, and he will like to take them to bed with him. If a puppy is given toys, they will keep him happy and amused, and they will also stop him destroying valuable objects that take his fancy. A puppy sees no difference between your best Gucci shoes and your old gardening pair. Your puppy must learn which are his own things and which are taboo. Your puppy's nose is very sensitive, and he must quickly learn that the items that are taboo smell strongly of you or of one of the family. His toys, however, have their own particular scent and, since they belong to the puppy, he may do what he likes with them.

It is important that you choose the toys carefully, and perhaps give the puppy a different one each day of the week. He will certainly have preferences: if he seems not to care for one in particular, let him have another one, but do not give him all his toys at once. Buy your puppy toys made of hard rubber, which he will find difficult to destroy. Soft rubber toys are extremely dangerous, especially if pieces of rubber are swallowed. When toys start to deteriorate, they must immediately be thrown away. All puppies adore toys that rattle, squeak or make some other interesting noise. A hard rubber ball with a bell inside provides endless pleasure, but great care must be taken that the apparatus cannot be broken by sharp puppy teeth.

Most dog owners know what fun a puppy can have with a simple toy. Puppies love an old towel knotted in the centre and at the four corners, or a pair of panty-hose knotted tightly, or a pair of thick bed-socks tied together. However, these last toys must not carry the scent of one of the family. Great fun and games can be had with such improvised toys, especially if one of the family plays with the toy too. There are also very good imitation bones of raw hide made for dogs. They come in all sizes from 7cm (3in) long to huge ones of 45cm (18in). Dogs adore them, and they have endless fun gnawing at them. One of the most satisfying pleasures for a puppy is the gift of a sawn-off, raw shin or knuckle bone of beef. He will enjoy tearing off the meat and licking out the delicious bone marrow. The bone will last for ages and will not go bad. These bones are particularly good for puppies when they are teething. Never give your dog rabbit or chicken bones, because they splinter. Uncooked bones are safer than cooked bones.

Grooming

All dogs require grooming every day regardless of their coat. Some long-coated breeds require several grooming sessions a day, for example a maltese terrier. Other breeds may require twenty minutes a day spent on grooming or clipping. Small, short-coated dogs, like the smoothcoat chihuahua, will only require a few minutes spent on their coats. Whichever breed you have, make the grooming session a routine, keeping to the same time each day and grooming your dog in the same order. Keep a grooming box with all the necessary grooming paraphernalia: brushes, combs, flea comb, flea powder, scissors, nail file and clippers, cotton wool buds, baking soda for teeth, ear powder, tooth scraper for tartar, and powdered permanganate of potash for nails accidently made to bleed when being clipped. If you make a routine of grooming it becomes a good habit and is never considered a chore. It should be at a time of day that both you and your dog enjoy together. Each day your dog will shed some hair and skin scales. If these are not removed daily, your dog will scratch himself in order to get rid of detritus, and it is better for you to do this.

Dogs do not really need to be bathed frequently, and most of them do not enjoy it. However, some breeds must be bathed before being exhibited in order to bring out the quality of their coats. The majority only require a dip against fleas, lice and ticks. When bathing your dog, smear a little vaseline round the eye-rims to prevent soap getting into the eyes, and plug the ears with cotton wool to prevent water entering the ear canal. Great care must be taken to rinse all the soap out of the coat, either with a shower nozzle or, for large breeds bathed outside, with a garden hose. Large breeds can be taught to step into a bath, and this is an easy way to bath them. It is essential to dry the dog well, and to prevent him from getting into draughts or catching a chill. Rub the coat down with a towel and later brush and comb it.

Areas Requiring Special Attention
Many breeds suffer from ear problems, particularly the drop-eared breeds. Ears must be kept clean and should be examined once a week, perhaps as a routine on a particular day. Cotton wool moistened in alcohol or diluted peroxide cleans ears easily. However, if your dog's ears smell, he may have canker. This is caused by ear mites or bacteria. If the ears look swollen or inflamed, take your dog to the veterinary clinic as quickly as possible. If your dog persistently rubs or shakes his head or scratches his ear, he has an infection. Ear problems are easy to cure in the early stages, but can become chronic if left without treatment.

Some dogs suffer from watery eyes, which should be bathed in weak saline solution. Eye ulcers are much more serious and require

35

immediate attention from the veterinary surgeon. A septic eye is exceedingly painful, and ulcers leave ugly scars. I always keep special antibiotic ointment for dogs with large or protruding eyes. Ointment put in the eye every hour at the first signs of blueness will probably clear up the beginnings of an ulcer within a day. Eye ulcers are generally caused by injuries going septic.

Puppies should have their nails clipped every week, just the tip being taken off each time. The quick in the nail is then kept short, and the puppy becomes used to the routine, provided that he is never hurt by having the quick cut. Should a nail bleed, put a little potassium permanganate, which has been well pulverised, on the tip of the bleeding nail to stop the haemorrhage.

It is easier to file the nails of large breeds, particularly if you train them to lie on their side in a comfortable place. You can have a little gossip with your dog whilst you file away, and some dogs are so unperturbed by the procedure that they almost go off to sleep in the process.

Anal glands are two sac-like glands on either side of the anus, which discharge their contents into the rectum. Dogs can release the fluid at will to demarcate their territorial boundaries. Occasionally, the sacs become blocked, and the secretions require to be expressed very gently. If your dog has this problem, your veterinary surgeon will show you how to express the sacs. The odour is most unpleasant, but, if the glands are not attended to, a septic abscess can form.

Puppies do not require their teeth to be cleaned before they are nine months old. After this age, the teeth should be rubbed over with a cotton cloth dipped in baking soda. Sometimes, when the teeth are neglected, tartar forms at the base. It is better, if the tartar is thick, to ask your veterinary surgeon to remove it. The dog may have to have an anaesthetic or just a sedative. However, it is not difficult to remove tartar yourself. You should give your dog a mild sedative, then gently hook the scaler just above the tartar rim on each tooth, give a sharp pull and the tartar should come away. If the tartar is light, it may be just scraped away.

Some breeds have a thick undercoat, which must be combed out when the dog is moulting. If the undercoat is left, it forms into mats of wool and may harbour parasites. Balls of wool may form between the pads and toes, and burrs and briars may become entangled in the matting. There are special shampoos which help in the unmatting of the coat, but when mats become bad they are better cut out. If you intend to ease out a mat in the coat, always start at the ends of the hair and gradually work in towards the skin. It is more comfortable for dogs to have the long hair removed from their toes and pads every few weeks, rather than to wait for the removal of large balls of hair.

Some long-coated breeds need to be given a spoonful of olive oil once a month, particularly dogs that lick and groom their coats a great deal. The hairs are swallowed and form balls in the stomach or intestines and may cause constipation. A spoonful of oil will help the dog to pass the unhealthy ball of wool.

Some dogs kept indoors under electric lights will shed their coat all the year round. If you wish to prevent this, put your dog to bed in a darkened room as soon as it becomes dark each evening. Nature will then take its course, and your dog will shed his coat twice a year, in the autumn and in the spring.

A dog's bed must be kept clean, and any blankets must be washed regularly in disinfectant. His kennel should also be sprayed with a pesticide, and faeces removed by using a special scoop or by putting a plastic bag over your hand. The stools should be buried or put down the lavatory, and the bag put in the waste bin.

It is quite normal for your dog to eat long blades of grass, in order to make himself sick, if he has a slight digestive upset. Milk of magnesia will quickly settle his stomach, but should he continue to eat grass he may have worms, so take him to the veterinary clinic for a worm test.

Parasites
Practically all puppies suffer from worm infestations and in some countries these parasites are worse than in others. The four most common worms found in dogs are roundworms, tapeworms, hookworms and whipworms.

The breeder should have wormed the puppy at the age of three weeks, and again at five weeks, for roundworms. Roundworms can cause a pot-belly, diarrhoea, anaemia and a dull coat. If the infestation is serious, the worms may reach the air sacs of the lungs, causing pneumonia and death. Roundworms may be vomited or passed in the stools. The eggs are laid in the stomach and the intestines, and some worms grow to the horrifying length of over 12cm (5in).

Tapeworms are not as dangerous for the dog as some of the other worms, but they may grow from a few centimetres to over a metre. They are, in fact, many worms joined together. The worms grow by new segments being added to the end. These segments contain the tapeworm eggs, and they will be seen in faeces passed by the dog— they look like grains of rice. When dry, the segments are eaten by fleas and also by lice. The fleas hop on to the dog, the dog may then catch a flea with his teeth and swallow it, and the tapeworm cycle starts once again. Dogs with tapeworm infestations have voracious appetites, but never gain weight. Some unfortunate dogs end up with chronic colitis. The danger of tapeworms is less for the dog than for a few unlucky people. In the wrong host, the tapeworm turns into a hydatid cyst. Should this occur in the brain, liver or eye it is very serious.

In New Zealand efforts are being made to eradicate the problem by a law, according to which all dogs must be dosed against tapeworm every six weeks. The dogs that are still causing problems are the sheepdogs on large farms, which are often away for several weeks at a time rounding up huge flocks. They are fed on raw sheep which may itself be infested with tapeworm, and so the danger to people is from the farm dogs and not the pet dogs. The fear of hydatids is so strong among New Zealanders and certain other sheep-rearing people that there is much cruelty to their dogs, and the majority of the three million population of New Zealand are dog haters or dog fearers. This is sad, because working dogs are of enormous importance to the New Zealand economy, but no doubt this prejudice will gradually disappear.

Any drug that is strong enough to dislodge and kill worms automatically does damage to the dog—in some cases it may even kill a dog or puppy. Dogs should not be wormed unless there really are worms present. If there is evidence of worms, then before worming ensure that the dog has not got a temperature, is not constipated and is not off colour or off his food. Feed the dog on a rice diet for a few days prior to worming him, giving him two meals a day instead of one. If the dog was given his last meal at 8pm, then worm him at 8am the following morning on an empty stomach. The dog's intestines will be sore and, where tapeworm heads have been buried in the intestines, the situation will be worse. Therefore, a wise precaution is to feed your dog for a few more days on soupy rice and a bland diet, adding some multi-vitamin drops and arrowroot.

If you are wise, you will take your puppy to the veterinary surgeon rather than dose him yourself: firstly, to make certain that he actually has a worm infestation; secondly, to ascertain which type of worm he has; and thirdly, to ensure that he is given the correct dosage by your knowing his actual weight. It is quite unbelievable how many puppies are killed, even by experienced breeders, by overdosing with worm drugs. Many veterinary surgeons do not have weighing machines. Therefore, if your dog is to be wormed or if he requires an anaesthetic, I strongly advise weighing him at home, especially if he belongs to a toy breed, and giving your veterinary surgeon his exact weight. A flotation test is a simple method for examining a dog's

38

stools for worm eggs, which, if present, may then be examined under a microscope. Detection of heartworms requires a blood test.

It is most important that your dog should be kept free from external parasites if he is to be kept healthy and in good condition. Fleas are the most common parasites and cause the most serious skin problems in dogs. They are also part of the life cycle of the tapeworm. In order to keep your dog free of fleas he should be groomed every day, and fleas and flea eggs should be removed with a flea comb. When the fleas become entangled in the hair pulled out by the comb, remove the hairs with the comb inside a plastic bag containing a little flea powder, and drop them to the bottom. The fleas will die and the bag can be discarded later. Place a little flea powder at the top of the dog's neck and also a little above his tail. The fleas will run through his coat and in due course will come in contact with the powder which will kill them. If you catch an individual flea, crush it between your two thumb nails until you hear it pop.

Flea infestations are more difficult to control in some parts of the world than in others. In some countries, I would give my dogs a flea wash with a special iodine solution to sooth the skin about every six weeks. A little flea powder in the daily grooming is always a great help. I have used flea collars and they certainly help most dogs, but unfortunately some dogs are allergic to the collars. Flea powder has the advantage that when it drops off the dog in his basket or on to the carpet it still continues to act as a flea deterrent, against the eggs, the larvae and the adult flea. Other methods of flea control include aerosol sprays, which most dogs dislike because of the noise and the cold. There are also anti-flea pills, which create a high level of insecticide in the dog's blood stream, thus killing the flea at its first bite. I, personally, do not care for this method of eradication because I feel that so much poison going round the dog's body cannot be good for him. It might, however, be suitable over a short period for a dog of a large long-coated breed with a really bad infestation of fleas.

To keep a house free from fleas, periodic powdering or spraying of crevices, cracks in the floorboards, bedding, chairs, carpets, airducts and so on should be carried out. This should be followed about half an hour later with thorough vacuum cleaning. It is a constant battle, as one female flea may lay as many as 500 eggs in the course of her life. Whatever flea poison you do decide to use, always read the instructions carefully, and take extra care when using any such poison on puppies.

Ticks are blood-sucking parasites, and an infestation can cause paralysis and anaemia. They are most debilitating. A tick may lay between 4,000 and 5,000 eggs, which is a horrifying thought. Remove individual ticks with eyebrow tweezers or forceps, getting at the head buried just below the skin. A spray will also make the tick drop off, as will the end of a burning cigarette, but the latter method is not recommended because the dog might get burnt. If a tick is pulled off by hand and the head left buried in the skin the area will go septic, so squeeze the skin to get the head out. If this method fails, use a sharp sterilised knife or razor blade to make a tiny slit in the skin so that you can remove the head with tweezers. When a tick head is removed, the skin should have a little antiseptic dabbed on the sore place.

There are two kinds of dog lice, those that suck and those that bite. The life cycle of both is short, only eight days. There are special insecticides against lice, which require weekly applications for a number of weeks.

In these modern days it is relatively simple to keep your dog practically free from all forms of parasites by vigilance, good grooming, correct feeding and the proper use of insecticides on bedding, blankets, kennels and dog runs.

NB In my book *Dogs and How to Groom Them,* there is an excellent recipe against ear complaints — it prevents most problems if used weekly.

4

House-training

House-training should be a matter of anticipation, vigilance, teaching and praise. It is never too early to start house-training your puppy, and it is also never too late. The only difference is in the time it will take you. It is not difficult to train a puppy to be clean in the house. The younger the puppy the longer it will take, because a tiny puppy does not have complete muscle control over his bowels and bladder. He will not have full control until he is twelve weeks old, and even then only for a limited period. A puppy may have an 'accident' if he becomes over-excited at seeing a member of the family returning home, or at the arrival of a new visitor, or perhaps after playing an exciting game. Complete house-training takes time, patience and perseverance. It is certainly a full-time job, and any puppy-training should be done by one person and one person only.

It is essential that a puppy should never be punished whilst he is being house-trained, and certainly never frightened or scolded for having an 'accident'. If you do forget yourself and admonish your puppy for what you believe is a misdemeanour, your puppy cannot possibly understand you. He naturally thinks that, for some terrible reason, you are cross with him for urinating, not that you are displeased with the place he has chosen.

Your puppy learns entirely by constant repetition which eventually forms a habit. Since he learns to urinate from odour associations, it is important that he should learn to relieve himself in a place of your choosing. Your puppy will learn more quickly if his outings are regular—all dogs know not only the time of day, but they also learn the days of the week and what events should take place on particular days.

When house-training your puppy you must learn to anticipate his needs, and these will vary according to his age. An eight- to nine-week-old puppy wants to relieve himself in the same place each time. You must take advantage of this natural behaviour by taking the puppy to the place of your choice. A puppy up to the age of twelve weeks will probably require to be taken out every two hours. No two puppies are identical in their requirements, and so you must watch your puppy's habits.

Your puppy should be picked up and taken out first thing in the morning (preferably just before he wakes up), after each meal, each time he wakes up, after playing, and last thing at night. It is better not to allow your puppy any drinking water after 5pm.

The length of time it takes to house-train a puppy depends on his age and on yourself. A puppy can be trained in any amount of time, varying between two days and three weeks. However, if an owner is not absolutely consistent and diligent in teaching his dog, it may take up to four to six weeks. No dog should take longer than this. There are a few breeds which are more difficult to house-train than others, dachshunds being one of them. If you choose a dachshund, which is a most delightful breed, make certain that he never has an opportunity to have an accident and you will have no problems.

The house-training time will be much faster if you can spend two weeks in concentrated effort to prevent your puppy from making any mistakes. Every accident he has is a retrograde step which will prolong the process of training. It is well worthwhile, therefore, to make the extra effort to avoid any mistakes. If a dog is not house-trained, it is inevitably the owner's fault and not the dog's.

Bitches are always easier to house-train than dogs. Both sexes will squat as puppies. A dog learns to lift his leg when he is about six months old, and this act is under the control of hormones. Some bitches too occasionally lift their legs when urinating. Mature male dogs urinate in special places, 'marking' their territory. When out of doors, dogs urinate at different places, leaving their 'calling cards'. By doing this they are leaving interesting information for other dogs, who then know of their presence, or how long ago they were in the area. Each new dog that passes the place also leaves his calling card. In no time, all the dogs in the neighbourhood know who is about and perhaps why. An older dog may have sensed a bitch coming into season. Soon there may be a pack of dogs in pursuit of this bitch who has left her calling cards in the area. After leaving his card on a bush or post, a dog will often scrape up the earth nearby with his hindlegs and then with his forelegs. This the dog does as an additional visual signal to other dogs who may pass by, so that they too may be aware of who has been there before them. Bitches coming into heat will urinate frequently and scratch the grass and rip up the earth just like dogs. They are informing the dog world nearby how interesting they are going to be in the not too distant future. So, if you wish to avoid a pack of dogs outside your home, never allow your bitch, when coming into season, to urinate in the road or in your front garden.

Some puppies can remain clean if their last meal is given at 8pm, whilst other puppies require their last meal between 11pm and mid-

42

night. It is really a matter of observation and experiment. Few puppies can manage to last from 10pm until 6am the following morning without relieving themselves before they are fourteen weeks old, especially if the weather is cold. So you must not expect too much too quickly. Keep your puppy in an area where it is not too disastrous if he does have the occasional 'accident'. Never let him see that you are upset. Just clean up the results of any mishaps rapidly—it is important that there should be no odour left, because if there is the puppy will undoubtedly use the same spot again.

If you do find a large wet patch on your good carpet the best thing for you to do is to mop up all the surplus moisture with an old towel, then put the towel into a bucket containing a little ammonia or nappy rinse. Rub the area with some soapy water to which you have added a little vinegar or lemon juice. Keep blotting up the extra moisture you are putting on the area. Pour some club soda over the stained area, place a dry towel which has been folded into a convenient shape on the wet place, and then stack some heavy books on top, or an iron. The weight will help to soak up the surplus moisture. Keep putting a dry towel down as soon as the old towel becomes moist. Finally, place an electric stove near the damp patch. The soda water prevents the carpet from becoming stained, provided that the urine is fresh and has not dried into the carpet.

Try to be one jump ahead of your puppy all the time he is awake. Watch him and look for any signs that indicate that he wants to relieve himself. He may whimper, start sniffing the ground, turn in circles, look agitated, run up and down by the door, or perhaps give you an expectant look. There is not a moment to be lost. Take the puppy out immediately to the place where he has been taught previously to relieve himself. Urge him as you always do to 'Hurry up!' Remember that puppies often need to urinate twice after a meal. The moment he has finished, praise your puppy gently and, if you feel you would like to hasten the training time, give him a titbit. He quickly realises that the sooner he is finished the sooner he will be rewarded. Praise was the first reward; the titbit is the reinforcement.

Gradually, as the puppy learns the meaning of 'Hurry up', the titbits may be eliminated and perhaps given only when you are in a hurry and first thing in the morning and last thing at night. He will soon accept your praise as sufficient reward. When your dog is fully grown he may only evacuate his bowels once a day or, if he is fed twice a day, he will do so twice. In order to hurry the process some people like to give their dog a small suppository. I personally do not like this idea.

It is perhaps worth bearing in mind that a young puppy remembers for only thirty seconds. When you want your puppy to relieve himself, you should always take him outside and wait there with him. Never just put your puppy outside and close the door on him. He may simply huddle by the door or may wander off, and the chances are he will have forgotten why he was put out. You, of course, when you let the puppy in, will have no idea whether he has performed or not. Rain, snow or a howling gale are no excuse for not going out with your dog. The dog's guard hairs will keep him dry, but when you go in again make certain that his tummy and feet are dried.

It is relatively simple to teach your puppy to be clean during the day when he is under direct supervision. It takes longer, however, for him to manage to last through the night, but it will help if the puppy is kept warm. Young puppies should, therefore, be paper-trained as well as being trained to go outside. For paper-training you need an indoor playpen—as important for a puppy as an outdoor run—unless you have a small room in the house, such as a lavatory, which you can make over to the puppy. The floor of either should be covered in tiles or vinyl with layers of newspaper laid flat on the floor. The pen should be divided into a larger and a smaller section, with the puppy's bed, which should be as small and as comfortable as possible, in the smaller section. The larger section, which is covered in newspaper, is the puppy's relieving area whilst he is tiny.

When you first put your puppy in his indoor pen he will explore everything—his bed, his toys, his water bowl—but this is not going to take very long. The puppy would much prefer to be out and about, being the centre of attraction. Harden your heart to his crying, barking, yapping and, finally, whimpering—he cannot go on for ever. Take no notice of him and continue with your occupation; stuff your ears with cotton wool if you cannot stand the noise. The puppy is bound to get tired of pestering and will probably soon curl up in his bed and fall asleep amongst his new toys. Do not give in to your puppy's heart-rending cries every time he is placed in his pen. Persevere and he will accept his new pen in two or three days without any more fuss.

Keep a very keen eye for any signs of waking up. The moment you hear him move—he will stretch himself and then probably give a big yawn—this is the time to pick him up immediately and to take him outside to his special run or the part of the garden where you wish him to relieve himself. Wait with the puppy, tell him to 'Hurry up' and, when he has finished, take him indoors. If it is playtime have a little game, then you might be wise to take him out again before putting him into his pen. He will be tired and will accept his pen more readily.

Your seven-week-old puppy will need to be taken out every two hours, but as he grows older the time can be lengthened. A sixteen-week-old puppy will probably have three bowel movements a day. Gradually, as he becomes older, the outings need be less frequent, until he only requires to be let out five times a day. By the time your puppy is seven or eight months old, you may find that you have trained him up to the stage of having to be let out only four times a day, with only two bowel movements, provided that the times you take him out are kept at regular intervals.

After you have had your puppy a few days, and he has learnt to use his newspaper at night, you will probably find that he has used the paper farthest from his bed. Gradually leave less and less newspaper on the floor until only one sheet is left in the furthest corner from his bed. Your puppy will only soil this one sheet of paper. You can encourage your puppy to use the same spot in his playpen each time by leaving a small sheet of soiled paper in one corner.

Your puppy is now trained to go out of doors during the daytime and he will use the one sheet of paper in his room or pen during the night. By the time he is four months old you should try taking away the last sheet of paper. The following morning you must make certain that you get up before your puppy's normal waking time so that you can take him outside before he has an accident. Now that your puppy is older he has control of his bladder and bowel movements, and he will very soon learn to wait for you to take him out.

Sometimes a puppy trained entirely on newspaper will not relieve himself outside. In such cases just take a sheet of soiled paper out with you and place it on the ground. As soon as the puppy starts to use it, very quietly remove the paper from under him, allowing him to urinate on the soil. Next time you take your puppy out, take him to the same spot; he will smell the urine in the ground. This never fails to make him use the same place another time.

We once had a beautiful longcoat chihuahua whom we sent to Canada and the USA to do the show circuit so that he would become the first British-bred chihuahua to be made up to champion in the New World. He had, of course, been paper-trained. When he returned to England he had to go through quarantine and spend six months in kennels. Luckily for us and for our little dog the kennels were only 5km (3 miles) away, so that we could visit him daily. I was amused to see this tiny fellow in a large concrete indoor kennel, with his little travelling box in one corner and in the opposite corner a tiny folded newspaper no larger than 30 by 15cm (12 by 6in) for his convenience. International Champion Aztec Star Golden Glory never once missed the paper or soiled the floor of his kennel.

45

An excellent method of training an older puppy, that is a puppy of at least four months old who is already lead-trained, to go through the night is to place his basket or bed by yours and to attach his lead to your bed. When the puppy becomes uncomfortable he will probably whine and become restless. He may jump up against the bed, but in any case he will disturb you. There is no time to be lost. Slip your shoes on—they should be at the ready—and, according to the age and size of the puppy, either carry or lead him outside without delay. Take him, as always, to the same spot and tell him to 'Hurry up', then praise him and lead him back to bed. The puppy will be just as anxious to return to his nice warm bed as you are.

Do not let the puppy sleep in or on your bed unless you intend to allow him to do so for the rest of his life. If your puppy is a great dane you may regret your early soft-heartedness, especially if you have a single bed. If his lead is tied to your bed your puppy will gradually learn to last through the night without having to relieve himself. Eventually you will find that he will not disturb you until you wake up at your normal time. Do not tempt providence: get up immediately and take your puppy out. This night training is a rapid method of general house-training and may be accomplished in as little as three nights. You should, however, allow the puppy to continue sleeping in your bedroom for at least two weeks, if not for ever. But you must remember that any accident is a retrograde step, so that it is up to you to spend sufficient time teaching your puppy and observing him in order to make certain that no accidents occur. It is wearying work, concentrating on your puppy for the requisite two or three weeks, but it is infinitely less frustrating than allowing frequent accidents to occur over a period of several months.

The Outdoor Run
Before you acquire your puppy, make sure that your garden, or at least the front or rear part of it, is completely fenced in so that your puppy is secure from roaming. If your garden is too large to enclose, then you should build a special run for your dog. This should include some form of warm kennel which should be just off the ground, in the shade and out of the wind. This becomes your dog's outdoor quarters and he should have his toys there to keep him occupied. Dog runs are far better if they are long and narrow. It is much more fun for a puppy to be able to rush up and down the long sides of his territorial fence than to have a square enclosure with hardly any run at all.

Of course, you should have your dog in the house most of the time, and all the time when you are at home. However, there are many times when you cannot take your dog out with you, and then it is useful to put your puppy in his run and to know that he will be perfectly safe while you are away. It is also a great comfort to know that, while you are out, the puppy will not be doing any damage in the house, to your precious furniture and good shoes, and at the same time to know that he will not be digging holes in your lawn in which to bury his favourite bone.

When the puppy is older, and a great deal larger and stronger, it will be a relief to know that he cannot roam on to your neighbour's farm, killing his chickens or sheep or chasing his cattle. Dogs on their own and without supervision are bound to roam and gang up with other dogs and go off hunting. Large, uncontrolled dogs can be most frightening for young children and elderly people who may be unsteady on their legs. Undisciplined dogs are liable to bite strangers and children and enter into dog fights. A roaming dog is also a hazard on the roads. No dog can learn on his own to be aware of the dangers of traffic and may be hit or nearly hit by a vehicle. He may be maimed or even killed, and in the process is liable to cause a serious road accident.

You should take your puppy for the occasional country walk, so that he can smell all the fascinating scents of the countryside, most of which we are totally unaware of ourselves—hedgehogs, mice, frogs, moles, pheasants and rabbits. Once you know that your puppy will respond to your call or whistle, let him off the lead for a splendid run.

Dogs in Flats
Dogs that live in flats have to be kerb-trained or entirely paper-trained. Obviously, it is better for tiny toy breeds to be paper-trained in the flat and only taught to use the kerb when they are out. It can be quite trying, rushing a tiny puppy up and down in a lift to the nearest kerb every time he wants to relieve himself, especially if you have to wait for a lift. It is easier to train large breeds to use paper indoors at night and the kerb during the day and, whilst they are small, paper in the flat during the whole or part of the day. Once the puppy of a large breed is four months old he can be entirely kerb-trained during the day and, provided that he is taken out at midnight and 6am, he will probably not have to use his paper again.

If your dog is to be house-trained to relieve himself all the time in a flat, without going outside, you should provide him with two pens, a small one to contain his bed and a larger one where you will teach him to relieve himself. The latter should be waterproofed and covered with layers of flat newspaper. To start with, when the puppy is young, the relieving pen should be placed where he can easily see it, but as far away from his bed as is convenient for him to use.

47

As soon as you arrive home with your puppy, give him a good drink of water, sit down quietly in a chair and stroke him gently. He will soon show signs of wanting to relieve himself. Take him to his RP (relieving pen) and place him gently on the paper, leaving him there until he has performed once. Leave him a little longer, since he will probably want to do so twice, then lift him out, telling him what a good boy he is. Do not clear up the wet paper but leave it down until the puppy wants to use the RP again. Cover the area with newspaper if you wish, but remove this top layer before you take the puppy back, as he needs the odour of the urine to reinforce his memory of what he is to do and where. Watch your puppy like a hawk and, the moment he moves, stretches or yawns, carry or lead him to his RP and put him down near the stained newspaper.

Once your puppy has accepted you and feels less strange in his new home, start to put him down a few centimetres from the door of his RP. If he does not walk in of his own accord give him a gentle nudge or even a little push and close the RP door behind him. Tell him to 'Hurry up', praise him when he has finished, open the door, encourage him with one of his noisy toys, or even a titbit, to come out and show him the way home to his bed, or have a little game with him first. You will be surprised how quickly your puppy will learn what his RP is for, and he will soon go there of his own accord. Gradually increase the distance between his bed and the RP, until you can place it on the balcony or in the bathroom or anywhere else you find convenient in your flat.

Keep your puppy's bedding dry and clean and wash his blanket regularly, rinsing it in Napisan or water with a little vinegar. Put some salt or flea powder in the crevices of the box or basket to keep away fleas. Fleas also dislike pine needles. If you are out walking, gather a few fresh pine needles and place them beneath the puppy's blanket or cushion.

When teething, puppies love to chew something hard to relieve their sore gums. Make certain that they are given their own things to chew and, if you have valuable furniture, just rub a little oil of cloves over the legs of chairs and tables with a cotton rag. The smell of the cloves generally stops puppies from gnawing the wood, and if the smell does not deter them they will certainly dislike the bitter taste.

Occasionally, one comes across a puppy who refuses to relieve himself when he is on a lead. He dislikes the restriction round his neck, which makes him feel inhibited. This is particularly awkward if you live in a flat and are trying to kerb-train your puppy in the street. Some puppies can be quite contrary and will only relieve themselves when they are back in the flat. There are two ways of helping your puppy. One is to leave the lead on in the house, after you have taken the puppy back to his indoor pen, until he has relieved himself. The other is to place a long, fine, light cord or fishing line round the puppy's neck when you take him outside. The first time you take him out, choose a time when there is little traffic about and few distractions. Without the heavier lead restraint the chances are that your puppy will relieve himself by the kerb without further problems. You may have to allow him a fair time to sniff around and, within limits, permit him to choose his own spot. Once the puppy has become accustomed to the light cord, upgrade him to the collar and lead. The moment he has learnt to relieve himself whilst wearing his collar and lead, then use the words 'Hurry up' and, if you like, reinforce your words with a titbit. This will save you many embarrassing minutes standing on the edge of the pavement (sidewalk) waiting for your dog to relieve himself and being an object of ridicule to the passers-by. Teaching your puppy to perform quickly will benefit you both, particularly if it happens to be pouring with rain.

If you have to take your puppy into the street at night to relieve himself make sure that his collar fits snugly and cannot slip over his head should he pull on the lead. Your dog should wear a good collar, with his name and your address or telephone number on it. Stick some good reflector tape round the collar so that, if your puppy should escape at night, it is easier for drivers to see him in the dark and for you to find him if he is hiding in the bushes (provided that you have a torch). A reflector tape on your puppy's collar could well prevent him from being run over should he be prowling across a road at night.

5

How to Train a Young Puppy

From the moment that your puppy arrives home with you he starts learning a completely new way of life. During his everyday routine he will learn many important words and numerous new experiences. He must learn what he may and must not do. He will learn this by associating certain good behaviour with praise and reward. He will quickly learn what constitutes bad or undesirable behaviour by receiving no praise and probably some discomfort, such as a jerk on a leash or a bump with your leg. He must be made to think that such unpleasantness has been caused only by himself and has no connection with you. You should never laugh at your puppy when training him or he will not consider that you are being serious.

Every time you notice your puppy starting to do something on his own that you will be wanting to teach him in the future, you must take the opportunity of saying the word for what he is doing or is about to do. By doing this your puppy learns naturally and rapidly, associating what he is doing with praise as his reward. Moreover, it is much more fun for him to do what he wants to do of his own accord than by being told to do it. Anything that a puppy does of his own volition he will absorb more easily than from formal training.

Each time you put your puppy in his bed, pat the bed and say encouragingly 'Jock, bed' (or whatever the puppy's name is). When you think he wants to relieve himself say 'Jock, out' or 'Would you like to go out?' He quickly learns the word 'Out'. Every time you go into the room and your puppy is awake, call him by name—'Jock, come!'. When you feed him, say 'Jock, dinner'. Your puppy quickly learns all the important, simple words and he understands by the tone of your voice all the terms of endearment and praise such as 'Clever boy', 'Good boy', as well as terms of urgency such as 'Stop it!' and 'Hurry up!'. When you notice your puppy about to sit, say 'Sit!', reinforcing your word by scratching his head or chest. When you happen to notice him about to lie down, say the magical words 'Lie down!'.

With your puppy's daily grooming he also learns 'Sit!', 'Stand!' and 'Stay'. Besides all the pleasant, encouraging words, your puppy must learn the very important 'No!', 'Gently', 'Give!', and so on. You

50

will be surprised how many words he will learn with very little effort on your part. Do not confuse him with too many new words at a time. Later, when you see him standing well, with his head up, say 'Stand!' or, if you prefer it, 'Stay!'.

When you see him doing something wrong, as with a small child, distract his attention by saying rather severely and in a deep voice 'No!' As he looks up, change your tone of voice immediately and call him to you in a high-pitched exciting tone, saying 'Jock, come!', and make a great fuss of him.

You can, of course, train your puppy or dog entirely by this method, by rewarding all required behaviour when your dog does it naturally and on his own volition, and by discomfort or unpleasant consequences when he is disobedient, although the latter must never be associated with you. He must always feel that any un-pleasantness is due to his own fault. For example, when you bump him with your leg, your puppy must feel that it was entirely his fault for bumping into you. Above all, never punish your puppy. Ad-monish him by other means.

Lead Training
Young puppies can easily be taught to walk on a lead from the age of seven weeks. Just before a meal put a very light crochet collar on the puppy, leaving a short end dangling down. Place the puppy on the floor for his dinner. You will find that he is so keen on his meal that he will not even notice that he is wearing a collar. If there are other young puppies about, they are bound to play with the loose end, giving it tugs, and the puppy will quickly become used to any pressure on his throat. The next step, on the following day, is to sit your puppy on your knee and replace his collar, to which has been attached a very light cord or piece of string. After the puppy has run around for a little and has become used to the trailing end you should pick up the end and nonchalantly start walking with the puppy in any direction he chooses. Coax and encourage him to follow you, using a titbit if you like, calling him by name, and praising him frequently when he is walking well. He will have no difficulty follow-ing you at this early age because you are now his pack leader.

If your puppy has not learnt to walk on a lead by the age of twelve to sixteen weeks you should now start to teach him. You will teach him to heel at a much later date, sometime after he is six or seven months old. No puppy should be given formal training before this age, and most trainers prefer to start when the puppy is about eight months old. Guide dogs do not start their training until they are four-teen months old, and circus dogs not until they are two years old.

51

Before you embark on your first lesson, read up exactly what you are going to do, and remember how important your tone of voice is. To teach your puppy to walk on a lead you will need a good, soft leather collar which the puppy will have worn for at least three or four days before his first lesson. Find a suitable light line or cord about 2m (6ft) in length, and decide on three or four different areas where you can take your puppy. You must choose places where he has never been before, and the area should be quiet and without distractions. If you happen to know of a quiet place with a wall down one side, or an alley, so much the better, but it is by no means essential. Choose a fine day and a time shortly before your puppy is due to have his next meal. During his lesson coax him and praise him whenever he is walking well, but you must never laugh at his antics.

Before you start the lesson, quietly pick up your puppy in your arms and place him on your knee. Talk to him gently in a normal manner, and quite unconcernedly attach a light cord or line to his collar. Then carry him to the area you have selected for his lesson and simply place him on the ground and ignore him. This unfamiliar place may be a little alarming, and the chances are that your puppy will walk towards you because he will want you to pick him up. If you are lucky and he does this, simply walk quietly away from him; make certain that the lead does not become entangled in the puppy's legs, and be sure that there is no pull on his collar. Encourage him by talking to him and, after about ten steps, bend down and keep coaxing him and pat him gently, at the same time praising him for being so clever. Hold the lead or cord in your right hand and encourage your puppy to walk on your left side; when you pat him, do so with your left hand. Follow this procedure, each time in a different place, for two or three days. If your puppy decides he would prefer to walk away from you, then just follow him, making certain that there is no pressure on his throat.

Occasionally a puppy will just sit down exactly where you place him and will refuse to move, not knowing what to do or because he does not like the feel of the cord on his collar. Ignore your puppy completely and stand quite still until he decides to move. Some puppies will sit for five minutes or more, but eventually he will get bored with sitting. When the puppy moves, simply follow him quietly, going wherever he leads you. Talk to him occasionally and, as soon as he moves well, praise him and pick him up and carry him home. If a puppy refuses to move altogether, wait ten or twelve minutes before picking him up and taking him home. Take your puppy to another place the following day and keep your lessons to the same time of day. Do not spend more than five minutes on the actual lesson. Wear shoes that are quiet so that your steps will not distract your puppy. Most puppies will move after a day or two, but do not try to hurry an obstinate or timid puppy. Continue to ignore him and have patience.

Now He Must Follow You

After two or three days your puppy will no longer be worried by his lead, so proceed to a new area. Put your puppy on the ground and walk away. If he follows, well and good, but if he is still reluctant to move, wait until you are as far away from him as the lead will permit and, without looking at him, give a gentle tug on the lead, bend down, pat your knee and encourage your puppy to come towards you, saying 'Good boy, well done'. If he delays, give another small tug and immediately follow the tug with gentle words of encouragement. It is important not to look at your puppy when you tug the lead, and never do so when he is actually coming towards you. In no way must your puppy associate you with the gentle tug; he must only associate you with words of praise and encouragement, and must think it is the collar and lead which are making him uncomfortable.

The first lesson in learning to follow you should not entail more than two or three gentle tugs. Your puppy is going through a new experience. He is now having to go where *you* want to go, and he is learning that the tug is stopping him from going where *he* would like to go. The puppy is really being taught by repetition of a negative stimulus by remote control, which he must never associate with you. His lessons must be happy and relaxed experiences.

If you can take your puppy to a new area for each lesson he is far more likely to want to follow you wherever you go, because of his fear of the unknown and of becoming lost. As soon as your puppy walks well on a lead and keeps close to your side and looks forward to his outings, then is the time to open his eyes to a larger, more noisy world. Take your puppy gradually through all kinds of situations, leaving the noisy ones until the end, because these are the most frightening and unnatural situations.

New Situations

When you start to introduce your puppy to new and, for him, perhaps frightening situations, take everything slowly and gradually, step by step, introducing him to this new world as if everything is perfectly natural. Let the puppy see that nothing is of concern to you and that nothing should be of concern to him. There is no need for particular encouragement or even reassurance, simply a calm, matter-of-fact attitude. Your puppy must learn about traffic on the roads, people in crowded shops, lifts, swing-doors, the noise of planes (especially Concorde), fire engines, steamrollers, railway stations, trains, other dogs, whistles, and also small noisy children.

If your puppy seems particularly apprehensive in any new situation, do not force him to go near the object that frightens him. Lead him quietly away and try again the following day. Each time you will find that you can persuade your puppy to approach the object a little closer until eventually he will accept it without further fear. It takes time and patience for puppies to accept such monsters as articulated lorries, thundering trains and double-decker buses without a qualm. In some cases holding a small puppy in your arms will give him a sense of security, especially if you talk to him soothingly until his fear has subsided. Do not expect too much from your puppy; he is very small and this new world might seem very alarming. It is up to you that he never becomes frightened. If your puppy is terrified by a bad experience he will be set back considerably, and it may then take you a very long time to overcome his fear.

Teaching a Puppy to Stay on His Own

Your puppy has learnt about the haven of his own bed in his playpen, and he has learnt that he must not cry and pester you when he wants to get out. Once your puppy has become house-trained, so that he may be permitted to have the run of even two rooms in the house, you must now start to teach him to remain alone without barking, crying, whimpering or scratching the door.

To Stop Him Barking and Scratching at the Door

As with all training, take everything slowly. Choose a time during the day after you have fed your puppy and he has been out to relieve himself. He will be feeling a little sleepy. Give him one or two of his favourite toys and put him into his bed. If he barks, say 'Bed, stay!' Sit quietly in a chair for a few minutes and, while he is quiet, get up and go out of the room. The moment the puppy starts to bark go up to him and, gently but firmly, hold his mouth shut and, because he cannot bark, praise him. You can do this with an adult dog too and it is probably the quickest way to stop a dog barking. If your puppy howls, bang on the door very loudly and say 'No! Stop it!'; use your hand or an old shoe or chain depending on how much noise you wish to make. As soon as the puppy has been quiet for a few minutes, return to the room and praise him. Gradually increase the time that you are away, until your puppy is quite happy to remain on his own. He will soon learn that you are coming back.

Another useful method, if you happen to have trouble when your dog is left alone, involves leaving the dog in a dark room. The moment he starts to bark, say 'Shhhhh!' firmly. When he starts to bark again, open the door and switch the electric light on and off several times. This sudden light and darkness takes the dog by surprise and distracts him from barking. After you have used this method you should be able to leave your dog alone anywhere, including the car, without his resorting to barking. Yet another useful deterrent is a water pistol squirted into his face while he is barking.

To stop a puppy scratching at the door when he is left alone, you should listen for the first sound of scratching. Open the door quickly and slap a rolled-up newspaper on your hand or on the door and say sharply 'No! Stop it!', or use one of the methods quoted above to stop him barking. Your puppy will soon learn that his scratching at the door does not please you and that he receives no praise. As soon as he stops misbehaving, return immediately and greet your puppy.

Destroying Your Possessions

Your possessions are never safe if a puppy is left alone with them. You must only chastise him when you actually catch him in the act of chewing or destroying one of your valuable belongings, as otherwise he will have absolutely no idea why you are cross with him. It is extremely wrong and cruel to scold your puppy unless you are sure that he can understand why he is displeasing you. It is far better to distract his attention and immediately call him to you and praise him for coming to you.

Even if the puppy has grabbed your beautiful new silk scarf or your best evening sandal is being quietly chewed to pieces, calm your obvious anger and approach your puppy quietly. Very gently remove the object from his mouth by tapping the top of his nose with one finger (try the force you should use on your own nose to do it and you will get the idea). While you are tapping, say in your most reproving manner 'No! Naughty!' If he does not let go, press his lips back against his upper teeth and this will make him open his mouth. When you have rescued the article, immediately put it down in front of your puppy. Quite naturally, he will make another attempt to grab the article, but you are ready for this new assault. Proceed to tap the puppy across his nose more forcefully than previously and also repeat 'No!' more emphatically, but do so without raising your voice. Repeat the lessons a few more times, and your puppy will know that his action displeases you.

Never rush at your puppy and try to grab something out of his mouth, never throw anything at him, and never scream or shout at him. You will only frighten the puppy and be ashamed of yourself for losing your temper. Of course, you must be forceful in your tone of voice, but you must not, on the other hand, be severe and frightening. Some puppies are very sensitive while others are quite tough, so you must use your discretion as to how far you should go. If you over-step the mark, it will take you a very long time to win your puppy's confidence back.

Jumping on Furniture

A dog must be taught to respect your furniture, so start your puppy off as you intend to go on. It is not really wise to allow your dog on your chairs and sofas. Hairs get left behind and cling not only to your clothes but also to your guests' clothes. Some people do not mind their small dogs on chairs, or even on their bed, and enjoy their dogs sitting on their laps. I admit I am one of them—I like my dogs all about me and in every room of the house. However, it is far easier to prohibit dogs from lying on chairs at the outset rather than to allow them to be on them at some times and not at others.

Every time your puppy tries to get on to a chair, remove him immediately before he actually gets on. If the puppy has never achieved his wish of lying in a chair, he will not know how comfort-able it is, and there will be no bad habit to break. Each time he makes the attempt just put him on the ground and, once he is there, make a fuss of him, stroking and patting him, and distract him with a toy or bone. Keep a sharp eye on the puppy and, the moment he puts his paws up on the edge of the chair, tap his toes sharply with the tips of your fingers. In your most reproving voice say 'No! Naughty!', and place the puppy immediately in his bed with his toys to distract him. It is, of course, unfair to leave your puppy alone in a room for more than a very short time—he is bound to get into mischief if he is left without supervision. Put temptation out of his way by placing objects on the chairs to make them uncomfortable for him to lie on. Furniture legs may be rubbed over with oil of cloves to deter the puppy from chewing them.

Teaching Your Puppy to Go to Bed

It is best to teach your puppy to go to his bed after he has had a good game in the garden and is really tired and ready for a nice long sleep. Because the puppy is tired, bed is exactly what he wants, so put him in his bed and, as you do so, say 'Bed' and he will settle down quickly and fall asleep. Repeat the word 'Bed' every time you place him in his bed, and also whenever you notice him going there on his own accord, and you will be astonished to find how quickly you will be able to send your puppy to his bed from any part of the house that he happens to be in simply by telling him 'Bed'. Never forget to praise him every time he goes there.

Teaching Your Puppy to be Gentle and Not to Bite
It is important to teach your puppy to be gentle, whatever his ultimate size will be—you cannot start too early. Offer him a small titbit and, if he tries to grab it roughly from your hand, say 'No! Ouch!', and do not let him have the treat. Wait a little and then re-offer the titbit. If the puppy again tries to snatch the morsel from your hand, tap his nose with your fingertips. Then offer him the titbit once again and this time, as you offer it, say in a quiet gentle voice 'Gentle!' The puppy will react to your soft voice and, as soon as he takes his much wanted titbit gently from your fingers, praise him quietly. You will have to repeat this lesson many, many times when your puppy is small, but it is an important part of his education. It is a lesson easily learnt, and will be retained all his life.

Many dogs, particularly the large breeds, go through a boisterous stage, but luckily this does not last long. However, if the puppy has been trained early to be gentle there should be no need for owners to resort to wearing thick leather gloves and boots. When a puppy is going through this boisterous stage and starts to play too roughly or to bite his toys, or perhaps becomes over-excited in any way, you will find that your soft, gentle voice saying 'Gentle!' will produce an immediate reaction. The intensity of his game will automatically diminish and you must follow this reaction with your usual quiet, gentle praise, keeping everything in a low key.

Your puppy must also learn from a very early age that he must never bite. The first time he nips your fingers or hand in play, tap him sharply on the nose with the tips of your fingers—the puppy will not like this. At the same time, using your most authoritative tone of voice, say 'No! Naughty!' and stop the game you were having. Call the puppy to you after a few minutes and start playing with him again. If he bites again, repeat the chastisement with a sharper tap on the nose than previously. He will soon learn not to bite in play.

Unfortunately, owners who enjoy playing with their dogs roughly and who tease them in the process are encouraging them to turn into biters. With a small puppy, biting may not hurt, but puppies grow fast and, with the large breeds, soon learn their strength. In only a short time such a puppy will become aggressive, using his strong jaws and large, sharp teeth. Every time he bites or nips, he becomes bolder; in due course the owner of the puppy will be in trouble and the poor dog—through no fault of his own—will have to be put down. Sometimes such dogs are sent to professional trainers to try to tame them, which at this stage is no easy task. Female hormone therapy is probably the only recourse to make the dog less aggressive, plus correct, firm training. I cannot stress too strongly that you must stop your puppy learning to bite before it becomes a habit. Make him play with you gently and never permit him to be rough, even if he is not attempting to bite or nip.

Teaching Your Puppy Not to Jump Up

It will, perhaps, be helpful for you in learning to understand your puppy if you realise that from the age of six weeks certain important characteristics of the puppy are established, and some of these typical features can be of help to you in training your puppy. All puppies by the time they are eight weeks old have what is known as the face-licking greeting response. They start first by face-licking their mother, then progress to other faces—their siblings, the cat, their owner, children and other people. Faces always have a tremendous fascination for all puppies and, in order to be nearer the face, they instinctively try to jump up. At this age the puppies also learn to make what is known as the inguinal approach, that is sniffing each other in the groin, investigating both the genital and the anal areas. You will notice that the puppy who is doing the investigating moves his head about sniffing gently, while the puppy that is being investigated will stand motionless and will be quite passive during the investigation. He cannot help this, because he is in what is known as a 'behavioural-inhibition' situation; in other words he is under an automatic social control. So deeply implanted is this characteristic in dogs that you can take advantage of it by simply placing your hand gently in the groin when training your puppy to stand or to stop him from jumping up.

Puppies will even react to a lifesize drawing of a dog if it is placed on the ground within their reach. An eight-week-old puppy will investigate the face first, whilst even a tiny five-week-old puppy, if he is sufficiently hungry, will investigate the ventral-groin area. However, once he uses his nose, the puppy soon realises that there is no response from the drawing, and he will go off and seek out something else more interesting. A puppy places far more importance in what he scents and hears than what he sees.

You should start teaching your puppy not to jump up from a very early age. If he is taught that jumping up displeases you he will learn to show his affection for you in other ways. You in turn must show the puppy how devoted you are and tell him how much you love him. If you have been away for some hours, or even a few minutes, your puppy may be so delighted and thrilled to see you that he may hurl himself at you and jump up, perhaps dirtying your new clothes or tearing your stockings. Never permit your puppy to jump up on some occasions and not on others. You must be consistent and never allow him to do so.

If your puppy rushes over to greet you when you first go into a room, before he is near enough to jump up, bend down over him and, the moment he has all four feet on the ground, start patting him gently and keep talking affectionately. With a very small puppy or dog you should kneel down. As soon as the puppy starts trying to leap up again, bend forward over him and keep up a running, re-assuring conversation with him in a quiet, low-key tone of voice. If he still persists in jumping up, wait till his feet are once again on terra firma, continue to pat him, but this time hold him down very gently and place one hand in his groin. Let the puppy know you really do appreciate his love, but that you do not appreciate being jumped on. Never make the mistake of patting and praising him unless he has stopped jumping up and all four feet are on the ground. Most puppies learn very quickly not to jump up.

In training a more exuberant, large puppy you will require patience and self-discipline, because you must remember that you may not scold your puppy for jumping up. You must keep your voice gentle and pleasant. What you have to do now is to try a more force-ful way of preventing him from wishing to jump up. The next time your puppy jumps up, keep talking to him kindly but at the same time hold his forepaws, one in each hand, and squeeze them. You must not hurt the puppy; just make your pressure strong enough to cause discomfort. You must not let him associate the discomfort on his paws in any way with you—you are talking so nicely to him that you could not possibly be the source of his discomfort. Every member of the family or any friend coming in to see you must react in the same way.

A puppy that does not respond to this method must be taught in another way. Wear a pair of soft shoes with rubber soles and follow exactly the previous method, but whilst you squeeze the puppy's forepaws, gently step on his hindpaws. It is imperative that you should not hurt your puppy in doing this—if you press too hard you could break a toe. The pressure you put on the hindtoes is for the puppy's discomfort and nothing more. As with all training it is just a matter of constant repetition, and your puppy will soon learn not to jump up.

It is most important that your puppy's affection for strangers should be curbed. Put a light check-chain collar on your puppy, one which fits well, just going over his head with ease, and attach a leash.

Ask a friend to enter the room and, as the puppy tries to jump up, tell the friend to bend over him and pat him, while gently telling him he is pleased to see him—but only when the puppy has four feet on the ground. Try to anticipate your puppy's jump and jerk him off balance with a jerk on the leash, saying as you do so 'No!' in the nicest possible way. A few practices like this with different people will soon teach your puppy not to jump up. He will learn that he is loved all the more for keeping all four feet on the ground.

If a dog has not been taught not to jump up on people when he was small and manageable you will have to resort to a stronger approach. When your dog comes bounding up to you, full of exuberance, instead of bending over him just before he reaches you, anticipate his leap and, as he makes it, lift your knee up so that it catches the dog full on the chest and throws him off balance. The dog is taken aback and given a strong jolt but, as soon as he has regained his balance, call him over to you in your most affectionate and loving voice and, the moment he stands still, pet him and make a fuss of him. The dog must never associate your knee with you.

Using your knee is a very strong method of training. However, it is better for a dog to be brought up sharply two or three times in this way than to use one of the other methods which have no effect on him. Once the dog gets the better of you then he automatically loses his respect for you. A strong, large dog can take quite a thump from your knee on his chest, and it is better to resort to two or three strong knee-jerks than lots of ineffectual ones. Very few dogs will not stop jumping up after a couple of bumps on the chest.

Another method of teaching a dog not to jump up is to anticipate his leap and, as he jumps up, to grab his collar under his throat and pull him sharply down. At the same time say very sharply 'No! Sit!' Once again, the moment your dog obeys, pet him and make a great fuss of him. You will find the method quite simple. As you grab the collar, drop on to one knee. In this way, you will reduce your height and increase the closeness of your fascinating face to your dog's own, thus eliminating his urge to jump up to you. You should remember that dogs like to show their affection by jumping up, and it is also a form of play and a way of attracting attention.

Teaching Your Puppy to Lie Down

Teaching your puppy to lie down is both useful and easy. Every time that you notice your puppy about to lie down of his own accord, say 'Lie down!' and, once the puppy is actually lying down, say 'Stay' and praise him. You will be surprised how, after a very short time, your puppy will connect the words with the act. It is best to start this lesson for the first time when you know your puppy is tired after playing, or after a meal when he will be feeling sleepy and ready for a nap.

The lesson is also useful if your puppy is inclined to bark or insists on barking at a stranger at the door, because you can then say 'Lie down' and this will stop the puppy barking, since no dog likes to bark when he is lying down.

The easiest way to teach an older puppy to lie down is to make him sit in front of you. Then, with both your hands pull his legs forward from under him. As you do so, say quite quietly 'Lie down!', putting the emphasis on 'down'. The moment the puppy is lying down, you should hold him down with one hand on his back, while with the other hand you pet him in his favourite way, probably by scratching his chest. At the same time reassure the puppy, saying something like 'Such a good boy'. The moment he stops struggling and is quiet, tell him in a gentle way to 'Stay!' and go on praising him.

As soon as your puppy understands the words 'Lie down' and conforms, you should start using the normal hand signal for 'Down' which is used in obedience training. To make the signal, you should stand in front of your dog, raise your *right* hand as high as you can above your head with your fingers outstretched and make a sweeping gesture down to below your puppy's eyes. It is well worth while teaching your puppy to lie down at an early age. Teaching an adult dog is generally much more difficult.

To Teach Your Puppy to Come When Called
After initially teaching your puppy to come to you when called in a room, call him in a passage, later in a small garden, and so on. Your puppy is being conditioned to the word and the word forms a habit. Next you should choose a quiet place he has never been in before, one with no distractions but with a few bushes or a hut you can hide behind. Carry your puppy to this place and put him down gently. Your puppy will no doubt become rather brave and sniff around the area, darting here and there at all the fascinating new scents. Let him enjoy himself, investigating everything on his own. Allow him to go quite far away from you and then suddenly hide when he is not looking. When the puppy discovers that he is alone, he will be quite upset and will probably rush back to the place where he last remembers seeing you. He will run around looking for you, becoming more and more worried. When the puppy is quite far from you and has his back turned to you, give him a friendly call—'Jasper, come!' He will hear your voice and, after you have called him several times, will run towards the place from where your voice comes. Most puppies will not use their nose to try to find your scent. However, just before he is

61

about to find you, come out of your hiding place and call 'Jasper, come!' The puppy will be delighted to find you and you should lavish him with praise, tell him what a clever dog he is and how delighted you are to see him too.

You will probably find that for a short time your puppy will not let you out of his sight, but gradually his confidence will return and his nose will direct him to something very exciting. Play the game of hide-and-seek a couple of times a day for several days, hiding in a different place each day.

For the next few days take your puppy for a normal walk in a different area and, when he is quite a long way ahead of you, call 'Jasper, come!' and proceed to run in the opposite direction. Repeat your call several times whilst running away. The moment your puppy has caught up with you praise him lavishly and talk to him. As with the previous game, repeat the running away only twice during each walk—you should not let your puppy become bored with the lesson. Your puppy by now is forming a good habit of coming when called. There is nothing more pleasing than to own a dog that you know will come the moment he is called.

Shy and Vicious Dogs
Well bred dogs, in spite of being highly intelligent, very sensitive and extremely perceptive, may be ruined by ignorant, impatient or bad-tempered owners. It is all too easy to spoil a puppy for life, for instance by expecting too much from him too soon or by frightening him into submission whether by voice, by a threatening hand raised in the air, or by throwing something at him. Never resort to slapping a puppy with your hand or even with a newspaper. Any form of unnecessary punishment is absolutely taboo. Never shout and scream at your puppy—he has very sensitive hearing. If you resort to any of these forms of intimidation, even if only once, you can turn your beautiful puppy into a shy, nervous, cowering dog, in spite of excellent breeding for temperament and self-confidence. Unfortunately, a shy dog quickly becomes timid, a timid dog becomes frightened, and a frightened dog may in turn become vicious.

Once a dog has begun to be vicious, he quickly learns to use his new-found power of frightening people and keeping them away, which is just what he wants. He may start with a small warning growl; next time he will progress to a teeth-showing snarl; and from there it will not be long before, the next time he is frightened, he will try a nasty nip. It could well be only a short time before he tries a full-blooded bite. A dog that bites is too much of a responsibility for any owner, whatever the cause, even if this behaviour is entirely the fault of a previous owner. Vicious dogs have to be destroyed, though sometimes castration is successful.

It often happens that puppies that are extremely sensitive are also very intelligent. These are the puppies that need exceptionally careful handling in their early days. They require much patience and understanding, and very gentle training, but the time spent on them is often the most rewarding of all. This type of dog frequently turns out in the end to be the most remarkable and affectionate, trusting pet, and a wonderful friend and companion.

Car Training

All dogs enjoy riding in a car, unless they have been frightened or have only been taken in a car to visit the veterinary surgeon (your dog will associate the veterinary surgeon with nasty smells and unpleasant happenings, rather like many people feel about a dental visit). If your puppy is seven weeks old or so when you collect him from the kennels he will happily settle down in your lap covered in a blanket, feeling perfectly secure and warm. He will be most unlikely at such an early age to be car sick. He will enjoy the motion of the car and will show no sign of fear. Keep the windows of the car open and the very young puppy is most unlikely even to drool. Take him for short car rides daily so that he will not forget the experience and he will quickly get his 'car legs'.

Take your puppy for his first drive about three hours after his last meal and, if possible, find someone else to drive the car so that you can concentrate on the puppy. Keep the windows down and take a large soft towel, some tissues and a plastic bag to put them in after use. Keep your puppy's head up. The car should not be driven at more than 50km (30 miles) an hour. Talk to your puppy reassuringly and stroke him. Make the first drive a short one, about five minutes in length, and gradually increase the speed. Your puppy will feel better on the front seat than in the back, because there is less swaying of the car in front. Do not allow your puppy to go to sleep, because this is a lesson. If all is well, let the puppy look out of the window and make him sit. You will have to repeat 'Sit' many, many times. Looking at the scene going past him may make the puppy feel sick, in which case cover the moving scene from his sight.

An older puppy or a grown dog requires to be taught his car etiquette. He will also need practice at learning about the strange movement, which may often make him feel slightly sick, in which case he will drool or even be sick—a most unpleasant experience!

Training an older dog or puppy to ride in a car follows the same procedure as described above, but put your dog on a leash as if he is

about to go for a special walk. Use an exciting tone of voice, saying something like 'Would you like to go in the car?' Take the dog to the car, which should have the front door ready open, and place his forefeet on the doorstep saying 'Into the car'. Give him a helping hand in and on to the front seat, which should be covered with the dog's own blanket or cushion. Then get into the car and sit beside him. Talk to him and pet him, stroking him in his favourite places, on his chest and behind the ears; hold his muzzle lovingly and make him feel the car is all great fun. Simply sit in the car for about ten minutes and then take him in for his meal. You could do this several times a day for two or three days until your dog is completely accustomed to the car and will get in on his own at your question and then your command 'Into the car'. The next stage is to tell your dog to 'Sit' and then start the car. Just leave the engine running, as if nothing unusual is taking place, and keep chatting to him all the time. Turn the engine off and then train your dog to remain sitting until you give him the command to get out of the car—'Out!' You should repeat this exercise for a few days.

Although you may find this a slow method, it is one well worth spending time on. Your dog is learning to get into the car, to sit in it and to get out of it. He is now well used to the car, so you should reverse the car slowly out of the garage and simply leave it parked. Keep talking and reassuring your dog. After about ten minutes drive the car back into the garage. Each day drive the car a little further until he is quite used to the motion of the car. Insist that your dog 'Sit' by tapping his rump sharply with your fingertips. If there is not room to do this just press his rear down until he conforms. If you have a long journey to make, you might be wise to give your dog some anti-car-sick pills about an hour before you plan to start. If you want your dog to get out of the car at any time, do make certain that he is on a leash before you allow him out.

If you have a dog that is particularly nervous of the car, you could give him a favourite titbit at the end of each journey, praising him for his courage and endurance. You will find it easy to teach your dog to sit by the car door before you give him the command 'Into the car!'

Dogs that are not trained to behave well in a car can be exceedingly dangerous, especially larger dogs that jump about from side to side or from the front to the back seat. Accidents are caused by such atrocious behaviour. Some dogs insist on barking their heads off at the sight of other dogs outside the car or even strange people. This can easily be stopped by the use of a child's water-pistol

---

An airedale trained to stay quietly in the car by the command 'Down-stay!'

squirted quite suddenly in the dog's face. At the same time say 'No! Stop it!' The dog does not associate the deed with you, as you are at a distance. The shock makes him stop barking momentarily and you must then praise him. Whenever your dog barks, repeat the lesson.

Once your dog has learnt to enjoy riding in a car, he will be happy to remain in the car when you are away. Start by leaving him for short periods, with an old sweater or his own rug for company. If your dog starts to bark, reprimand him sharply and give him a quick squirt with the water-pistol. Leave him for only a few minutes at first, gradually lengthening the time you are away. The dog soon learns that you will always come back. A dog in your car, whatever his size, is a good deterrent against car thieves or burglars.

When you leave your car, it is extremely important that you lock the doors and leave the window down a little so that your dog has plenty of fresh air. If the weather is warm, make certain that your car will be in the shade all the time you intend to be away. In hot weather or in hot climates it can be extremely dangerous for dogs to be left in cars unless the windows are opened sufficiently for enough air to circulate. Numbers of dogs die every year from heat stroke, because thoughtless owners do not realise the fearful heat that can build up in a car on a hot day when the windows have been closed.

Cars on the Road
All dogs should know about cars on a road and they must never be permitted to chase a car or a bicycle.

The best way to teach a dog or a puppy that roads are dangerous is to find someone who will drive a car slowly down a quiet road behind your dog and you and, when the car is just a short distance from your dog, give a loud blast on the horn. You, in the meantime, will walk down the centre of the road with your dog heeling nicely. The moment the horn is blown, jerk-release the leash and get your dog on to the side of the road immediately. Proceed to walk down the road again and repeat the lesson. After two or three blasts on the horn your dog will have learnt his lesson and will go in to the side of his own volition. Then repeat the exercise with the car coming towards you.

Quick Guide to Training a Young Puppy

This is a guide to what you should teach your puppy between the ages of seven weeks and seven months. If you make this list, you can cross off all the lessons your puppy has learnt as you go along. Your dog will be able to learn a tremendous number of words. Guide dogs for the blind are taught a particular vocabulary, as are gundogs, working hounds and tracking dogs. You decide what your dog should learn and you will have enormous fun teaching him.

Positive Training
His name.
'Bed!'
'Hurry up!'
House-training.
To be groomed.
Nails cut or filed.
To stay on his own.
To wait for his food.
'Sit!'
'Stand!'
'Stay!' } whilst being groomed.
'Lie down!'
To walk on a lead.
To ride in a car.
To know his own toys.
To learn to be gentle.
To come when called.
To wait to come into the house.
To sit at the kerb.
'Leave!'
'Give!'
'Take!'
'Go back!'
'Quiet!'

Negative Training
Not to bark and howl.
Not to scratch at the door.
Not to destroy your possessions.
Not to gnaw furniture.
Not to jump up.
Not to get up on chairs.

Not to bite.
Not to chase the cat.
Not to chase cars.

Useful, Practical Tricks
(Use food for inducement.)
'Shake hands!'
'Roll over!'
'Die for your country!'
'Beg!'
'Say your prayers!'
'Catch!'
'Sit' when throwing a ball.

Conversational Commands
'Fetch your lead!'
'Carry the basket!'
'Fetch the newspaper!'
'Bring your dish!'
'Where is your ball?'
'Go and fetch the trowel!'
'Go and find the golf ball!'
'Where are Missus's slippers?'

6

Trick Training

The Value of Trick Training

The more you teach your dog and the more you talk to him, the better. This is particularly important when he is a puppy. Although it is never too late to teach an old dog new tricks, it may take a little longer and it would be unwise to expect an old dog to jump.

If you teach your puppy to perform useful tricks, he will not only develop faster both mentally and physically, but his co-ordination will improve as well as his agility. He will also learn to look for hand signals and will understand a number of commands. Your puppy will never be bored with his daily life; in fact he will glow with brightness and intelligence and you will be able to bask in his reflected glory. You will also get great satisfaction and fun from teaching your puppy, and friends will admire your clever dog for bringing your slippers—when no one else will—for fetching the newspaper and for dying for his country.

All trick training, like all other training, is done by kindness; rewards take the form of titbits and you should never admonish your dog. As with normal training, give your puppy his lesson about three hours after his last meal and when he has been confined in his bed or kennel for a couple of hours. The latter is not essential, but may help with some dogs. Trick training may start at six months.

Shake Hands

This is an extremely easy trick to teach your puppy and it is excellent for shy or timid dogs. Once they have learnt the trick and will shake hands with all the family when asked, then they must learn to do so with strangers. From there they will progress to being stroked and touched by people they do not know. This is a first lesson towards show training, together with the stand for examination by a judge.

Place your puppy so that he is sitting in a corner; if he is of a small breed put a table in the corner and say in a kind voice 'Shake hands', and as you do so touch his right foreleg with your *right* hand and with your *left* hand push his shoulder very gently, so that he is just thrown off balance with his weight now on his left foreleg. Whether your dog raises his paw on his own or not, just pick up his paw and shake it

69

gently, reward him with a piece of baked liver or other titbit and praise him. If you do the exercise two or three times a day before his meals your puppy should learn to shake hands in a couple of days.

Roll Over

This is another trick which is most useful for puppies that are inclined to be tense and nervous. Asking a dog to lie down or to roll over is requesting him to put himself in a vulnerable position, one that no dog really likes until he has full confidence in his owner. Learning this trick automatically increases a puppy's self-confidence and thus reduces his nervousness. The best time to teach this lesson is after your puppy has been playing, so that he is naturally tired and would like nothing better than to lie down and have a little nap.

Start by making your puppy sit, then lift his left foreleg with your *right* hand, gently push his opposite shoulder with your *left* hand until he is lying down, and then continue pushing gently until your puppy is lying flat on his side. Do this on a soft carpet or lawn. Grasp both his right legs, one in each hand and just flip your puppy over on to his other side. As you do so say 'Roll over'. Allow your puppy to get up immediately and have a game with him. If he is lazy and does not get up at once, just hold his legs again and flip him towards you, saying 'Roll back'. Praise your puppy and play with him again. Do this several times a day when your puppy is tired.

Try making only a circular movement with your hand in the direction in which your puppy is to roll, telling him as usual 'Roll over'. He will soon manage to roll over without a helping hand. Later he will learn to comply with your request without the hand signal. He will soon learn to roll over and over and over, then roll back and over and over. You will notice that your puppy will roll over in the opposite direction to that in which his forelegs are pointing because he needs the impetus given by the swing of his legs. Keep a happy tone of voice and give lavish praise when he does the trick correctly.

Beg

Most puppies learn to beg easily, although there are some that find balancing difficult, whilst others have weak spines and long backs, and require a great deal of practice until the backbone becomes stronger. When teaching your puppy to beg you should make certain that he sits firmly and squarely on his haunches with the weight of his chest directly above his hindquarters and his forelegs tucked well in. His head should be nearly parallel to the ground. To help your puppy to keep his balance his tail should be straight out behind.

The easiest place for the lesson is probably in a corner of a room which has a soft carpet. For a small breed place a table in the corner. Give the lesson just before a meal is due. Place your puppy in the corner and make him sit. Hold a morsel of food above his nose and, when he starts to sit up, say 'Beg'. If the puppy does not sit up high enough or starts to overbalance, support his forelegs carefully. Once he is in the correct position, give him the titbit and praise him joyfully. The two walls on either side of your puppy give him a sense of security. Do not give your bait unless your puppy really is sitting up correctly, and then be generous with his titbit. Practise the lesson several times a day before your puppy's meals. He will learn this trick very quickly. Once he has understood what you want him to do, start to eliminate the titbit, only giving it occasionally. Most dogs learn to beg very quickly without either being asked or being offered the bait. It is a short step from here to teach a small dog to dance on his hindlegs, although large breeds are often too heavy in the head and shoulder to do this trick.

Trust and Paid For
This is a variation of 'Beg'. Find some flat, equal-sized biscuits or pieces of cheese. Ask your puppy to beg and place a biscuit just behind his nose, holding his muzzle between your thumb and third finger and balancing the biscuit with your index finger so that it does not fall off. Say 'Trust!' The biscuit on the puppy's nose will soon start to make him drool. Quickly say 'Paid for', and release your fingers from the titbit. 'Paid for' should be said in a low, drawn-out manner, because you do not want your puppy to become too excited. The moment you let go of the biscuit your puppy will toss his head, and no doubt the biscuit will fly across the room. Praise him and allow him to eat the titbit. Repeat the exercise in an unexciting manner. Your dog will soon learn, with practice, how to toss the titbit and catch it in his mouth. He will accomplish this more by scent than by sight. It is important that the titbits should always weigh the same because your puppy must learn how much of a toss is required in order for him to catch the biscuit before it flies across the room.

Say Your Prayers
This is another useful exercise, making your puppy obedient and at the same time giving you more control over him, because no dog likes to have his eyes covered, since this makes him feel vulnerable. Your dog will probably come over to you when you are eating and may, quite of his own accord, sit up and beg or put his paws on your lap. If he does, say 'Stay!' and gently push his head down for a few

Trick training, such as 'Fetch the newspaper', helps a dog to develop mentally and physically, and gives him a feeling of achievement

---

seconds. If he does not put his paws on your lap naturally, start the lesson with the sit and beg and then persuade your puppy to put his paws on your lap. When he does so, hold a piece of bait in your fingers below his nose so that he has to bend his head in order to get it. At that moment say 'Say your prayers', praise your dog quietly and give the release word 'Amen!'

Fetch the Newspaper
This is a useful accomplishment. Roll a newspaper tightly and put on an elastic band or piece of Sellotape to keep the paper rolled up neatly. Throw the newspaper on the floor a few feet in front of your puppy and say 'Fetch the newspaper'. If your puppy has not yet been taught to retrieve, place the paper in his mouth and put your free

hand under his chin. If he does not grip the paper strongly enough, tap it and he will automatically tighten his grip. Praise him when he brings it to you, say 'Thank you' and take it. Once your puppy is good at this accomplishment in the house, take the newspaper outside and increase the distance that the puppy has to carry the newspaper. Finally, place the newspaper wherever the paper boy usually drops it and tell your puppy to fetch the newspaper for you. If you live in a street, you may have to take care that he does not bring you all your neighbours' newspapers too!

Catching a Ball

Most dogs enjoy catching a ball, but many do not seem to see it until it is almost in front of their nose. First make certain that the ball is not so small that it could be swallowed. It should, on the other hand, not be too large for your puppy to catch and carry in his mouth.

Start by playing a game with your puppy's ball. Then make him stand. Pretend to throw the ball a few times so that your puppy will learn to keep his eye on the ball and on your hand. Throw the ball gently in a low arc, aiming towards his mouth so that he can see it. He may miss several times; if he finds it difficult, use a biscuit as he can smell this. When he does catch it, praise him and get him to bring the ball back to you. Once he has become clever at catching the ball, go into the garden and play catch there. Throwing a ball for a dog is a wonderfully easy way of exercising him with very little effort on your part. Once he has learnt to catch a ball easily, make him start the game from a sitting position. If you live near a golf course it is great fun and quite lucrative to teach your dog to find and retrieve golf balls.

Later, if your dog enjoys water, you can throw a stick into the sea or a river or pond. Always start off by throwing the stick only a short distance from the water's edge until your dog will go further and further out, when he will have to swim to retrieve his stick. Swimming, of course, is an excellent exercise for a dog. Some breeds adore water whilst others hate it. A dog should be hosed down after swimming in salt water.

Go Back

If he has not learnt to sit on command, this is a handy exercise for your puppy once he knows how to catch a ball.

Although your puppy may know how to heel and sit, he may well not have any inclination to sit anywhere you ask him except at heel. So, make your puppy sit by giving him the command. Throw the ball and, when he returns with it, take it and with your *right* hand wave

your puppy back saying 'Go back!' The moment he takes a few steps back give the command 'Sit!', then, the instant he complies, throw the ball for him.

Some puppies may be a little slow moving away from you. If your puppy just sits expectantly, walk over to him and shove him back gently with your leg. Once he has gone back a few steps, command him to 'Sit!' but, before throwing the ball for him, you should return to the exact place from which you threw the ball last time. Keep praising and encouraging your puppy and he will soon learn to sit anywhere on command, even when he is some distance away.

Wait at the Door

This is a sensible lesson to teach your puppy, particularly if you live in a street or road where there is likely to be traffic.

Put your puppy on his lead in the hall by your front door. Ask a friend to open the door for you and, if your puppy darts out, give a sharp jerk-release on the lead. As you do so say 'No! Sit!' Ask your friend to open the door several times and repeat the command. Next time when the door is opened, walk out with your puppy, giving him the command 'Out!' Then lavish him with praise. Repeat this several times. Ask your friend, after opening the door, to whistle for your puppy. It would be unfair to call him by name, since he should respond to his name. If your puppy attempts to go out before you give the release command 'Out!' jerk-release him back saying 'No! Sit!' When the door is next opened, go through it, giving your puppy the command 'Out!' You should then take him for an enjoyable walk and have a game with him. Every time you want to go out of the door for any reason, take your puppy with you on his lead. Give the command 'Sit-stay!' before you open the door, wait a moment, and then give him the release word 'Out!'

Once your puppy understands that he must wait at the door with his lead on, try the exercise without holding the lead. Let the lead trail on the ground. If your puppy tries to dart out, step on the lead, bringing him up sharply. When you progress to the lesson without a lead, keep your hand on the door knob so that, if by chance your puppy tries to run out before the release word, you can pull the door to and the puppy will bump his nose against it. He will have no idea that you were the cause of his discomfort and will think that it was his own fault. However, you must take care that your puppy is not frightened by the door.

Balls are an easy means of exercising dogs,.but they should be fairly hard and large enough not to be swallowed

Fetch Your Dish
This is another useful lesson for your puppy to learn and one that is very simple to teach. Find a light dish that your puppy can pick up and carry with ease. Throw the dish a short distance and say 'Fetch it!' When your dog retrieves the dish for you, drop in a little baked liver or other titbit and tell the puppy 'It's yours!'. Allow him to gobble up his titbit. Practise this a few times before his meals, then just put the dish down without throwing it and say to your puppy 'Fetch your dish!' The moment he brings it to you, place a succulent morsel in the dish and say 'It's yours!' If you are using dog biscuits as bait, rattle the tin for encouragement. At mealtimes always say to your puppy 'Fetch your dish!' and you will be surprised how quickly he learns this task, not only for you but for himself.

Jumping
It is probably better not to teach a dog to jump until he is a year old, particularly if he is of a large and heavy breed. Dogs enjoy jumping. One very good way of teaching him is to place a board not too high in a doorway. Put a collar and leash on your dog and take a good run up to the board. As you jump it yourself, lift the leash upwards and slightly forwards and give the command 'Simba over!', or, if you prefer it, 'Simba, hup!'. If the dog does not jump, lift him over with the leash. The jump should be so low that he really is only stepping over it with some encouragement from you. Practise this a few times, praising him profusely each time.

The next part of the lesson is also easy. Make your dog 'Sit-stay!' so that he is facing the doorway. Step over the jump quite quietly and enter the other room, then turn and face your dog. Hold the leash in your *right* hand and give the hand signal with your *left* hand, patting your chest or stomach or, for a small dog, your thigh. Give the command 'Simba, hup!' and, the moment he has gone over the jump, lavish him with praise. The next step is to send your dog over the jump into the next room by standing quite close to the jump. In no time at all you should be able to make your dog jump backwards and forwards from room to room. Praise him profusely each time, using an exciting tone of voice, but do not allow your dog to become bored.

Jumping Through a Hoop
This trick is fun for your dog and not difficult for him to do. Place the hoop in the doorway and bring your dog's leash through the hoop. Give him great encouragement and say 'Simba, hup!'. At first your dog may not care for the top of the hoop. If so place the hoop near the ground, so that your dog can just walk over the bottom of it so that he

becomes used to the arch above him. Gradually raise the hoop so that your dog has to jump. If he tries to go underneath the hoop, quickly lower it to prevent him from doing so. Go on practising the trick and eventually take the hoop right into the room, so that your dog no longer has the aid of the doorway.

To teach your dog to jump outside, set up a small jump about 30cm (1ft) high and, with your dog on a leash, run to the jump. As you get there say 'Simba, hup!' and jump over the obstacle with your dog. Practise a number of times, then teach your dog to make the jump on his own. This is quite easy. Make your dog 'Sit-stay!' about 2m (7ft) from the jump. Go to the other side of the jump and clap your hands, making the hand signal 'Come!' by patting your chest, and say 'Simba, come!' or 'Hup!'. Do not pat your thigh, because you want your dog to jump higher so that he will clear the obstacle. After a little more practice you will soon be able to teach your dog to jump over a stick held in your hand and later to jump over your arm. Whenever your dog performs correctly, lavish him with praise and affection and tell him what a clever dog he is and how proud you are of him.

7

Basic Obedience Training

There is, of course, no single method for training dogs. Each dog must be treated as an individual. Surprisingly, it is not the size of the dog, nor even the breed, that will determine the way in which he should be handled. It is the temperament of the dog which is the paramount consideration. Small, headstrong terriers may well require stronger handling than the more malleable labrador. On the other hand, shy, nervous or stubborn dogs will require quite different treatment. Dogs learn more by what they see than by what they hear; they absorb 75 per cent of their training from signals and 25 per cent from voice.

In general, working breeds like the ubiquitous german shepherd, the dobermann and the little sheltie are the easiest to train. Gundogs are not so easy to train for obedience work; they lack concentration because they are easily distracted by birds and animals. This is not at all surprising when you consider that a gundog can scent a man at a distance of 200 metres; perhaps even more surprising, he can scent a bird 75 metres away and can even distinguish what species it is. There is no excuse, therefore, for a trained gundog to flush and chase a hare or a rabbit. Terriers are difficult to train, because they are too individualistic. They normally require more patience and firmness owing to their headstrong character.

The easiest of all dogs to train is the non-sporting poodle, the standard poodle coming top of the list, followed closely by the miniature poodle. The little toy poodle, however, is not far behind. All dogs, nevertheless, can and should be taught normal basic training; some simply learn more quickly than others. A dog, of course, has far more patience than his trainer.

There is really nothing difficult in learning to train a dog. Anyone can do it, even a child. People who are good with children and animals will have no difficulty. Some people do have a natural rapport with dogs, and they therefore have a better understanding of what is required. Training, with experience, then becomes an art.

There is a great deal of difference between training your own much-loved dog, companion and friend, and having him trained by a professional obedience trainer who may have many dogs in training

Even a child can learn to train a dog. Note that the child's left hand should have been through the loop of the leash. Show dogs are exhibited with the leash in the left hand

at the same time. He will train your dog more precisely and faster, and he will be far stricter with your dog, both physically and verbally, than ever you will be. Your dog will be most beautifully trained for *him*, but you will find that your dog will not even begin to work well for *you* because he has to adjust his habit training to your ways. Your command tones, corrections and whistle will be quite different from the trainer's.

After such strict lessons, your dog is more than likely to become a great opportunist and to try to get away with all sort of antics. If he discovers that he can do what he wants whenever he feels like it, instead of doing what you have commanded, he will play up unless you take firm steps to prevent this. A dog will always obey a professional trainer, because he senses at once that the trainer knows what he is doing and will stand no nonsense, and the dog understands and respects this. The same dog may not obey his owner, however, if he finds that he is inconsistent or incompetent. He will detect the lack of authority and knowledge immediately.

A trainer should have authority, firmness and self-control. He must have endless patience and perseverance, kindness and consistency. He must know how to keep the lessons interesting and when to stop. He must know when to be firm and when to coax his dog. He must be one step ahead of him all the time and anticipate every move the dog is likely to make, so that a correction can be made before the dog has had time to make the mistake. A trainer must remember at all times that he is teaching the dog; he must never lose his temper, because the dog will not understand the cause of his anger. He must never repeat a command before a correction has been made. He must also never shout at the dog, particularly when he is running free, because he quickly becomes conditioned to not obeying a command unless it is shouted (how often this is seen out shooting!).

Dogs have very sensitive hearing. It is 140 per cent more acute than a man's. Moreover, they can detect exceedingly high frequencies which are inaudible to people; this is why the silent whistle is used for training dogs. A dog becomes trained to one whistle only, and so it is important that, if the dog changes hands, the whistle should go with him. The trainer's tones of voice are exceedingly important; he should use a coaxing voice, a normal voice and a commanding one. If the dog is nervous he should use an encouraging tone. If he is too excited, the trainer's voice should change to a quiet tone. The most important voice of all is the voice of genuine praise. All dogs, like people, adore praise, and so, in the early stages, a good trainer lavishes praise on his dog instantly at every genuine opportunity. A trainer must, above all, have the determination to succeed.

Never, never hit your dog in temper—dogs, like elephants, have exceedingly long memories. All corrections should only be made through the check-chain collar. It is absolutely taboo to throw chains at your dog or to use spiked collars as, I am afraid to say, some trainers do. This is totally unnecessary.

A good trainer is strict when he has to be, he is understanding of genuine mistakes made by the dog, and he is always consistent both with commands and with the leash corrections. Training should be enjoyable both for the trainer and the dog. This is made all the more so if the trainer has a good romp and play with the dog both before and after the training lesson.

However well a dog has been trained, it is absolutely essential that he should be given regular practice in what he has been taught. This applies equally to gundogs, obedience-trained dogs and pets. Like spoilt children, dogs that are permitted to disobey and roam on some occasions will quickly learn to take full advantage of the situation and will do so at every possible opportunity. Male dogs can scent a bitch on heat 3km (2 miles) away. When they get to her they may well find that there is the scent of a much more interesting bitch a further 3km on. It is grossly unfair to punish a dog that has been allowed to roam. If he is beaten for the same offence sometimes and not at other times, he will have no idea what he has done wrong. However, he will think that he is being beaten for coming home.

There is one simple way of preventing this confusion in a dog's mind and it does not cost very much. This is to make a long, narrow run so that the dog can get plenty of exercise on his own. Provide him with toys and a large knucklebone so that he does not become bored. His way of life, which soon becomes a habit, is divided between hours spent in the house, time in the run, and being out for exercise, training or shooting. You will be happier, your dog will certainly be much happier, the neighbourhood will be relieved, and the game-keepers and farmers will be delighted.

Training a dog is not only good for the dog, but it probably makes for happier relationships with neighbours and friends. One of the lovely things about training a dog is the wonderful rapport that is built up between you both. There is tremendous satisfaction in watching your dog work well and happily for you, not to mention the respect, love and affection that is so genuinely given. Your dog talks to you with every fibre of his being, as well as with his eyes, ears and tail. You are delighted when he has done well and the dog in turn shows his immense pleasure in having pleased you. A twenty-minute lesson every day is of the most marvellous therapeutic value. It is, in my opinion, far better than a session of meditation.

Training a dog improves your self-discipline and strengthens your character, perseverance and patience. You become more under-standing and at the same time acquire greater calm and serenity. You cannot possibly worry about your problems while you are train-ing a dog; the sheer concentration that is necessary precludes all other thoughts. It therefore provides excellent mental relaxation.

Formal Training
Once your puppy has reached the age of seven or eight months he is ready for more formal training. If you would like to train him for obedience work then this is the time to start. Personally, I do not care for this exacting, military-style, precision training for obedience tests. I feel sure that not all dogs enjoy this work, particularly if their trainer is not outstandingly proficient and extremely patient. The

time taken to train a dog to a high standard is about eighteen months of continuous work.

Hand Signals

During normal basic obedience training your dog is taught the various hand signals which go with the commands. This makes his training faster. Once your dog is really proficient, he can learn to obey in complete silence without any verbal commands. In the signal exercise in obedience tests the handler may use any signal he wishes, with movement of his hands, provided that they do not touch his body as part of the signal. The handler usually waits a full thirty seconds between any two signals.

It can be most confusing to the novice to know which hand is used for the various hand signals. It is quite obvious which hand must be used for certain signals; in other cases, it may depend on whether you are training your dog for exhibition or obedience. The important factor is that, whichever signals you decide to use, you must be consistent and always use only those signals. Throw the signal at your dog showing the position of the palm of your hand, so that the dog can recognise the signal with ease.

Quick Guide to Hand Signals

Sit! Use your *left* hand, fingers towards the ground, if your dog is at heel. At a distance stretch your fingers out.

Sit-stay! If you are standing in front of your dog, use your *left* hand, palm in front of your dog's eyes, fingers slightly raised. If you are standing sideways in front of your dog, use your *left* hand, fingers towards the ground, palm towards your dog.

Stand-stay! Throw the palm of your *left* hand towards your dog.

Down! Use your *right* hand, arm up and out level with your head, and keep your fingers spread if your dog is at a distance. When your dog is at the end of the leash, use your *right* hand, palm lower down, in front of your dog.

Come! This is known as the 'recall'. Place the palm of your *left* hand in front of your chest, or your stomach if the dog is small. It is better than patting your thigh or making a sweeping gesture past your leg, as it makes your dog raise his head and look happier as he comes in.

The Finish Use your *left* hand, fingers towards the ground. Swing

your palm round behind you and back to your side
for 'Heel!' (This is 'Go to Heel')

Stand for examination	*Right* hand, fingers slightly raised.
Between signals	Keep your arms at your sides. Allow thirty seconds between signals.

The Leash
During training the leash is sometimes held in the right hand and
sometimes in the left and occasionally in both hands. It is held in the
left hand for 'Stand for examination' (by a judge), for conformation
classes, and also when signals are made with the *right* hand, as with
the two commands 'Down!' and 'Down-stay!'. Both hands may be
used for a severe correction. The leash is held in the *right* hand for
the heeling exercise, so that the left hand is free to make corrections
on the leash and for petting and encouraging the dog.

The leash should be held with the palm of the hand through the
loop at one end and, unless the leash is required to be loose or
looped, the slack should be folded loosely in the palm of the hand, so
that there is nothing dangling in front of the dog's head. When the
leash is required to be held so that it is just taut and short it should be
folded more tightly. All corrections are made through the leash by a
quick snap-jerk-release action, either forwards or sideways and
always across you. The dog must, however, never associate the
correction with you, so do not look at him when you make the correction. He must only think that the sharp jerk on his throat that is
uncomfortable and which throws him off balance is entirely his own
fault. If you have an extremely difficult dog, one strong correction
with the leash is better than many weak, ineffectual ones.

Footwork
Footwork is important in dog training, so that you should wear soft-
soled shoes. When heeling, always start off with your *left* foot. The
dog learns that this means action. Once he is trained, it will not
matter which foot you start off with. For the 'Stand-stay!' exercise,
move forward with the *right* foot. The dog learns that this means no
action on his own part—he must stay still. If the dog moves too far to
the side when heeling, you must take a step to the opposite side. If he
goes too far ahead, take several steps backwards as you snap-jerk-
release the leash. You can make corrections by taking small steps or
large strides, or by pivoting on one foot. You should also alter your
speed from time to time, to keep your dog alert.

To sum up, your dog will learn more easily if you give the correct verbal commands in the right tone of voice, and make exaggeratedly precise hand signals with the hand not holding the leash. Aid your dog by starting off with your *left* foot if you want action or with your *right* foot if he is to remain where he is. For the Finish you move your *right* foot back to help you balance when you swing your dog behind you.

Quick Guide To Training

1   The key to all training is praise, kindness and consistency, and it is based on trust, affection and the correct use of the leash.
2   You will require much more patience than you think you will.
3   Your dog has much more patience than you have.
4   You must think both for yourself and for your dog.
5   Your dog learns by constant repetition and by conditioning his reflexes over a long period of time.
6   You will achieve the best results if your dog learns slowly over a long period.
7   Training does not advance evenly: there are periods of rapid progress, difficult periods, and times when seemingly no progress is made at all.
8   Your dog must never connect you, the trainer, with unpleasant experiences. He must think that they are entirely due to his own fault, such as bumping into you when heeling, or the pressure on his throat from the collar.
9   He learns that certain consequences are pleasing while others are displeasing.
10   He must learn that your *left* side provides his refuge: nothing unpleasant happens there.
11   He learns that your *left* hand is for caressing and for certain signals. He must never know that it is used for imparting corrections on the leash. Hand signals make training faster.
12   Your dog learns that correct behaviour leads to praise and comfort, whereas incorrect behaviour unaccountably results in discomfort and no praise or caresses.
13   Once your dog understands a lesson he will learn more rapidly if he is praised intermittently: he will be trying to earn his next praise.
14   Your dog must learn his lesson well before starting a new one.
15   If a new lesson is difficult, revert to an easy one where he will receive praise instead of being corrected.

16 Your dog will find training enjoyable at first. Keep it so, or else the novelty may soon wear off.

17 Vary the training to avoid your dog becoming bored.

18 Do assess your dog's temperament, so that you do not use too strong or too weak corrections.

19 Keep the lessons relaxed. If you find you are losing your temper stop immediately. Nothing will be achieved.

20 Never damp your dog's enthusiasm, and do not make him resentful.

21 Never laugh at your dog; he will not take the lesson seriously.

22 Do not allow your dog to sniff the ground; he will not be paying attention to you.

23 Keep the training sessions short; one twenty-minute period or two ten-minute periods, in the same place and at the same time each day for a minimum of five days a week.

24 Keep to your dog's vocabulary; same commands, same signals, same tones of voice, and same whistle. If you vary any of these you will confuse your dog.

25 Do not use your dog's name unnecessarily; it will confuse him and lead to mistakes. Never use his name for passive commands such as 'Sit!', 'Stay!', 'Down!'.

26 Try to avoid using negative terms such as 'No!', 'Stop it!'. Rather use positive terms such as 'Stay!', 'Come!'.

27 Anticipate your dog's mistakes and prevent them before he makes them, so that you can give praise instead of a correction.

28 Watch your dog's reactions; if he backs away from you he is afraid of you, or if his tail is down he is unhappy. He should obey you because he loves and trusts you, not because he is afraid of you.

29 Beating a dog may make him obey you because he is afraid of you, but it will take you many months to regain his confidence and trust, and you may never do so.

30 Never reprimand your dog when he comes to you, even if he has just misbehaved himself. He will think he is being scolded for the act of coming to you. Coming to you must be a pleasure to him.

31 If you have an excitable dog, use slow movements and quiet, low tones.

32 If your dog is sluggish, move faster and use enthusiastic and exciting tones.

33 Do not touch your dog except when necessary.

34 All training is common sense; do not call 'Come' when you see your dog running after another dog (he is unlikely to obey you).

35 Before you start training you must learn how to use and crack your leash like a whip. It is a snap-jerk-release action with your *left* hand palm down which you must make with authority. It is useless if it is too weak, and it is cruel if too strong. You must not look at your dog when you make the snap-jerk-release; it is done to startle him and to take him off balance. If you are walking do not stop nor alter your speed.

36 Keep your eye on your dog except when making a correction.

37 Be sure to keep his attention and to make him concentrate.

38 Be fair, but firm; we all have our off days and so do dogs.

39 Make a pause between each correction, praise and command.

40 *Never* repeat a command before correcting your dog, ie a double command.

41 If you have to repeat a command after making a correction, each command must be given more demandingly, and each leash correction more forcefully. If your dog continues not to respond, go through his repertoire so that you can take the opportunity of praising him.

42 In the early lessons give praise and encouragement at every opportunity. Later give praise intermittently.

43 Give adequate praise after each command, as soon as your dog is in the correct position.

44 On accepting any object from a retrieve keep your head down and do not stare at your dog, and then thank him.

45 When your dog is heeling, if he goes ahead of you take a step backwards. If he is too far to your left take a step to your right. If he is slow coming in to you run backwards.

46 If your dog makes a mistake when he is close to you, allow him to move from you and continue the mistake so that you have sufficient room to crack the leash.

47 Confine your dog for two hours before a lesson.

48 Play and romp with your dog before and after a lesson.

49 Never end a lesson *before* your dog is performing correctly, so that he can earn praise. He must finish every lesson happily so that he will look forward to the next one.

50 Resist the temptation to give your dog endless, unnecessary commands in the house when he is off duty. If you do, he will become bored and not work with alacrity.

51 Learn the places where your dog enjoys being scratched or patted.

52 When you use titbits as bait, choose something your dog enjoys, like baked liver.

8

'Heel!'

This is a dog term which means teaching your dog to walk on your left side with his head close to your leg. The command—which is the first command of formal training that your dog will learn—does not mean that his head should be near your heel. However, this is of no consequence to your dog; he simply has to learn the command 'Heel!'

If you have had your puppy from an early age, he will already have had some basic training and will know how to 'Sit', 'Stand', 'Stay' and 'Lie down'. This he will have learnt from his first grooming training and from the natural, spontaneous, behavioural words that you will have used whenever you have seen him about to do something which will form part of his training. He will also know how to walk on a lead. All this will make his future training much easier. If, on the other hand, your new puppy is already over seven months old and has had no previous training, then his formal training will take a little longer and you will need to be more patient and understanding, but you can still use the behavioural words.

To train your dog to heel you will require a metal check-chain collar, a 1.5m (5ft) leash, and a suitable, quiet, flat area, preferably without trees and fenced in, about 15m (50ft) square. You can also train your dog in a park or a quiet road.

Try to train your dog five days a week in the same place and at the same time and preferably some three hours after a meal. No lesson should last more than twenty minutes; alternatively use two sessions of ten minutes. The first lesson, depending on how well your dog does, should not be more than five or ten minutes. Your dog should be performing reasonably well in four days, and he can then start to learn the automatic sit. This should take about a week. To make training faster, you should also incorporate hand signals.

The Check-Chain Collar
The check-chain collar should be the correct size for your dog and should be made of good metal. On the whole, the broader the links of the chain, the more comfortable the collar will be for your dog, provided that the collar is not too heavy and that the links slide

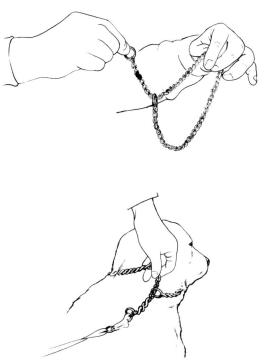

(a) Correct way of putting on a check-chain collar

through the ring with ease. On an average-sized dog the collar should slip over the head easily and, when the collar is tightened round the dog's throat, there should be 75mm (3in) of collar to spare. To make up the collar, simply hold one of the rings in each hand, lift one hand immediately above the other and then drop the top part of the chain slowly through the ring held in the lower hand until the two rings meet. You have now formed a collar from the original straight chain, with the large rings at either end.

Dogs are normally trained to walk on the left-hand side of the handler, in which case you must put the collar over your dog's head so that the chain pulls in an upward direction from left to right. The leash is fastened to the end of the chain which passes over the top of the dog's neck, not under it. It is most important that the collar be put on correctly. When you attach the leash to the collar you will notice that the moment you release all pressure on the leash the whole chain will drop, and there will be no pressure on your dog's throat. Always permit your dog to become used to this new slip-collar for a few days before you actually start teaching him to heel. Take him for a few walks with his new collar so that be becomes accustomed to it.

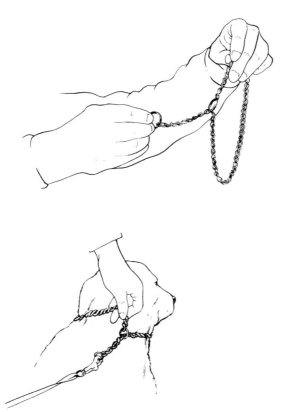

(b) Incorrect check-chain collar (NB The links should be larger — these would hurt the dog

The Leash
You will need a light, strong 1.5m (5ft) leash about 12mm to 20mm ($\frac{1}{2}$-$\frac{3}{4}$in) in width. It should be made either of soft pliable leather, which should be kept soft with saddle soap, or of cotton webbing. A soft leather one will hurt your hand less should you have a strong, unruly dog, but whichever type of leash you choose it should have a strong spring hook. The most suitable length and width for the leash will depend on the size and strength of the dog you are training. The lighter the leash the better.

Before the Lesson
Before teaching your dog to walk at heel you should prepare your lesson carefully, and make sure that you thoroughly understand what and how you are going to teach: your tones of voice commands (the command for heeling should be given in a pleasant, encouraging voice); when the commands are to be given; and, most importantly, the manipulation of the leash and check-chain collar.

Also decide on the time your lesson should last.

You should practise the sideways flick of the wrist and the jerk and let go' with the leash, either by finding someone to hold the collar, or by tying it round the side of a chair. The sharp jerk on the collar is the only admonishment you may give your dog whilst you are teaching him to heel. It is the split-second jerk on the check-chain collar that takes the dog by surprise and throws him off balance. A jerk is not a pull. The leash must be loose at all times except when the split-second snap-jerk-release for the 'correction' is made with authority. It is same movement as cracking a whip across you.

Never use a command as a correction. The moment your dog is walking by your side correctly, praise him and, whilst he is still doing so and has responded to the 'correction', then give the command 'Heel!' in an encouraging voice. Keep practising the split-second jerk-and-let-go, which is done with your left hand on the leash, palm down. The force you require to use will depend upon your dog. If your dog does not react, then you are not using enough force in your jerk. If, on the other hand, your dog suddenly whimpers or cowers, then you are using far too much strength.

Dog and Trainer Mistakes
The most common mistake that you are likely to make in your training is to allow the leash to become taut. This means, either that you have not reacted quickly enough to start the jerk-release before your dog has got to the end of the leash, so that you are pulling your dog back to the correct position instead of jerking him back, or that you are altering your pace when you make the jerk-release. You may, on the other hand, be holding the leash too loosely so that valuable time is lost in taking up the slack, or snapping the leash up and down.

Other likely mistakes are that you are applying too much or too little force with the leash; that you are not leaving enough time between corrections, praise and commands; and, finally, that you are not keeping your eye on your dog at all times (except when you correct him). In this way you will lose many opportunities to correct your dog.

The common mistakes that your dog is likely to make are to lunge ahead of you or to lag behind; to try to jump up and play; to insist on sniffing the ground; or to heel wide. If your dog insists on sniffing the ground, move to another area or jerk-release his head upwards. If he persists, scuff your foot along the ground between his nose and the scent that he finds so enticing.

In order to make lessons more enjoyable for your dog have a good romp and play with him both before you start the lesson and afterwards. When you want the training session to start, get your dog's attention and tell him 'Simba, now it is training time'.

Teaching Your Dog to Heel

You should start your lesson by making your dog sit close to you on your left side. Adjust the length of the leash, which you should hold in your *right* hand. Your right hand should be held comfortably, slightly in front of your body, so that the leash hangs in a loop between your hand and the check-collar. The check-chain collar is then loose round your dog's neck and there is no pressure at all round his throat.

Your left hand is used for correcting. You must not take your eyes

———————————————

(below left) 'Heel!' The lesson starts, the dog is sitting. The loop of the leash is in the right hand. The spring hook is attached to the ring in the check-chain collar which goes over the back of the dog's neck. The right hand is held at the side and slightly in front of the waist. Dog and trainer's feet are in a straight line. The command is 'Heel!' in a pleasant, encouraging voice. The trainer will step forward with the left foot and slap her leg with her left hand

(below right) Trainer and dog move off at a brisk pace. The trainer walks towards a spot straight ahead; the dog has pulled her off course and is heeling wide. She will now slap her left thigh to encourage him to come in

off your dog. Get your dog's attention by saying in an inviting voice 'Simba, heel!' Slap your hand on your left side and walk forward with your *left* foot. If your dog does not know how to walk on a lead, he will probably lunge ahead of you. Allow him to get almost to the end of the leash and, *before* the leash becomes taut, grip it with your *left* hand with the palm facing the ground and give it a smart jerk across you. This will bring your dog back to your side. You must release the leash immediately; the action is a smart 'crack' on the leash followed by a 'jerk-release'. The check-chain automatically tightens on your dog's throat and impedes his breathing momentarily, so that the jerk takes him by surprise and throws him off balance. The moment your dog is at your side once again, praise him saying 'Good boy' or 'Clever girl'.

Whilst your dog is walking correctly in the heeling position, command him by name, thus alerting him for action, with 'Simba, heel!' Keep walking at the same pace and do not slow down or stop when you make the jerk-release action. After each jerk-release the check-chain collar loosens and the leash will once again fall in a loop. Always make the jerk-release action before your dog gets to the end of the leash and it becomes taut. If this happens, it is

Encourage the lagger by patting your left thigh. Jerk-release the leash with your left hand, flicking it across your thighs

92

impossible to crack the leash and jerk it, and you will end up committing the unforgivable sin of pulling on the leash instead of jerking and then releasing it. If you pull on the leash you are throttling your dog and putting him in grave discomfort.

Start walking slowly (stepping off with the *left* foot) and increase your speed to a brisk walk, so that your dog can trot beside you at a comfortable pace. Keep encouraging him with kind words, coax him and, if he strays too far from your side, slap your left leg with the palm of your hand. Occasionally, bend down and pat your dog. If he wants to jump up and play, say 'No!' firmly. If he lags behind, encourage him to come to you by taking quick short steps; use an exciting tone of voice to give more encouragement, jerk your dog forward with a light, forward movement and praise him the moment he is beside you. Keep patting, talking to and praising your dog and you will soon have him walking happily beside you with his head in line with your left leg. Remember that the leash is jerked across you, not up and down.

When to Give a Command
When your dog walks beside you of his own accord, with the leash quite slack, and responds to your light jerk-release, this is the moment when you give the command 'Simba, heel!'

If your dog has not learnt to sit during his puppy training, you can start his heel training when you have got him standing calmly on your left side. Get your dog's attention by calling his name, then give the command 'Simba, heel!' and start walking immediately after the word 'heel'. Give the leash a sharp jerk-release forward in the direction you are going to walk. Do not make the mistake of making the jerk-release in an upward direction. If your dog is a long-legged dog, then you should take longer steps; if he is small, then you should take shorter steps. Your speed in either case may be brisk because both small and large dogs can trot along quite happily at a good speed. If your dog is inclined to be excited, then walk a little more slowly; if he is sluggish, urge him to move more briskly. Always walk towards a definite spot so that he cannot pull you off course.

Walking in Different Directions
If your dog continues to rush ahead of you instead of heeling, let him do so, but just before he gets to the end of the leash, make your short, sharp jerk-release movement with your *left* hand and, as you do so, keep your *right* hand held into your body. Turn and walk in the opposite direction, guide your dog into the correct heel position and praise him with 'Well done! Good boy!' You may have to do this half

If he lunges ahead, take him off balance by turning round with a sharp jerk-release, keep your right hand hard into your waist and walk in the opposite direction

As you turn, jerk-release the leash sharply with the left hand. The novice makes the mistake of not giving the correction with her left hand and is caught off balance, so that she is unable to bring the dog into the heel position

a dozen times before your dog responds. If your dog is being difficult you will have to make a series of sharp jerk-release movements, increasing the strength of each jerk. On the final jerk-release, turn round and once again walk in the opposite direction.

Walking Wide

If your dog keeps walking wide, slap your leg and encourage him to come close. You may have to jerk him to your side, praising him immediately he is there. The moment the check-chain slackens your dog will feel more comfortable and he will also soon realise that this is pleasant and is followed by praise. If you can find a wall it is quite helpful to walk close to it, so that your dog has no opportunity to walk wide of you. If he walks too close, bump him hard with your knee or leg, which he will find unpleasant; he will soon learn that he prefers the comfort and praise of walking correctly to heel (see page 96).

Difficult Dogs

If your dog insists on being difficult and keeps darting ahead of you, make a series of very fast about-turns. You will be surprised how effective this is. As a variation, instead of turning and walking in the opposite direction, as you make the jerk-release movement, take three quick steps backwards and immediately walk forward again without stopping. Guide your dog back to his correct position by the side of your left leg, praise him while you continue walking and give the command 'Heel!' (see page 97).

Do Not be Impatient

Keep your first lesson down to ten minutes, stopping the lesson when your dog is moving well at heel. Praise him and make much of him. You must now let your dog know that his lesson is over by saying something like 'Lesson over' or 'You are free now' in a happy tone. At the same time release your dog and have a game and a romp with him. He will enjoy this and will look forward to it.

You should increase the length of subsequent heeling lessons to twenty minutes. As soon as your dog is heeling correctly, keep walking briskly, make a right-angle turn to your left and guide your dog into position. Next take a step to your right and make a right-angle turn to your right. To make your lesson more interesting and to keep your dog's attention on you, keep making turns to the left and to the right and about-turns. Remember to leave suitable gaps between your commands, corrections and praise. If your dog insists on jumping up, speak in a sharp and reproving manner, saying 'No!' or 'No! naughty!' and, at the same moment as a punishment, but still

(above) 'Heel!' The correction is made by taking a step to the side away from the dog. The left hand grasps the leash and makes a quick jerk-release which brings the dog into the correct heeling position. The moment the dog is walking correctly, say 'Heel!', praise and pat him

(left) If your dog moves too close, take up the slack with your left hand (which the novice here has failed to do), bump him hard with your left knee between his neck and shoulder. Keep right hand close to waist. If he is in front of you, bump him hard with your right knee, hitting his chest

If your dog forges ahead, before the leash becomes taut, the left hand gives a sharp jerk-release on the leash and at the same time you take a step backwards, jerking him to the heel position. When your dog is moving correctly, give the command 'Heel!' and praise him

keeping the same brisk pace, jerk the leash straight up. Your dog will not care for this. The moment he has all four feet on the ground again, make a sharp turn to the left and make sure you praise him.

You must not over-tire your dog during his lessons, and you must never frighten him or scold him. He will be trying his utmost to please you, but he may not understand what you want from him. It is up to you to teach your dog and, if he does not understand, then perhaps you are doing something wrong and are not teaching him correctly. You are learning too, and you may find that lessons do not always go as smoothly as you wish.

In all your dog's training, you will find that there are periods when his progress is rapid and times when he seems to make no progress at all. Take heart. Teaching your dog to heel correctly is the most difficult lesson you will have to teach him. It should not be more than four days before your dog gets the idea. From then on it will be a question of practice and more practice, varying your speed from a slow walk to running, walking in a circle to the right several times and then to the left. Try zigzagging a three-quarter turn to the right and then to the left. By doing these exercises you will keep your dog alert and having to keep his attention on you; he must be on the ball to keep up with you, to slow down with you and not to bump into you.

Quick Guide to Heeling

Place	Quiet area 15m (50ft) square, or quiet road or park.
Requirements	Check-chain collar of good metal with strong links. Leather or webbing leash 1.5m (5ft) in length with spring hook.
Select point	Decide to walk to a particular point such as a tree or post.
Tone of voice	Pleasant and encouraging and with authority.
Name	Alert your dog before command by calling him by name.
Leash	Hold in *right* hand close to and slightly in front of your waist. Leash is loose and looped in front of your body. No pressure on your dog's throat.
Lesson time	Tell your dog in a serious tone 'Lesson time'.
Start of lesson	Dog sits on your *left* in line with your leg.
Command	'Simba, heel!'
Signal	Slap your *left* leg with your *left* hand.
Walk forward	Start off with your *left* foot.
Speed	Start slowly, increase to a brisk walk. Keep the same pace and walk to your pre-decided point.
Pace	Do not change your pace or stop when you make the 'jerk-release' correction (this can be difficult).
Correction	A sufficiently strong jerk-release action with your *left* hand grasping the leash before it becomes taut. Do not look at your dog when you do this. If your dog darts ahead, the only correction you may make is through the leash (it takes the dog off balance by jerking him sideways).
Dog in correct position, head by your left leg	Only now may you praise your dog, ie when his head is by your *left* side.

First correct steps	Only when your dog is moving correctly by your side may you give the command 'Heel!'
Never repeat a command before making a correction	Make any correction with your *left* hand through the leash. Help your dog with the hand signal. Jerk him back to his correct position, head by your leg.
Praise	Praise and pat your dog at every opportunity in the early lessons, provided that everything is correct. Say 'Good boy' or 'Clever girl'.
Jumping up	If your dog jumps up or wants to play, say 'No!' in a sharp, reproving tone.
Pulling on leash	Never pull on the leash; *always* use a sharp jerk-release with the necessary strength with your *left* hand.
About-turn	When your dog darts forward, jerk-release the leash with your *left* hand and turn and walk in the opposite direction.
No verbal reprimand	Do not reprimand your dog for not heeling correctly. Use the leash jerk-release correction only, whipping it across your thighs.
No talking	Do not talk to your dog except for commands, praise and encouragement. *Never* laugh at him.
Ten about-turns	Eight or ten about-turns in the first lesson.
Vary procedure	Give jerk-release with *left* hand, at the same time take three rapid steps backwards without halting. Continue forward, guide your dog to heel position and praise him.
Dog walks wide	Jerk-release leash, at the same time step to the *right*.
Let dog out	If your dog is too close you cannot jerk-release. If you pull your dog, it is an unforgivable sin on your part.
Right-angle turns	If your dog is slow on the *left* turn, bump into him smartly.
After jerk-release	Step backwards or sideways, or bump into him with your leg, to help correction.
Punishment	Your dog must never realise that the admonishment comes from you; he must think that the discomfort on his throat is his own fault.
Dog lags behind	Encourage your dog, jerk-release him forward gently, pat your leg, praise him. Increase your speed taking *short steps*. Encouraging voice more important than anything else.

99

Bounding about	If your dog bounds about, keep to the same pace, say: 'No!' emphatically, jerk-release leash straight up in the air, keep walking, get your dog's attention and do some turns.
End of lesson	Tell your dog 'Lesson over' or 'Off you go'.
Romp and play with dog	It is important that your dog should enjoy and look forward to his training. Make a great fuss of him.
Extra aids	Give lesson not less than three hours after your dog's meal. Confine him to a room or kennel two hours before lesson. Walk along the side of a long wall. Vary your speeds, prevent boredom and over-tiredness. Once your dog understands your command, he will learn more rapidly if you praise him intermittently.
Jerk-release	The leash must be slack at all times except when the split-second·snap-jerk-release is made for a correction. The movements are: *left* palm on leash; sideways flick of the wrist; jerk the leash across you, letting it go immediately so that you avoid pulling on the leash. The object is to startle your dog and take him off balance.

9

Automatic Sit, 'Sit!' and 'Sit-stay!'

Automatic Sit

Teaching your dog to sit automatically is an easy lesson for him to learn, and you may start teaching him after two or three heeling lessons. The command 'Sit!' is given without using your dog's name, in a sharp, clear manner. Never repeat the command before making a correction. At the same time as you give your dog the command 'Sit!' tap him sharply and smartly on his rump with your fingertips. Practise tapping your fingers on the back of your hand or low down on your own back, and you will soon get the idea. Tap your dog near his tail, never near his shoulders. You should practise the movements you will be required to use with a leash tied to a chair before you actually start trying to teach your dog to sit. If your dog is a large, thick-coated breed, you may need to slap his rump, but what you must not do is to push your dog into a sitting position.

Tap your dog sharply and praise him immediately, petting him with your *left* hand. Your dog will learn to sit very quickly, because he will be waiting for his praise. Most dogs will learn the automatic sit in a week, which is very encouraging for the trainer.

Practise the Leash Movements

To practise the leash movements for the automatic sit, tie your leash to a chair about the height of your dog's neck. Imagine that after heeling you have come to an abrupt stop; the leash is looped between your dog's collar and your *right* hand, and your dog's head is in line with your *left* leg (your dog must not be in front of you). Now, raise your *right* hand immediately above your dog's collar, making the leash reasonably taut. Grasp the middle of the leash with your *left* hand, letting it go with your *right* hand, then, keeping your *left* hand immediately above your dog's collar, grasp the leash a few centimetres above your dog's head with your *right* hand. Let go of the leash with your *left* hand, and with the same hand tap your dog on his rump. As you do so, pull the leash in your *right* hand upwards and slightly backwards, and at the same time give the command 'Sit!' sharply. The leash should be in a straight line immediately above your dog's head (see page 102).

101

Automatic sit, dog is on trainer's left. Leash folded up and taut. Give the command sharply and clearly: 'Sit!' Pull leash straight up and slightly backwards and with left hand tap the dog sharply with finger tips on his rump

The Correct Sitting Position

What you are trying to do is, a fraction of a second before you halt, to pull up on the leash and tap your dog down, saying 'Sit!' Your dog should sit about 25cm (10in) away from your leg with his toes and your toes in the same straight line. He must sit squarely on his haunches. The timing of each movement is most important. To make your dog sit correctly, tap him down and pull upwards on the leash, thus guiding him into the correct position. If he sits wide, tap him lightly on the outer side of his left hip. If he sits too close, tap the opposite hip. If he rushes ahead, be very quick with your correction; give the command 'Sit!' and tap your dog's croup sharply to make him sit quickly. As he starts to sit, release all pressure on the leash, give him lavish praise, and pet him with your *left* hand. If he sits too far behind, you can either hold your fingers a little in front of his nose and encourage him to move forward—if he does, praise and pet him—or you can take a couple of steps forward and, as soon as your dog is level with your left leg, command him to 'Sit!'

Some dogs are inclined to lean on your legs, in which case step smartly to the side so that he will overbalance and tell him to 'Sit!', making certain that he does so correctly. A slight push with your knee may straighten your dog, but it is probably better to guide him into the required position entirely with the leash.

As your dog learns to sit every time you stop, he expects the praise and petting with your left hand. Gradually, you can stop the aids as he becomes more proficient: first eliminate the pull upwards on the leash, giving only the command and the praise-and-pat; next leave out the finger-tap; then, once your dog understands that when you halt this means he must sit, give up the command 'Sit!' altogether.

If your dog is the type that likes to rush ahead of you, you will need to give him the automatic sit exercise very frequently, somewhere between every six or ten steps. On the other hand, if your dog is slow and is inclined to lag behind you, do not halt so frequently. Keep walking for perhaps thirty or forty steps before you again give the command 'Sit!'

It is important that you should vary the procedure as much as possible in order to keep the lesson interesting and to make your dog pay attention. Keep your eyes on your dog all the time and try to be one jump ahead of him, recognising the fault he is about to make, so that you can guide him into the correct position with the leash before he sits incorrectly. Walk a distance of perhaps thirty steps before giving the command to sit; then move only a few paces before giving the 'Sit!' command. Then try fifteen paces and a quick succession of sits with odd numbers of paces between them. Walk in several circles to the right, then straight ahead, then circle to the left, and so on.

About the beginning of your second week of training, ascertain whether your dog really does understand the command 'Sit!' If he stands when you halt, give him the command 'Sit!' in a quiet voice. If he sits immediately, without any guidance from the leash or your fingers, then you will know that he has learnt the command but was not concentrating when you stopped.

During the automatic sit exercise it is important to vary your speed, especially as your dog becomes more proficient. He should, however, never be permitted to break into a gallop—a fast trot is the quickest speed you should expect. If your dog breaks into a gallop, jerk-release the leash and at the same time take a step backwards. This will bring him to your left side again.

A Fun Method
You can have fun teaching your dog to heel and sit automatically if you have two people to join in the training. This is particularly enjoyable when you have a family dog because a husband or wife or child can help with the proceedings.

The person who is actually training the dog walks as usual with him on his left, while the other person walks quite close to the dog on his other side. The trainer gives the commands and the extra person makes the corrections. The dog walking between the two people receives lavish praise from them both!

The Figure of Eight
A most useful exercise is the figure of eight, which teaches your dog to stay close to your side in a crowded street. If you intend to pass a person on your right and your dog decides he prefers to pass the person on his left, the three of you can become unnecessarily entangled, even perhaps tripping the pedestrian up.

Find two posts or objects which you should place 2–3m (7–8ft) apart. Take the first time round at a reasonable speed. Start by standing to the left of the first post. Give the command 'Simba, heel!', walk to the centre and go round the post turning to the left and keeping as close to the post as possible. Return to the centre and then proceed round the other post, again keeping as close to the post as you can, moving round to the right and back to the centre. Give the command, without your dog's name, 'Sit!'

You will find that with this exercise your dog will probably lag behind you. Coax him, praise him, talk to him and encourage him. You may have to jerk-release the leash several times. Try to anticipate the place your dog is likely to lag behind you. Do not alter your pace on the turns (you will find a fairly brisk pace the best). When your dog starts to crowd you on the inside turn, bump him (by accident!) with your knee. If he tries to go on the wrong side of the post, tighten the leash until your dog corrects his position and praise him lavishly when he does. To begin with you can help your dog when turning to the right by taking small steps, so that he does not get too far behind; similarly, when turning to the left take long steps when your dog is on the inside, so that he will not have to alter his pace.

Once your dog has the idea of staying close to you, incorporate the automatic sit and varying distances and try to keep to a brisk pace all the time. As your dog becomes even more proficient, instead of using posts try using people, and then people holding their dogs on leashes. This experience will teach your dog to concentrate on you and to take no notice of other dogs, and he will keep his mind on the lesson. Remember, constant praise and encouragement and keep your lesson short and interesting, only stopping when your dog is doing well. Then release him from his lesson and have a good romp and play with him.

Quick Guide to the Automatic Sit

Dog's position	About 25cm (10in) from your *left* side.
Tone of voice	Clear and sharp.
No name	Do not use your dog's name.
Command	'Sit!'
Speed	Brisk.
Start of exercise	With the command 'Simba, heel!' Leash in *right* hand.
Halt	Suddenly stop when your dog is going well.
Hand movements	*Right* hand, with leash over dog's head, held high. *Left* hand, grasp middle of leash. *Right* hand, take leash 15cm (6in) above collar and pull straight up.
Tap or slap	*Left* hand, tap with fingers, or slap dog's rump smartly.
Give command	'Sit!' at the same time as the leash is pulled up and croup is tapped sharply down by the tail.
Dog sits wide	Tap with *left* hand on your dog's *left* hip.
Dog sits close	Tap with *left* hand on your dog's *right* hip.
Dog sits in front	Take several steps forward, encourage your dog to follow. When your dog is level with your leg, give command 'Sit!'
Dog leans on your leg	Step to side so that your dog overbalances.
Praise and pet	Praise and pet your dog at every opportunity.
Eliminate aids	Give up the upward pull on leash. Stop the finger tap or slap on rump.
Stop command	After halting, stop giving the command when your dog sits automatically.
Dog stands instead of sits	Because he is not concentrating. Give the command 'Sit!' in a *quiet* voice.
Vary pace	Vary pace and strides, make figures of eight.

'Sit!'

If your dog was not taught to sit when he was a young puppy then you will have to teach him to sit in situations other than the automatic sit when heeling. He must learn to sit whenever you tell him.

Stand in front of your dog and get his attention. Remember you must only tap your dog close to his tail once; any correction is done with the leash. With the leash held fairly short in your *right* hand, so

'Sit!' Trainer stands in front of dog, leash in right hand, folded and just taut. Give command 'Sit!', pull up on leash and tap croup down

that you can keep it just taut above your dog's collar (the latter is brought up high on his throat and under his chin) give the command to sit and pull the leash straight up above your dog's collar. Extend your *left* hand over his back and smartly tap your fingers just above his tail, at the same moment giving the command, 'Sit!' without using your dog's name. Practise this in different areas, but start by choosing comfortable places for your dog to do the exercise, eg a smooth lawn rather than a wet muddy field. Practise the 'Sit!' command standing in front of your dog, to the side of him or to his rear, each time pulling the leash up straight above his collar and tapping his rump down sharply with the fingers of your *left* hand. The moment you see that your dog is going to sit of his own accord and not at your command, do not tap him down. Do not forget your immediate praise.

In this first important week of his training, your dog has learnt to heel, the automatic sit and the sit command. That shows you that it is not too difficult for either you or your dog. Neither of you will be perfect, but you should both be coming along well with a great deal of regular practice.

Quick Guide to Sit in All Situations

Dog's position	Standing in front of you.
Tone of voice	Sharp and clear.
No name	Do not use your dog's name.
Command	'Sit!'
Start of exercise	Stand in front of your dog.
Leash	Held fairly short in your *right* hand, just taut above your dog's collar, which is brought up under his chin.
Movements	Pull leash straight up above your dog's collar with your *right* hand.
Tap or slap	Lean over your dog and tap his rump sharply with the fingers of your *left* hand.
Give command	'Sit!' at the same time as leash is pulled up and croup is tapped down.
Practise	Practise the 'Sit!' and vary the place where you stand.
Vary your position	Sometimes give the 'Sit!' lesson standing at the side, in front, or behind your dog.
Praise and pet	Praise and pet your dog at every opportunity. Scratch his chest.
Aids	Choose a good area and conditions for sitting—soft grass, not a hard wet road, a windy day or when pouring with rain.
All exercises	Continue to practise all exercises so far covered —'Heel!', automatic sit and 'Sit!' Once your dog understands the commands, give intermittent praise. He will work better.

'Sit-stay!'

The 'Sit-stay!' lesson should take you about a week. You are going to teach your dog to sit anywhere you wish by himself. Until this stage you have always had close contact with your dog, but now you are going to teach him to become used to your leaving him on his own and to stay on command.

Hold the leash in your *right* hand and remember that you must keep your eye on your dog all the time. You will give the hand signal using the palm of your *left* hand, which you throw in front of your dog's eyes with your fingers down so that your dog can see it. When you move you will start off with your *right* foot. Previously, when heeling, you started with your *left* foot. In this way your dog quickly learns that when you start with your *left* foot he will be going *with* you, but when you start with your *right* foot he will have to *stay* where he is. Once your dog is trained, which foot you start with will be of no consequence. Without using your dog's name, you will give the command 'Sit!' sharply and emphasise 'Stay!' in a deep voice, giving the hand signal at the same time with your *left* hand.

Start your lesson with some heeling work together with the automatic sit, with the leash in your *right* hand and your dog on your left side, his head in line with your *left* leg. When you halt, your dog will be sitting correctly and squarely. Place the palm of your *left* hand, fingers towards the ground, directly in front of your dog's eyes. Do not touch your dog, but give the command 'Stay!' at the same time as the hand signal. Move several steps forward. Be ready to make the correction with your *left* hand, should your dog move, by a gentle corrective jerk upwards. Your dog will understand that he is not complying with your wishes. You must make the correction the split second your dog moves and before he has had time to reach the standing position. Do not expect your dog to sit for more than fifteen or twenty seconds. As soon as your dog is sitting correctly, show him the palm of your *left* hand and at the same time, if your dog appears about to move, repeat the word 'Stay!' several times (this is not so

'Sit-stay!' After heeling, say 'Sit!' sharply and clearly. Command 'Stay!' in a deep voice. Leash in right hand close to waist. Throw hand signal close to dog's face with left hand, step off with right foot, and move to end of leash

(above) 'Sit-stay!' Move to end of leash, still holding it in the right hand. Face your dog and give the hand signal with the left hand palm towards dog with fingers slightly raised. Give the command 'Stay!'. Emphasise 'Stay!' in a deep voice

(right) 'Sit-stay!' Walk round your dog, giving him the hand signal with the left hand and the command 'Stay!' He will follow you round with his eyes

much a command as a discouragement). Return to your dog's side and give him the praise that is due to him, quietly and without fuss. You should only give your praise when you are standing by the side of your dog, not when you are standing away from him; if you praise him when he is sitting on his own this will only encourage him to move towards you. Do not repeat the word 'Stay!' when your dog is sitting quietly and does not appear to intend to move. If you do, the command ceases to have any meaning for your dog.

Repeat the exercise several times and remember not to talk to your dog or praise him until you have returned to his side. If your dog starts to break position, use the gentle jerk-release correction or try flipping the leash with your *left* hand so that it hits him under his chin as you move away. This should restrain him from getting up. Do not speak as you do this; he must not associate the discomfort with you. If your dog does not sit, bend forward and tap his rump in the usual way. Each time you walk away from your dog make the distance a little greater, until you can walk to the end of the leash, turn round facing your dog and say 'Stay!' in a deep tone. The palm signal will have to be repeated several times; there must be no talking or encouragement. Your dog will not be perfect, but will be beginning to understand. The whole procedure must be taken in a quiet, relaxed and unexciting way.

After perhaps thirty seconds, walk towards your dog in a casual manner and walk round him. Keep him on your left side until you return to the correct heeling position. Let your dog remain quietly by your side in the sitting position; do not make him excited or he will jump up. If he tries to come towards you as you return to him, reprove him by saying 'No! Bad dog!' or 'Naughty!' Make the correction gently with your leash and, when all is going well again and your dog is once more sitting quietly, praise him gently and tell him what a good dog he is. If your dog breaks while you are walking round him, or when you are behind him, use the same leash correction as previously. You must remember that, when you are standing at the end of the leash, there must be no pressure on your dog's collar. If you jerk the leash in any way your dog will automatically break and come towards you. On the first day do not try to do this lesson from the end of the leash more than a few times, certainly not more than four. Continue your training with the rest of your dog's repertoire.

After three days you can start to vary the exercise. Walk up and down in front of your dog; walk round your dog one way and then the other way, and then round him several times. Make the corrections when necessary and end up in the heeling position with your dog on your left. Give him lavish praise.

Training on a Long Cord

Your dog is probably not as good as you think he is, so the next stage of the 'Sit-stay!' exercise, which you should reach by the second week—but do not worry if you do not—will be taught with the aid of a 6m (20ft) cord (you could use a 5m (15ft) cord, if your dog is small). You are going to perform some antics yourself, trying to distract your dog—clap your hands, jump up and down, stamp around. You will undoubtedly succeed in your objective. The moment your dog breaks his sitting position and moves away, you must correct him and take him back to the *exact* spot where he had been told to sit previously. If he is small, carry him back. Exact means exact, not somewhere near. As you take your dog back to the place, use a scolding tone with a few quick, jerk-release corrections with the leash as you go, saying 'No! Bad dog!' or 'Naughty!' Once your dog has been returned to the *exact* place, cease all scolding. Give the command 'Sit-stay!' and use the palm of your *left* hand for the hand signal at the same time. Keep practising this until you can get to the end of the cord without your dog breaking his position.

A warning here: you may have to keep your dog working on a long cord for several months. Do not let him off the cord until you are absolutely sure you have your dog under full control. Once your dog is off the cord, all you are left with is your commanding voice! If he does break when he is off the cord, return him to the *exact* place as before and restart your lessons with the cord control. Novices always make the mistake of working without a cord before their dog is fully trained.

As soon as you feel confident that you have your dog under full control, walk to the end of the cord and drop it surreptitiously. Turn round and walk a few paces towards your dog along the cord. Keep your eyes on your dog all the time. Should he break, step on the cord and pick it up. Continue with the corrective routine. Progress slowly until you can drop the cord and walk further and further away from your dog, up to about 30–35m (33–38yd), while your dog still remains quietly in the 'Sit-stay' position.

The efforts of all your training are now to be realised. Go through your dog's repertoire, ending up with the automatic sit. Gently remove the leash or cord from your dog's collar. With your *left* hand hold the end of the check-chain collar and with a jerk-release (your dog thinks that he is still on the leash) give the command 'Stay!' Use the palm of your hand for your hand signal and walk off smartly, starting with your *right* foot. You are not only giving your dog his commands correctly, but you must act with confidence to show that you know he is going to stay. You are getting the message across. If you will your dog to stay, he will stay.

111

The object of the 'Sit-stay' exercise is to make your dog remain sitting until you give him the command to do something else. You can make the exercise more difficult by going out of sight or by sitting on a seat behind him, pretending to read a newspaper. If he thinks that you are not watching him he will naturally try to break, and you must be quick to prevent him doing this. This part of your dog's training often seems to be at a standstill. Do not be discouraged, because what he has learnt is becoming ingrained as an unforgettable and permanent habit. He is being conditioned.

Quick Guide to 'Sit-stay!'

Dog's position	About 25cm (10in) from your *left* side. A comfortable place.
Tone of voice	Deep tone with emphasis on the word 'Stay!'
No name	Do not use your dog's name.
Command	'Sit-stay!' given before you move. 'Sit!' said sharply.
Signal	Palm of *left* hand is thrown in front of your dog's eyes. Do not touch him. Keep your fingers outstretched, pointing towards the ground. Give the command and signal together.
Correction	Made by jerking the leash up with *left* hand and with minimum of force, just before your dog starts to move and before he gets up.
Leash	Held in your *right* hand.
Exercise	Start lesson with heeling and automatic sit.
Move off	With *right* foot for 'Sit-stay!' (*left* foot for 'Heel').
Praise	Lavishly, but only when your dog is by your side.
If dog breaks	Gentle upward jerk-release action with *left* hand.
Move several steps	Give command and signal. Return to your dog's side. And praise him.
Dog refuses to sit	Tap rump, give command and signal and jerk up on the leash.
No collar pressure	Move in front of your dog and face him. Give command and hand signal. Do not jerk leash or put pressure on your dog's collar or he will walk towards you.
Walk to and fro	After three days move to and fro in front of your dog. Walk round him. Later, kneel on one knee,

bend down, turn your back, sit down behind him. Use correction if your dog moves.

Using long light cord

If your dog moves, take him back to *exact* place each time. Later drop cord, and each lesson walk further away. Remove cord, jerk-release the check-chain collar, give the command 'Sit-stay!' and move off with your *right* foot. Later go out of sight.

Practise all exercises

Return to your dog's side, wait a few seconds and praise him quietly. Give the command 'Simba, heel!' and start off with your *left* foot. Once your dog understands what to do and knows the command, give praise intermittently.

10

'Stand-stay!'

Your dog has progressed remarkably fast. You taught him to heel in four days (but not perfectly) and then started the automatic sit lessons. In the third week you started his 'Sit-stay!' exercises and by the end of the first week of these lessons you progressed to using the long cord. The 'Stand-stay!' should take you about three days. However, if your dog is taking longer to learn any of these lessons, do not worry. There is no hurry. It is far more important that what you teach your dog should be thoroughly learnt; the time he takes is of no consequence. The important factor is that both you and your dog should enjoy your training sessions together, and this will not happen if you become impatient.

The 'Stand-stay!' command is a most useful one for your dog to learn because it has many practical applications. It is useful, for example, when your dog has to visit the veterinary surgeon; when his temperature is taken; when he has a grooming session at the beauty parlour; when his ears or eyes are being attended to; and it is very useful in bad weather when you do not wish your dog to dirty his long coat by automatically sitting in the mud each time you stop in the street. But most important of all, it is the 'Stand-stay!' command which is so essential in the show ring.

Once your dog has learnt to 'Stand-stay!' he has progressed to the real understanding of obedience. Obviously, when your dog is on his four legs he reasons that his legs have been made to move on, so in heaven's name why should he not use them at will? Previously during training when commanded to 'Sit!' your dog has been quite comfortable sitting when he has been told to do so. Now it is a different matter.

Your dog has been trained to sit automatically each time that you have halted. Now when you wish him to stand you must give him a command and a hand signal to assist him. You will also assist your dog if you swing out away from him and stand in front of him sideways on (your dog will not confuse this movement with the halt by his side, for which he has previously been conditioned to sit automatically).

The Stand-stay Lesson for Obedience

Using your normal 1.5m (5ft) leash, commence your lesson by commanding your dog to heel, using his name. Take care at no stage to jerk the leash. Keep the leash in your *right* hand as usual; grasp it with your *left* hand about 30cm (1ft) above your dog's head, pulling it up and slightly forward. Step out with your *right* foot and swing sideways on to your dog giving the command 'Stand-stay!' as you do so, firmly, putting the stress on 'stay'. As you do this relinquish the leash from your *left* hand. You end up standing about 60cm (2ft) in front of your dog. Quickly bring your *left* hand down, fingers pointing to the ground, and tap your dog gently on his nose. You may have to repeat this several times, a little harder each time. By tapping your dog's nose you will prevent him moving forward (see page 116).

The leash by this time will be slack from your dog's collar to your *right* hand. Repeat your command 'Stay!' several times in a firm manner. (This is regarded as a warning rather than a command, and is given in order to avoid having to make a correction.) Do not expect your dog to stand for more than a few seconds the first time. It is important that he receives praise before he makes a mistake. Only increase the time your dog stands when you are sure that you have time to give him praise before he moves. You must take enormous care not to jerk the leash upwards or you will make your dog sit. Keep your hands still, the palm about 8cm (3in) in front of your dog.

Hand Signal and Leash Method

If you fail to stop your dog moving with the palm of your hand, you must resort to wielding the leash. Take a long stride forward with your *right* foot, swing in front of your dog, and face him. Now, with your *left* hand grasp and pull the leash steadily straight up and very slightly forward from your dog and towards you. At the same time give the command 'Stand-stay!'; give the signal with your *right* hand (instead of the usual *left* hand). It will not matter to your dog whether you use your left or right hand for the signal, but the *right* is more convenient because the leash is in the *left* hand. Your dog may possibly become a little confused with the signal and the 'Stand-stay!' commands when he has been previously conditioned to the 'Sit-stay!' when you halt beside him.

Start the exercise again from the beginning, swinging out in front of your dog and each time moving further away until you are as far away as the leash will permit. Keep to the same methods as you used for the 'Sit-stay!' lesson, moving about in front of your dog. Your dog will find the next part of his training easy because he already knows how to stay, and of course he understands the command. So, as with

(above left) 'Stand-stay!' After heeling say 'Stand-stay!', step in front and to the side of your dog, leash in right hand having released the grasp with the left hand. If your dog tries to move forward, tap him on the nose with the left hand and say 'Stay!' If he moves again tap him more sharply still. If he tries to sit keep the leash taut

(above right) 'Stand-stay!' Walk round your dog with the loose leash in your right hand, giving the hand signal 'Stay!'. His eyes will follow you round. The dog reacts better for a smile than for a severe expression

the 'Sit-stay!' lesson, walk round your dog in the usual anti-clockwise direction until you come to the heeling position with your dog on your left side. As you reach the position, give both the verbal command 'Stay!' and the hand signal with your *left* hand, with your palm 8cm (3in) in front of your dog. Pause a moment or two, then praise your dog quietly. Give the command 'Simba, heel!', let your dog heel for a short way and then repeat the 'Stand-stay!' lesson, this time moving round your dog in a clockwise direction until you reach the heeling position once more.

Should your dog break position at any time during the lesson, give the leash a quick *upward* jerk and at the same moment say 'No!' firmly. Then restart the whole lesson from the beginning. It is important that you do not give the command 'Stay!' when you stop in the heel position by your dog. You have been teaching your dog to sit when you come to a halt beside him. In order not to confuse him, make absolutely certain that you swing out in front of him with your *right* foot before you give the command 'Stay!' If your dog attempts to sit or succeeds in doing so, whatever you do, *do not jerk* him to his

116

feet. You must pull on the leash steadily, until you get your dog standing on all four feet, and only then may you give a forceful command 'Stay!' Circle round your dog until he stands well and repeat 'Stay!' Halt in the heel position for a short time. Your dog learns that he may only move when he is given the command 'Heel!'

The Groin Method for Conformation Classes

There are various methods of teaching your dog to stand. It can be taught by making use of natural canine behaviour. As mentioned in an earlier section of this book, when a dog makes an inguinal contact with another dog, the second dog or puppy automatically becomes passive and will stand quite still without moving whilst the investigation continues. The dog is under an instinctive behavioural inhibition or, as it is sometimes expressed, under 'social control'. The groin touch is a useful method for a handler or trainer to use in teaching a dog to stand, particularly for a show.

'Stand-stay!', groin method for exhibition. Fold the leash in the left hand, so that it is just taut, with a forward pull to prevent the dog from sitting. Bend over the dog and place the palm of right hand in his groin (inguinal region) so that he is under social control. Stand on your dog's left, so that he does not confuse this with the automatic sit

In order not to confuse your dog with the automatic sit, stand quite quietly on his left, with the leash folded short in your *left* hand. Move your *left* hand forward in front of your dog and as you do so bend over him and place your *right* hand gently in his *right* groin saying 'Stand-stay!' in a firm, low voice. Do not jerk the leash or he will sit. Practise the exercise moving round your dog the opposite way, reversing your hands. Many dogs are inclined to swing their hindquarters out away from the trainer. In this case, all you do is to bend slightly over your dog and touch his *right* groin very lightly with your *left* hand. If you have been too slow and your dog sits, you may have to lift him to a standing position. Some dogs enjoy having their rump scratched so much that you may be able to make your dog stand by doing this. How you get your dog to stand is not so important. What you must remember is to give the command 'Stand!' the moment your dog stands, otherwise he will be unable to associate the command with the act (see page 117).

Circling
Occasionally, a dog may turn in a circle when the handler starts to walk round him. If you are moving round your dog on his left side, gently place your *left* hand on his groin by his right hindleg as you move. This will stop your dog following you round. If you are moving round from right to left, use your *right* hand and place it on your dog's left groin by the top of his hindleg (see page 119).

Use of the Trainer's Foot
Another method of teaching your dog to stand involves using your foot. As your dog comes to a halt you can prevent him from sitting if you quickly place your *left* foot, with your toes pointing upwards, underneath him. As your dog starts to sit, he will feel this strange, unexpected thing beneath him and he will be most unlikely to sit on it. Your dog will therefore stand. The moment he does so, give him the command 'Stand!' and follow this with the hand signal with your *left* hand and the word 'Stay!'

To Help Your Dog Stand in Line
In order to help your dog to end the exercise so that his two forefeet are in line with each other, you must watch him carefully and time his stride. As your dog starts to bring his left foreleg forward give the hand signal for 'Stay!' with your *left* hand as your dog's foot comes in line with his right leg. This will ensure that your dog puts his foot down immediately instead of carrying it forward slightly in front of his right forepaw. This precision is not really necessary unless you

To prevent your dog from circling, place the left hand holding the leash in the groin (inguinal region) on the dog's right side as you walk round him

intend to go in for obedience work. Nevertheless, this little extra attention to detail does make the exercise look good. It is also extra training for your dog, making him keep his attention upon you. Once you have given the command 'Stay!' your dog should stand quite still. While he is learning the lesson he is bound to move a little; when he does move, say 'No!' with great firmness and in a low tone, and as soon as he is still give the command 'Stay!' and praise him quietly.

Teaching a Small Dog to Stand on a Table

The easiest way to train a small dog (or a puppy of a large breed) to stand, is to teach him on a table. This saves a great deal of bending. It is also essential if your dog belongs to a breed which, when exhibited at a conformation show, is judged on a table. You can even train your dog on a table while you sit on a chair. For a show, you should set your dog up on the table so that his forelegs are a few centimetres from the right-hand end as you face the ring. This is done so that the judge can go over your dog easily. Keep his head facing straight forward with your right hand. Lift your dog up under his brisket and just behind his elbows, high enough above the table so that you can direct his forepaws on to the table, taking care as you do so that they are in line with each other and that his forelegs are also parallel and well under your dog. To adjust the hindlegs, you simply place your fingers in the crutch below his tail, lift his hindquarters off the ground and drop both hindfeet on to the table in the required position for your particular breed. The moment your dog has his four legs on the table correctly, give the command 'Stay!' If he moves, repeat the exercise. To adjust the forelegs you can also lift the dog gently just off the ground with your two hands placed on either side of his jaw, or by lifting him by his leash. You can also see-saw your dog into position.

If you are handling your dog for a judge, keep your slip lead neatly rolled up in the palm of your right hand, and stand behind the table. The lead should be just taut enough not to sag, and, whatever you do, do not drop your lead on to the table. To encourage your dog to stand still, just place your hand gently at the side of his groin. Once your dog has learnt to 'Stand-stay!' on the table he will have no difficulty on the ground.

Quick Guide to 'Stand-stay!' for Obedience

Leash	Normal 1.5m (5ft) leash. Hold in *right* hand.
Tone of voice	Firm and low.
Command	'Stand-stay!', with the emphasis on 'stay!'
No name	Do not use your dog's name.
Position	Heel, grasp leash in *left* hand, swing out in front of your dog and stand 60cm (2ft) in front of him. Relinquish leash and stand sideways on to your dog.
Signal	Hand signal with your *left* palm towards your dog, fingers open and pointing down.
If dog moves	Tap your dog's nose if he moves, several times if necessary and harder at each tap to stop him moving forward.
Leash	In *right* hand. Slack unless dog is inclined to sit. Command 'Stay!' several times firmly as a warning.
Palm	Palm of your *left* hand held still, 8cm (3in) from

your dog's face. Signal and leash reversed when in front of dog.

No jerk   Do *not* jerk the leash upwards or your dog will sit. Do not command 'Stay!' in the heel position.

If dog sits   If he sits, standing in front of your dog, *pull* towards you on the leash until he stands, then give command 'Stay!'

Jerk-up   If your dog breaks at any time, give sharp jerk upwards, saying 'No!' and restart the lesson. Give intermittent praise once your dog understands the command.

Stand for Examination

Your dog must become accustomed to being handled, not only by you, but by a stranger. This exercise is useful if your dog has to go to a veterinary surgeon at any time or if he needs to go to a beauty parlour for a grooming session. It is essential if you intend to show your dog.

Give the command 'Stand-stay!' using the *right* hand signal, and walk to the end of the leash. After a moment return to your dog; repeat 'Stay!' then stroke his head, scratch him gently behind his ears and scratch his chest. Your dog will love this. *Do not talk to him at all.* Go back to the end of the leash and only then may you praise your dog, *never whilst you are touching him.* Return to your dog, scratch behind his ears, run your hands soothingly down his neck, back and rump and finally down his hindleg and tail. Once you have touched your dog, do not at any time lose body contact with him. Return to the end of the leash once again, saying something like 'What a good boy!' The leash is held in the *left* hand for exhibiting.

Your dog must get used to all kinds of handling. Occasionally, you may come across an inexperienced judge who will press down on your dog's rump, erroneously thinking he is testing the strength of your dog's back. All dogs will brace against such a touch. Some judges may do this to watch the reaction on a dog's stifles. In any case, you must make certain in the show ring that, should a judge press down on your dog's rump, he will not sit, but will brace himself against the push. This is why, when you were teaching your dog to sit, you taught him by tapping him sharply on his rump with your fingers and not by pushing him down.

Finally, go up to your dog and move your hand down one foreleg. Bend his foot back so that you can examine his pads. Lift a leg forward and let it drop back into position. Examine his ears. Open his

Stand for examination and for showing. Move to the end of the leash. Give command 'Stand-stay!' firmly, emphasising 'Stay!' Do not use his name. Give the hand signal with the right hand, palm down, fingers slightly raised so that your dog can see them. For obedience, leash and signals are reversed. He must not move before the command 'Heel!'

---

mouth to examine his teeth and lift his lip to count them. Once your dog has learnt to be touched by his trainer, then you should find friends, both male and female, to go over him.

The biggest mistake you are likely to make, and must avoid at all costs, is to *jerk* on the leash when you have given the command 'Stand-stay!' If you do, your dog, quite correctly, will sit.

Occasionally it is difficult to make a dog stand for examination when you move away from him. There are several ways in which you can help him to learn. If your dog is of a small variety, then place an uncomfortable object just beneath him, such as a small pot of plants or a long narrow box. When you go to the end of the leash, should your dog attempt to sit, he will be restrained by the object beneath him. For large breeds you could try making your dog straddle a

122

ladder lying on its side or a solid jump made, for instance, from a broom balanced on two boxes and covered with a towel. Change the leash for a long cord so that you can gradually move further away from your dog. Some dogs will learn to stand immediately, if their rump is scratched and their head is patted.

Once your dog has become reasonably proficient with the 'Sit-stay!' and the 'Stand-stay!' exercises, you should alternate them so that your dog really does understand them and is able to distinguish the commands for each without making a mistake.

Quick Guide to Stand for Examination for Conformation Classes

Leash	The leash is always held folded up in the *left* hand for conformation classes. Hold it straight above the collar, just taut. Some breeds are exhibited on a loose leash. When standing behind the judging table, hold the leash in the *right* hand; when the dog is placed on the ground change the leash to the *left* hand.
Command	'Stand-stay!' firmly. Later just say 'Stay!'
Tone of voice	Low.
Move	Move to the end of the leash, which is in the *left* hand. After a few seconds return to your dog and at the same time give the hand signal.
Signal	'Stay!' with your *right* hand. Give the verbal command.
Leash	Extend the *left* hand over your dog so that the leash is on his *right*.
Walk	Walk round your dog anticlockwise. Stay a few moments, heel and praise.
If your dog sits, circles or moves	As you move round your dog, place your *left* hand, which is holding the leash, in his *right* groin. This prevents him from circling or sitting. Then move round in the opposite direction.
Stand	Stand behind your dog and then in front of him, for a minute, as if a judge were going over him. *NB* In Obedience, leash and signals are reversed.

11

'Down!' and 'Down-stay!'

It is quite simple to teach a young puppy to lie down. The older a dog becomes the more difficulty you will find in making him obey this command. However, many a dog's life has been saved by it when he was about to rush across a road to investigate or chase another dog or to go after a bitch in season. The dog may be oblivious to an on-coming car or lorry, but at the owner's command 'Down!', if he has been well preconditioned to the command 'Down-stay!', the dog drops like a stone to the ground and stays where he is until his owner gives him another command. In a case such as this, you may not have time to give the hand signal too.

For some reason, dogs do not like lying down to this command, probably because in itself it is a vulnerable position. Also, the signal given for 'Down' is a most aggressive one—an arm raised in an unnatural position, with the hand pointing towards the dog. Any dog at first would instinctively feel that he was going to be hit, and if he is going to be hit, he would much rather be standing on all four legs.

The Nose Tap 'Down!' or Leash Tap
A tap on the nose while giving the 'Down!' command can be quite successful, provided that you make the tap hard enough and in the correct place and also fast enough. But lavish praise must be given the split second that your dog is lying down. The first time you do the exercise, give the command 'Heel!' After a few steps halt, and as your dog sits give the command 'Stay!' and grasp the leash in your *left* hand as you move to stand in front of him. You are taking your dog by surprise. Raise your *right* arm, hand towards your dog where he can see it easily, say 'Simba, down!' and drop your hand quickly, giving your dog a very sharp tap on his nose with your finger tips. Follow through and, using both hands, pull your dog's forelegs by the pasterns towards you. In the same split second—and this is very important—you must pet and praise your dog and reassure him. You have just done something unexpected and not very pleasant to him and you want to put it across to your dog that the end result is well worth while. Whilst your dog is still lying down, walk round to the left and when you return to the heel position say 'Sit!'. Instead of tap-

124

ping his·nose you may hit the leash near his collar.

Repeat the lesson, only this time raise your hand quickly but hold it in position for a little longer than previously, just above your dog's head and where he can see it easily (this is a frightening position of your hand). Give the command 'Simba, down!' If your dog is going to drop of his own accord do not tap his nose, but praise him lavishly as he goes down. Depending on your dog's temperament and on how accurate you are with the tap on his nose, your dog should go down on his own by the fourth time. The same applies if you hit the leash.

If your dog moves or tries to crawl away, just put your hand on his body and say quite quietly 'Stay!' Start the lesson again, only this time hold the leash quite close to the collar in your *left* hand and give the signal for 'Stay!' with your *right* hand, restraining your dog from moving with the leash taut. Sometimes a dog tries to play or roll over. If yours does this, just push him over by his shoulder into a dog's normal lying-down, slightly curled-up position, which is far more comfortable than the correct and upright, more formal 'Down!' position. (The former is the position you should leave your dog in when you go shopping.) If he plays up, just give him a quick jerk-release with the leash, putting him into a sitting posture, then give the hand signal with the *right* hand for 'Down!' and simply walk away. Your dog will be so surprised at no notice being taken of him that the chances are extremely good that he will lie down of his own accord.

The Weaving Method
I was shown a further method of teaching a dog to lie down many years ago when I was in Hawaii. The idea is that you place your dog in the 'Down!' position, showing him what you want him to do, using the minimum of force on your dog's body and without giving him the opportunity or the idea of bracing his legs and resisting. Your dog could very easily fight back with all the extra power gained from going into this new position, but luckily he does not realise this. You are going to put your dog in a lying-down position for the first time by kneeling beside him on your *left* knee and holding the end of his check-collar in your *left* hand. This whole procedure is far less menacing for a dog than the threatening 'Down!' signal made with the *right* arm held high and the palm of the hand held towards your dog.

It is important that you should hold the check-collar between the spring hook of the leash and the other ring on the collar. Take great care that your finger cannot get caught up in the ring because obviously, should it do so, it would be extremely painful. Your *left* hand should be held with the thumb uppermost and you should hold

the end of the chain sufficiently far down to prevent your dog from being able to twist and turn his neck. Do not hold the collar too tightly so that it chokes him and makes him uncomfortable.

All you need is control. You will be putting your weight, or as much as you need, on the top of your dog's shoulders with your *left* arm. Weave your *right* arm beneath the pastern of your dog's *right* foreleg and hold his *left* foreleg just above the pastern with your *right* hand, keeping your thumb on top. When you want your dog to lie down, exert a downward pressure on your dog's withers with your *left* arm and at the same time pull his legs forward from under him with your *right* arm and hand. If you and your dog collapse, do not laugh (it is difficult not to). If your dog is small and you have large hands, you can pull both his forelegs from under him with your *right* hand. With a large dog you may find that you need to hold his *left* leg well above his pastern in order to prevent him from being able to unthread his *right* leg from over your *right* arm. Look carefully at the photographs and you will easily understand this simple manoeuvre.

Because your dog cannot understand what you are doing, or what you want him to do in this ridiculous position, it is most important that you regain his confidence by reassuring him and by praising him lavishly. Tell him how clever he is and allow him to get up immediately. Continue with the normal heeling lesson and all the exercises your dog has learnt to date. After the automatic sit repeat the 'Down' lesson. If you divide the lesson into ten-minute periods, your dog should practise the 'Down!' half a dozen times each lesson. If you have a difficult dog you can make the lesson much easier by confining him between you and a wall during the exercise.

The Shoulder-Shove Method
The shoulder-shove method is a very easy way of making your dog lie down. It is excellent for all dogs that are not required to do obedience work. The down position here is a natural curled-round position, which is far better if you want your dog to stay down for a

---

(left, above) 'Down!', weaving method. Trainer kneels on left knee. Holds leash end of check-chain collar in left hand with the thumb up and dog sitting on the left. Right hand weaves between dog's forelegs, grips the leg above pastern with thumb on top. Pull forelegs forward with right hand and arm. Say 'Down!' in a firm low tone. Praise. Put hand on withers and stroke the dog saying quietly 'Good dog', bend over him, and let him get up immediately

(left, below) 'Down!', weaving method. Viewed from the front, the dog is going down easily. If he resists, bear down with all your weight on his withers with your left forearm. Praise him and let him get up immediately

long time, such as while he waits outside shops during a morning's shopping expedition.

As with all the other 'Down' methods, start your dog in the sit position and stand or kneel beside him. With one hand grasp the further foreleg above the pastern and lift it, then place your other hand on your dog's opposite shoulder and give him a steady shove quite quickly towards the lifted foreleg. Once again your dog is off balance. Do not lose body contact with your dog with the shoving hand nor with the leg-raising hand until your dog is lying happily and naturally. Reassure him, scratch his chest, pet him, tell him how clever he is and let him get up again.

'Down-stay!'

As soon as your dog is lying down, give him the command 'Stay!' and the signal with the palm of your *right* hand held in front of his face. The rest of the lesson is almost identical to the 'Sit-stay!' lesson, first

---

'Down!', shoulder shove. Trainer kneels or stands. Lifts further foreleg and pushes dog firmly on nearer shoulder. Dog loses his balance and lies down. Say 'Down!' in a firm, low tone and then command the dog to 'Stay!'

'Down-stay!' Trainer moves to end of leash in left hand and with right hand gives the signal 'Down-stay!', palm towards the dog and fingers slightly raised. The rest of the exercises for the 'Down-stay!' are similar to those for the 'Sit-stay!', walking round your dog, and to and fro in front of him. You may also walk over him

with the leash and then with the long cord, increasing your distance gradually and walking round your dog and even over him. Your dog will finally graduate to doing the lesson off the leash.

Return to your dog and stay by his side. Do not let him move. If he tries to get up, jerk him straight down to the ground and say 'No! Naughty!' Leave your dog immediately and then return to him. By doing this you are teaching your dog that once he is down, he may not move before you give him another command.

Getting Up from the 'Down!' Position

When you want your dog to get up from the down position, do not use any force with the leash. Return to the right side of your dog as usual and stand beside him for a few seconds. Call him by his name and at the same time pretend to walk forward with your *left* foot or just bend your *left* knee, but instead of actually walking forward stay where you are. Your dog will start to get up and as he does so give him the command 'Sit!' Praise him quietly and do not excite him. Repeat the whole exercise.

Quick Guide to 'Down-stay!'—Weaving Method

Position	Start with the automatic sit. Kneel by your dog on your *left* knee. Place the leash over your *right* knee. Hold the end of the check-chain in your *left* hand, *thumb* up. Weave *right* arm through your dog's forelegs. Hold his *left* leg above the pastern, thumb on top. Lean on dog's shoulders with your *left* arm and *pull* his legs forward with your *right* arm and hand. Reassure and praise your dog lavishly.
Tone of voice	Firm and low, with authority. Much encouragement and reassurance essential.
No name	Do not use your dog's name, except when getting up.
Command	'Down-stay!'
Signal	*Right* hand, fingers slightly up, extended in front of your dog's head. Distant signal: *right* hand, fingers splayed, arm out and hand in line with your head.
Leash	Hold in your *left* hand, ends folded, about 30cm (1ft) in length and just taut. Stand to the side and kneel on left knee.
Lesson	Choose a quiet place and a comfortable one.
Correction	When your dog is down, place a gentle, restraining hand on his withers to prevent him from getting up. Say 'Stay!' Stroke your dog gently on his withers and bend down and over him as you do so. Say 'Good boy!' If your dog gets up, restart the lesson.
Repeat and practise	The lesson is as for the 'Sit-stay!' Walk round your dog, in front of him, on a leash and on a cord, etc. In addition, walk over your dog when he is 'Down'. Extend distances and time gradually until your dog will obey without the cord. To get up, bend left knee, say 'Simba, sit!'.

12

The Recall, 'Come!'

The most important command that your dog must learn is to come promptly the moment he is called. Any puppy who has been taught to come when he was young will have no problem with the recall exercise. A great deal more patience is required for an older dog who has fallen into the bad habit of coming only when it is convenient for him to do so or even not at all.

The lesson must take place in a quiet area with which your dog is already familiar and where there are no distractions of any kind. Run through the lessons that you have already taught him. Give him the 'Sit-stay!' command, walk forward with your *right* foot and face your dog. Make him stay for at least half a minute, then give the command 'Simba, come!', using an excited, encouraging tone. At the same moment give the leash, which is in your *right* hand, a sharp jerk-release towards you and, as you do so, walk backwards six steps. Encourage your dog to come towards you by patting your chest or stomach (depending on the size of your dog). Make the hand signal with your *left* hand. Coax your dog affectionately and do not jerk the leash. Encourage him to come towards you by gently reeling him in; gather up the leash hand over hand until you have your dog about 30–45cm (12–18in) away from you. Give the command 'Sit!' (without using your dog's name and in a sharp tone). Hold the gathered-up leash in your *right* hand. If your dog fails to sit, pull the leash up directly above his head and bend over and tap his rump smartly with your *left* hand. You must be as kind to your dog as possible in order to encourage him to come to you. Your dog must sit squarely in front of you in what is called the 'Come-fore' position. Do not pat your leg or thigh on the recall as this encourages your dog to move forward with his head down.

The moment your dog is sitting correctly, give him the command 'Sit-stay!' Do not allow him to break his position, and give him quiet profuse praise. Rub his chest, fondle his ears, pat him and really let him know how good he is. After thirty seconds or so, give the command 'Stay!' using the hand signal with the palm of your *left* hand in front of your dog's eyes. Walk round him and then return to the correct heeling position. With your dog on your *left* side, follow this recall lesson with some heeling and then repeat the exercise. Do this about half a dozen times during the first lesson.

After about a week teaching the recall on the normal leash, or a slightly longer one, start using a 5m (15ft) light cord or washing line and continue the lessons as previously. Timing is tremendously important. The exercise is a sequence of name, 'Come!', jerk-release, *praise*—almost all at the same time.

If your dog is inclined to be excitable, keep everything in a low key, with low-tone commands and quiet praise. Step back slowly. On the other hand, if your dog is slow and lazy, use a very exciting voice for his name, a high pitch for the command and several quick jerk-releases on the leash to get him up on his legs. Run backwards as fast as you can until your dog has reached the speed of trotting towards you. You may have to run backwards about 20 metres.

The recall exercise is probably the only time you should use any form of bait whilst training your dog, other than in trick-training and sometimes perhaps in the retrieve. If he knows that you have a piece of baked liver in your pocket and that, every time he comes when called and sits correctly in front of you, he will be rewarded not only with lavish praise but with a tempting piece of liver, he will be only too happy to come with alacrity when called. It is essential that your dog should enjoy coming to you, and bribing him through his stomach is a very quick way of teaching him!

Once your dog comes instantly when called, start to eliminate first the bait, by only giving it occasionally and soon not at all, then the jerk-release with the leash, and finally your backing up, or in other words running or stepping backwards.

Once you are sure of your dog's reaction to your command 'Come!', go to an enclosed area, put him in the automatic sit position, and quite casually remove his leash. Hold the end of the check-chain collar and give it a straight pull upwards. Give the command 'Stay!' and move three steps in front of your dog, saying 'Stay!' and giving the hand signal with your *left* hand. Then give the command 'Simba, come!' Praise your dog immediately. Spend about ten minutes each day on this lesson and each time move back only one step more. Do not go farther than six steps for the first few days. Extend the distance you move from your dog step by step, day by day, until you can call him to you from a distance. If your dog disobeys, put him on the leash again.

You must now teach your dog to come to you not only from the 'Sit-stay!' position but from wherever he happens to be—running free, playing or whatever he is doing.

Start teaching your dog in a different area, such as a park or large field, and use a long cord. When your dog is not paying any attention to you and has forgotten your presence, call him by name—'Simba, come!'—give the cord at the same moment a sharp jerk-release and proceed to run as fast as you can in the opposite direction. This practically always has the marvellous effect of making your dog run after you. As soon as he catches up with you, turn and face him and give him the command 'Sit-stay!' making the hand signal with your *left* hand. The moment your dog is sitting correctly, praise him. Tell him he is free and allow him to go off again. Wait for about four or five minutes and, when your dog is least expecting it, give him the command using his name, jerk-release the cord and run in the opposite direction. Keep practising the lesson for four or five days.

Some dogs will not run after you when you take off. In this case, reel him in slowly, but do not pull on the leash. Encourage him to come to you with a series of rapid jerk-releases. As you do this, keep walking backwards using your most encouraging voice.

You should progress to eliminating the remaining aids, and only give the command 'Come!'. Stop running away from your dog and just stand still. Later stop using his name.

Your dog must learn to come to you immediately you command 'Come!', even when he is intensely interested in something else. Find something to distract your dog, such as a friend with a dog on a leash or cows in a field. Let your dog go towards the attraction and, before he reaches the end of the leash, give the command 'Simba, come!' and give a fast jerk-release on the leash with your *left* hand. If your dog is more interested in the attraction of the cows or the other dog, make a quick series of jerk-releases on the leash, strong enough and sharp enough to bring him to you. As with all training, coming immediately when called becomes a habit from constant repetition, but in this exercise your dog has got to love to come to you; therefore you must never rebuke him or get cross with him. If you do, why ever should he want to come to you if he feels that you are going to reprimand him? Your tone of voice must be firm, high-pitched, exciting and encouraging.

The Tail Position
It is most important that, whilst training your dog, you should watch the position of his tail, because the position in which he holds it reveals more than anything else the way your dog is feeling. If his tail is up and held gaily, then your dog is enjoying his lessons and you are not being too severe. You can then proceed with more firmness when required. However, if your dog's tail is held low or between his legs, he is showing extreme unhappiness or even fear. If you want

133

your dog to work happily, willingly and with alacrity, you must be warned by this sign and treat your dog gently, both with the leash and in your commands. Shouting at your dog achieves nothing. You must remember that your dog is your friend and companion and should be treated as such.

Quick Guide to the Recall, 'Come!'

Place	Quiet area.
Tone of voice	Exciting and encouraging. Coax, *never* scold.
Name	Use your dog's name to begin with.
Command	'Simba, come!' Later only use the command 'Come!'
Leash	Hold the leash in your *right* hand.
Signal	With your *left* hand pat your chest for a large dog or your stomach for a small dog. Off leash, use *right* hand.
'Sit-stay!'	Walk forward with your *right* foot and face your dog. Give the leash a sharp jerk-release towards you. Take six steps backwards. *Do not* jerk the leash now, but encourage your dog to come to you.
Reel your dog in	Gather the leash in hand over hand. When your dog is about 30cm (1ft) from you, with the leash in your *right* hand give the command 'Sit!' (no name) in a *sharp* tone.
If your dog fails to sit	Pull the leash up sharply above your dog's head, bend over and tap his rump with your *left* hand. When your dog sits, say 'Stay!'
Praise	Lavishly scratch your dog's chest and make a fuss of him.
Wait	Wait about thirty seconds, give the hand signal to stay and walk round your dog.
'Heel!'	Return to the heel position. Do some heel exercises and repeat the lesson half a dozen times.
Important	Use 5m (15ft) cord. Follow the sequence of name, 'Come!', jerk-release, praise, all almost at the same time.
For excited dog	Use low-toned commands and quiet praise. Move gently.

For lazy dog	Use high-pitched commands and make several quick jerk-releases with the leash. Run backwards until your dog trots.
Bribe	Bribe your dog with a titbit when he comes to you.
Aids	Bait, jerk-release and moving backwards. Gradually eliminate these aids. Then stop running away, stand still, stop reeling him in and finally stop using his name. The command is 'Come!'
New area (off leash)	Eliminate all the aids. Run in the opposite direction.
Distractions	Make distractions, eg use of a friend.
Withdrawal of praise	Once your dog understands what you wish him to do, he will learn faster if you praise him intermittently, until finally you need not praise him at all.

13

'Heel!' Off Leash and The Finish

'Heel!' Off Leash

It is unwise to allow your dog to heel off the leash unless you are quite sure that you have him under control and that he will not run away. It may take anything from four to twelve weeks, depending on your dog, to reach this stage. When you first try, start by tucking the leash into your belt or pocket and pretend that you have your dog free. Should he be not quite as good as you had hoped, you can grab the leash if your dog starts to make off. Go through the repertoire of exercises for several days without holding the leash at all. If you find that your dog is doing well, progress to the next stage. Fold the leash

(below left) Off-leash automatic sit. The trainer is calm and serious, the lesson has started and the dog knows that he is off the leash

(below right) Off-leash 'Sit-stay!' Hand signal is made with the left hand, elbow in and arm out to the side, palm towards dog and fingers extended. The trainer looks at her dog and wills him to stay

Off-leash. Hand should be placed down by your side for thirty seconds after each signal

Off-leash 'Down-stay!' Hand signal is made with the right hand, arm out and up by head, palm towards dog, with fingers spread

Off-leash 'Come!' Encourage your dog to come to you. Smile at him. The hand signal is palm of left hand in front of chest. This makes your dog look up and happy. If the dog is small, pat your stomach. If your dog is on a leash it is easier to give the signal with the right hand. He will react to either hand

in half and hold it in your *left* hand with the two ends hanging down. Pretend to fasten the leash on your dog's collar and start off in the normal way. Strangely enough, your dog, having been conditioned to the leash for so long, will automatically think that he is still attached to it.

Whatever you do, should your dog move away from you, do not start to panic and relay your feelings to your dog, who will pick up your reactions as quick as lightning, which will, in turn, make him take off. Give your command 'Heel!' in the same calm manner as you did when your dog was on the leash. Do not use any exaggerated gestures. Your dog has been conditioned to certain tones and signals and it is most important that you do not vary these.

Rather than permit your dog to break or run off when heeling off the leash, it is far better that you should continue the heeling exercise on the leash, even for several months. Follow the old adage

'Do not allow your dog to make a mistake.' If he makes a mistake, it will take you many hours to rectify it. When you first make your dog heel off the leash, only do so for a short time. Your dog is not going to mind in the least being on the leash for a longer period. During the exercise he is having to concentrate on you; he is watching you, listening for your commands and looking for your hand signals.

Whether your dog is on or off the leash is important only to you. As long as your dog receives lavish praise for his work at every possible opportunity during his early lessons, and is given an enjoyable game and romp after each lesson, he will be perfectly content. Once he understands what he is meant to do, give your praises intermittently and he will work better, striving harder as he will for further praise, until finally no praise at all will be required.

———————————————

(below left) The Finish, off leash. Hand signal is with the left hand, palm down, fingers extended, moved round to the side and behind you and to your side again to bring your dog from sitting in front of you to the automatic sit position by your left side. The dog turns round at your left side. The command is 'Heel!'

(below right) Lesson is over. Have a romp with your dog. It is important that you both enjoy the lesson and the romp

a

The Finish (see page 142): (a) Dog is in sit position. Stand in front of dog, grasp leash in left hand, palm down, just taut. Look at dog; (b) Step back with right foot and keep weight on it. As you do so command 'Heel!' and give a sharp jerk, swinging your dog past your left side. As the dog comes past you, give a second jerk-release towards you, which will bring him round;

b

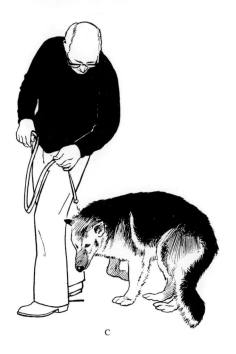

c

(c) Bring your right foot back in line with your left foot and your dog will be in the correct heeling position; (d) Once in the heel position, your dog should sit automatically. If not, tap his croup with your fingers

d

The Finish

The finish or 'Go to heel!' exercise is the finish of the recall or 'Come!', and it is one that the dog naturally enjoys doing. However, it is wiser to teach the lesson as an exercise separate from the recall. Previously your dog has been taught that after the command 'Come!' he must sit in front of you. Now he must learn that, to end the exercise, he must sit in the heel position by your *left* leg.

Start the normal training session. After heeling normally, give your dog the command 'Sit-stay!' and with the leash in your *right* hand as usual, turn and stand in front of your dog about 45cm (18in) from him, keeping the leash slack. You must now work rather fast. In a pleasant tone call your dog by name, 'Simba, heel!', and, grasping the middle of the leash with your *left* hand, swing your dog round in a half circle behind you. As you do this, step back with your *right* foot, keeping your *left* foot in the same position. Your dog has been swung behind you (on your left) and you must now bring him up to the correct heeling position, which is of course on your left side. As you do this, bring your *right* foot forward to its previous position. You may find it easier to incorporate a jerk-release at the start and at the end of the swing movement.

The moment your dog's head is in line with your *left* leg, give the command 'Sit!' (without using his name, since this is a passive command). If your dog does not comply with the command immediately, simply pull up on the leash and tap him smartly on the rump. Praise him profusely. This lesson is much easier than it sounds.

14

Retrieving and Scent Discrimination

Teaching your dog to retrieve is the most difficult of all the training exercises. It is also one of the most enjoyable both for the owner and for his dog. Once your dog has learnt to bring back objects on command, or to seek out objects which have been hidden, he has acquired a degree of responsibility and delights in the knowledge of a job well done. Both the trainer and the dog then have a tremendous sense of achievement. Retrieving is taught step by step and requires enormous patience. Your dog must never be hurried and he must never, never be forced. Retrieving is neither force nor play; it is very serious work performed on command.

A trainer's voice is very important; it must range from high-pitched and enthusiastic to low, firm and pleasant. There is no need ever to shout at your dog. He has extremely sensitive hearing. In the early lessons it is important to use your dog's name frequently, (everyone likes to hear their name spoken), to give lavish praise, to talk to him and to show enthusiasm. The first lesson your dog must learn, which is the most difficult, is to take an object on command. Later he must be taught to hold the object and then to give it up. The earlier a puppy starts to learn to retrieve, the easier it will be later on when he has his formal training.

There are really two kinds of retriever: one is the natural retriever, who retrieves in play without ever having been taught to do so; and the second is a well trained dog who will retrieve an object under any circumstances on command. Some breeds, such as gundogs, are natural retrievers by instinct and as puppies they adore carrying objects around. Other breeds, such as chihuahuas, on the whole dislike carrying things in their mouths and are therefore much more difficult to train. Nevertheless, all dogs can be trained to retrieve, but it will require much more time and a great deal of patience to train dogs in the difficult breeds.

Methods of Retrieving
As with all training, there is no one method of teaching to retrieve: some methods, for example using a dumb-bell, are solely for

RETRIEVING AND SCENT DISCRIMINATION

obedience training; others are for police work, etc. It is probably best to use a method which can be applied to any breed, in the town or the country, and regardless of whether the dog will eventually be used as a gundog, for police work, or for obedience tests. It is essential for a gundog to have a good mouth, and so all training must be done with something soft rather than with a dumb-bell. It should be remembered that a dog that has retrieved something regards the object as his own. In the dog's eyes, he ran after the object and found it and he now has it in his mouth, so why should he give it up at all, let alone for nothing? For this reason, I like to give a puppy a titbit on taking a dummy out of his mouth, to show him how pleased I am. Every time your dog gives you an object, whether it is a dumb-bell or a pheasant, he should be praised and thanked, using a phrase such as 'Good boy!' as if you really meant it. Retrieving is really team work; your dog has played his part, so you must play your part and give him his due.

Teaching a Young Puppy to Retrieve

A young puppy can be taught to retrieve for fun whilst he is playing. Teach him in a narrow passage leading to his bed. Shut all the doors so that there is only one exit. Use his favourite soft toy or an old leather glove tied round with string, making it small enough to fit in the puppy's mouth. An old woollen sock stuffed with wood wool is equally as good—a child's sock for a small dog or a man's sock for a large one. Whatever you decide to use, though, it must be soft and it must not roll.

Half an hour before your puppy is due to be fed, take him outside to relieve himself. Bring him to where you are going to teach him to retrieve and put him down beside you; if he knows how to sit make him sit. Then toss his toy about 2–3m (6–8ft) and in a high-pitched, exciting tone say 'Get it!' or 'Fetch it!' The puppy will chase it and pick it up, and his instinct will be to take it back to his bed. In order to do this he will have to pass you in the passage. The second your puppy picks up his toy start to praise him profusely, as if he is quite the cleverest dog in the world. Increase your praise as he comes towards you, then nonchalantly, but very gently, take his toy from him, praising him and making a tremendous fuss of him as you do so. Then, without any delay, throw the toy again, saying as you do so 'Fetch it!' Each time you do this allow your puppy to hold his cherished toy a little longer. His toy is very important to him. This lesson should be repeated only three times, but it should be practised every day at the same time and in the same place for at least a week. It is most important that your puppy should not become bored with the game and that he should look forward to it. He will very quickly become conditioned to the time, the place and the action.

In the second week of play training, begin by throwing your puppy's toy in a different place—try doing it in a room. If the puppy brings his toy back to you immediately, continue the lesson in the room. If he hesitates, or does not return directly to you, his habit training has not been absorbed sufficiently, so return your puppy to the passage routine for a few more days. Gradually choose different rooms and places for the lesson until it becomes second nature for your puppy to return to you every time he retrieves his toy and until he completely understands the words 'Fetch it!' (or 'Get it!').

Exchanging the Dummy for a Titbit

An excellent method of coping with a reluctant puppy is to exchange a titbit, which you will be holding in your *right* hand, for the dummy, which you must receive with your *left* hand as he drops the one in order to be given the other. At first you may have to make the exchange at only a short distance from the ground, increasing the distance and the height as your puppy gains proficiency. Start by kneeling on the ground and then bending over your puppy as you make the exchange, not forgetting to praise and thank him each time. Gradually, as you increase the distance, wait until your puppy has licked his lips before throwing the dummy again. Never give him the titbit before he brings the dummy back to you. He has to drop the dummy into your waiting hand, which should be ready by his mouth, in order to take the titbit. Your puppy is being conditioned to retrieve. Once he understands what you expect him to do, give him only intermittent praise and titbits, but never fail to thank him.

If your puppy refuses to pick up the dummy, put a very small piece of bait inside it or use a length of bamboo covered in something soft as a dummy and stuff a small piece of bait into the centre. (The titbit in your hand should smell stronger than the bait in the dummy.) This method can be used for an adult dog as it is also a process of conditioning.

You will notice that very often your puppy may not see the dummy as you throw it. However, he will have seen the movement of your arm and he will have heard the dummy strike the ground. From both these indications he will know in which direction to go. Later he will understand arm and hand signals as trained gundogs and sheepdogs do.

The False Throw

A throw is known as 'false' or 'empty' when the motions of throwing are made but nothing is thrown. The dog rushes off in the direction of the 'throw motion'. He does this because he has already learnt the arm signal for the retrieve and, although he may be facing in the wrong direction, he will see the signal out of the corner of his eye. Later he will learn to watch for the signal from a distance.

Formal Training for Holding an Object

Teaching your dog to hold an object is part of his formal training and there are several methods of doing this. The training is done with a check-chain collar and a normal-length leash.

One method is to leave your dog in his kennel for two hours before starting his lesson and to give the lesson about three hours after his last meal. Select a quiet spot where there will be no distractions; use the normal leash and check-chain collar. Heel your dog to a corner and give him the command 'Sit!' Place the leash on the ground in front of your dog, step forward with either foot and stand on the leash, making it taut. This allows you to have both hands free and

Step on the leash, bend down with the glove or dummy in your right hand and tap your dog's upper lip with it. If your dog shows no interest after several attempts open his mouth gently with your left hand

your dog under control. It is most important that you should now talk to your dog encouragingly, use his name frequently and keep your voice low and firm; above all, be exceedingly gentle and very patient.

Take a suitable soft object such as an old soft leather glove, rolled up and tightly bound round with string. If your dog is small you can kneel down to him, pinning the leash under your knee. If he is large place your foot on the leash and simply bend down to him with the glove in your *right* hand. Hold it about 30cm (1ft) in front of your dog's muzzle and then very gently tap your dog's upper lip with the glove, saying persuasively 'Get it!' Your dog will probably reach out for the glove, open his mouth and take it. If he takes no interest after several taps on the lip, draw the glove straight out in front of him, pretending that you are going to take it away from him; then gently tap your dog's lip again and use your most persuasive voice, saying 'Get it!' If your dog still shows no interest in taking the glove of his own accord after several attempts, you must quite gently open his mouth for him with your left hand.

Place your hand over your dog's muzzle and, with your thumb on the right side of his upper lip and your middle finger on his left side, press very gently on his back teeth until he opens his mouth wide enough for you to slip the glove in quickly. As your dog opens his mouth, say 'Get it!' Immediately stroke your dog under the chin in a forward direction with your *right* hand, keeping his muzzle up and, with your *left* hand, stroke his muzzle from the back of his nose towards his stop (where the muzzle meets the skull). This will keep your dog's head up and his mouth closed so that he will be unable to drop the glove. As you stroke, say quietly and firmly in a low tone 'Stay!—Stay!—Stay!' Do not let your dog hold the glove for more than a few seconds before you say, in a very kind voice, 'Give!' Take the glove out of your dog's mouth gently with your *left* hand, palm up—never, never snatch the glove away from him. Give your dog a small titbit, then, when he has eaten it, put the dummy back in his mouth. You must praise your dog instantly and make him feel that he has been tremendously clever. Should your dog fail to give up the glove, open his mouth very gently with your thumb and third finger by pressing his lips on his back teeth and say pleasantly but firmly 'Give!' Some trainers like to blow up the dog's nostrils as they give the command. Always take the glove.

If your dog tries to spit the glove out and refuses to hold it, place both hands above and below his muzzle, keeping his mouth closed, and firmly and quietly say 'Stay!' If your dog still tries to get rid of the glove with his forefeet, hold his muzzle in one hand and give a sharp jerk-release on the leash the split second that he starts to lift a foot off the ground. If you can manage to hold your dog's mouth shut with your left hand, scratch his chest soothingly with your right hand. This invariably has a very calming effect on a dog, particularly if you talk quietly to him all the time and use his name frequently. Dogs, like people, love to hear the sound of their own name.

Whether your dog takes the glove in his mouth himself or you have to open his mouth to slide it in, the split second that the object is in his mouth praise your dog profusely. It is your voice which is going to make the real impact on him more than anything else.

The Check-chain Method

Occasionally, one finds a dog who does not want to hold anything in his mouth. Some trainers spend many weeks working every day before they succeed in making a particular dog take an object of his own volition. Rather than spend weeks trying to persuade a difficult dog to take and hold an object in his mouth, you can make him take it by the use of the check-chain collar. Personally, I would only use this method as a last resort. It is essential that you use the collar correctly and smoothly and release your hold on the collar the split second after it has been tightened. It is imperative that, while you are tightening the collar, you keep talking to your dog in the most pleasant, reassuring manner, so that he cannot possibly connect you with the unpleasant sensation on his throat.

With your dog sitting on your left side and the glove held in your *right* hand, place the object in his mouth two or three times. Now you are going to teach him to take the glove of his own volition. To do this, first pull the check-chain collar so that it is drawn up high on your dog's neck behind his ears and at the top of his throat. Now slide your *left* hand gently beneath the collar between your dog's right ear and mouth. With your fingers against his cheek, hold the dead-ring in the cleft of your thumb and the surplus chain and the tightened collar in the palm of your hand; then, clenching your fist, turn it smoothly and quickly in an anticlockwise direction taking great care not to jerk the collar in any way. But, most important of all, you must talk to your dog, using his name and saying gentle, encouraging words.

The anticlockwise action of your hand tightening the collar makes your dog thrust his head forward towards the object which you are holding in your right hand in front of his upper lip. At the same time the restriction on your dog's throat automatically makes him open his mouth. As he reaches forward and opens his mouth slide the glove in, releasing the pressure the moment your dog has taken it, and say 'Simba, Stay!—Stay!—Stay!' Then say 'Give!', and receive the article in your *left* hand, palm up. Reward your dog with a titbit. Later if you teach your dog to work with a dumb-bell you should receive it in both hands.

Most dogs will learn to take an object of their own volition after the second or third tightening of the collar (this, of course, is negative training). However, the collar should be kept high on his neck for the rest of the training as a reminder. A reward of a titbit lets your dog know that you are pleased with him. If your dog shows no wish to drop the glove, try making him walk by your side for a few steps, still carrying the dummy, then bend down and take the glove from him and give him his reward.

The Check-chain and Leash Method

In this method of training the dog sits at heel and the collar is placed high up and under his throat. The collar is then pulled forward between your dog's ears and held taut with the leash, which should be folded up and very short. The dog is supported against the trainer's left leg so that he cannot get away. The command 'Get it!' is given and the trainer tightens the collar by lifting the *left* hand up slowly until the dog has to open his mouth. If your dog rears up he is given a quick jerk-release to the left so that he is taken off balance. On no account should you push the object into your dog's mouth, knock his teeth or in any way hurt or frighten him. If he fails to take the object, each jerk should be more severe than the previous one. But you must keep up your encouraging praise and remember to keep the glove near your dog's lips all the time.

Some dogs learn the give-and-take exercises very quickly; others do not, and much patience is required. Keep practising the lesson, interspersing it a few times between the regular training exercises. Gradually move the object further and further away from your dog and hold it lower each time. This will help him when he eventually learns to pick the object off the ground. If he drops the glove take no notice, but stop giving the profuse praise that you give when your dog is holding the dummy correctly.

Reaching for the Dummy

Once your dog has become accustomed to reaching forward and opening his mouth to get the glove, he must learn to stretch his neck out further and further. To start with he may only stretch his neck out a few centimetres, but this is real progress. Let out a little more of the leash, but still keep it just taut. Gradually increase the distance and lower the glove until, after a time, your dog will have stretched the full length of his neck, while still sitting at heel, and you will have stretched your *right* arm out as far as it will go. For each little bit of progress praise your dog profusely with the usual commands and titbits. Do not bore your dog but keep repeating other exercises during the lesson.

Eventually, in order to reach the glove, your dog will have to get up off his haunches. As he does so, loosen the leash a little so that your dog can actually go for the dummy. Say 'Get it!' and, as your dog picks up the dummy, give the usual encouraging praise, then step back saying 'Come!' This will make your dog turn and come towards you. As soon as he is in front of you give him the command 'Sit!', and place your hand under his chin to prevent him from dropping the glove. If he looks like holding the glove correctly do not touch him, but have your fingers in readiness. You must praise your dog excitedly and, as he comes in to you and sits, say 'Stay!—Stay!—Stay!—Give!' Take the glove in your *left* hand with your palm up and keep your head down. Do not look directly at your dog as you accept the dummy. Dogs, like people, feel uncomfortable and threatened when they are stared at from close quarters, and doing so might stop him relinquishing his dummy. Then praise him and give him his titbit.

Continue practising, each time dropping your arm lower until finally you can place the dummy on the ground. To begin with you should keep your hand on the dummy. Step by step increase the distance between your hand and the dummy, until finally you can actually place the glove a metre in front of you, as you do so giving the command 'Stay!' Your dog must not move until you give the command 'Get it!' Take your usual step back and, as your dog comes in to you, say 'Sit!' (later you can run back). After a few seconds command 'Give!' To finish the exercise neatly give the command 'Heel!' with the hand signal for the finish and, when your dog has completed his turn, start off with your *left* foot and end with an automatic sit. Praise and praise your dog.

Retrieving With the Help of a Friend

A quick method of teaching your dog to retrieve involves asking a friend to help you. Start with the usual exercises that your dog now knows well and end with your dog on the leash, sitting and staying in the heel position on your left side. Throw the same article that you have been using throughout the training about a metre or so in front of you. Give the command 'Get it!' If your dog hesitates or does not move at all, first point towards the glove, then take a few steps forward to encourage your dog and give a couple of sharp jerk-

150

releases forward with the leash. If your dog has absorbed all his previous lessons, which have been taken slowly step by step, he will retrieve the glove and return and sit in front of you. If he does so, repeat the exercise two or three times, throwing the glove a little further each time. Your dog will be retrieving the glove purely through sight by watching the article being thrown. Later, of course, he will retrieve by scent entirely, trusting to what his nose tells him.

If your dog fails to go for the thrown glove immediately, put a long cord on him and ask your friend to hold the end. With your dog sitting by your left side, throw the glove a metre or so and give the command 'Get it!' If your dog hesitates, your friend should pull your dog towards the object. As he moves, encourage him and praise him more and more as he picks up the glove and increase your praise even more as your dog returns towards you and exchanges the dummy for a titbit. Repeat the exercise with your friend's help, increasing the distance each time your dog makes a successful retrieve. It is very important that you give extra praise just as your dog reaches down towards the dummy, to encourage him and to keep up his interest in retrieving.

Retrieving off the Leash
This is done in the same way as when the dog was on the leash, except that the dog is controlled entirely by voice commands 'Heel!', 'Sit!', 'Stay!', 'Get it!', 'Come!', 'Sit!', 'Give!', 'Heel!' (later he will understand arm signals and the whistle). Gradually, as the dog becomes more proficient, the commands are reduced to 'Get it!' and 'Heel!' Praise should become intermittent, but thanks must always be given when receiving the dummy.

Your dog should practise all his obedience training exercises, carrying the dummy first with the leash and later without. He should be able to accomplish all the lessons with ease. The one he will find the most difficult is the 'Down!' with the dummy in his mouth. If you use a dumb-bell and you find that your dog is inclined to chew it, glue a strip of Velcro along the stem. This will stop him doing so.

The Many Uses of Retrieving
Once you have trained your dog to retrieve on command, there is no end to the uses to which the training can be put. A dog can learn to take messages, which can be very useful; for instance, if a husband is at the far end of the farm and has forgotten his pipe, and his wife is in the kitchen cooking dinner. Your dog can learn to take his exercise by retrieving a ball. The ball is thrown, and the command is given 'Get the ball!' The number of things that you can teach your dog are

151

almost unending. They are well worth the hours that you have spent in teaching him, as they are such fun and so useful.

The extent of a dog's vision is very interesting. If he is on flat ground he can see 20–60° below the horizon, 100–125° to the side, 30–45° on the nasal side of either eye, and 50–70° above the horizon. He is very often aware of your signals, even when he may not be looking in your direction.

Responding to a Whistle

Dogs learn to respond to whistles very easily. The Galton or so-called silent whistle has the advantage of carrying a great distance. When you buy one it is important to have it set so that in the event of your losing it you can buy another identical one. A dog is automatically trained to the use of one particular whistle, so that if you sell your dog his whistle should accompany him.

One blow on the whistle is to alert your dog. It is the equivalent of calling your dog by name or getting him to pay attention and look at you. If you want your dog to sit, one whistle and the command 'Sit!' is all that is necessary. Two whistles mean 'Come!', and so on. The whistle signal is reinforced with the arm signal.

Scent Discrimination

A dog's sense of smell is his most important sense. You cannot teach him how to discriminate between different scents. This he already knows. But what you do teach your dog is when to discriminate and what he should do about it. He has a memory of smells and he can unscramble mixed scents both on a trail and in his food. This is not surprising when you realise that the area inside a dog's head over which scent passes is about the size of the skin on his whole body, whilst our own equivalent area is as small as a postage stamp. For this reason you should not be too hasty in correcting your dog on a line of scent.

Teaching your dog to discriminate scents is both useful and fun. Practise for only three or four minutes a day and, after four days, most dogs understand and enjoy the work. To start with, train your dog inside the house and later outside; three times a week should be sufficient. Select three identical articles of old leather and carry one round in your pocket for a week in order to get it well impregnated with your scent.

With your dog in the 'Sit-stay!' position, place the untouched articles with a pair of tongs about 3m (10ft) from your dog. Then handle the one from your pocket well. Allow your dog to sniff it, but do not let him take it in his mouth or it will destroy your scent. Throw

152

the object about 15cm (6in) from the other one (but it must not touch it). Then place the palm of your hand over your dog's nose so that he can identify your scent and say 'Fetch it!' As he picks up the correct article say 'Good boy!', and he should return to sit in front of you. Let him hold the article a moment before you say 'Give!'; do not look at him as you receive it, and keep your head down. Then thank him. Add another similar article to the others (with the tongs). If your dog starts to pick up the wrong object, say 'No!' quietly and point to the correct one. Your dog may be looking at the article instead of using his nose.

Once your dog becomes more proficient, use wooden objects such as 10cm (4in) lengths of broom handle, mix them up with the leather ones, and finally add metal objects. This last test is more difficult since dogs do not care for metal in their mouths. Gradually increase the distance and then go outside.

If your dog has difficulty selecting the correct object, try placing a clothes line on the ground and get a friend to clip the articles at 10cm (4in) intervals on to the line. The only unclipped one will be your scented object which, when he comes to it, will be the only one that is easy to pick up. When he does so, give him lavish praise.

Your dog next progresses to the seek back. You can play games with him, starting off with the 'Sit-stay!' command and laying the object behind your dog. Place the palm of your hand over his nose and tell him to 'Go seek!' Progress to hiding the object in the passage or upstairs, and later in the garden. He must use his nose and you must make sure that he brings the article back to you each time. Gradually add more articles to the original scented one. Do not over-do the game or your dog will become bored. Later he will be more than useful looking for things you have genuinely lost.

You can help your dog by impregnating the object with your scent by placing it under your armpit (before you use a deodorant).

Part II
THE SHOW DOG

15

Clubs, Shows and Judges

When you refer to the Kennel Club it always means the English Kennel Club. All other kennel clubs are prefixed by the name of the country in which they operate, eg American Kennel Club, Malaysian Kennel Club, etc.

Breed Clubs
A newcomer to the dog world should write to the Kennel Club, enclosing a stamped addressed envelope, and ask for a list of breed club societies in the breed in which he or she is interested. All exhibitors should support at least one of their breed clubs, and it is of course better if you can support more. There are many and varied club activities such as lectures, teach-ins and judge-ins, as well as less serious social activities, coffee mornings, garden parties and dinners. Every year there is the excitement of the annual general meeting, which can be quite lively and a great eye-opener in some popular breed clubs. Popular and numerically strong breeds often have a great number of breed clubs. A breed like the german shepherd, for instance, has no less than forty-four clubs of various kinds. Spaniels are not far behind in the number of clubs, and retrievers have about two dozen clubs.

There are many well run and happy specialist clubs, mostly in the less popular breeds. Unfortunately, in the over-popular breeds specialist clubs are often notoriously tendentious, and they may well become completely controlled for many years by a strong-minded chairman or by a group forming a committee. The power that these people wield is often directed towards their own ends. Tears and tantrums and ganging up on some unsuspecting individual, generally instigated by jealousy, are by no means unheard of, but this is all part and parcel of the dog 'game'. If you, the newcomer, can have a calming influence in such circumstances and put your breed before dog politics you can contribute towards a happier club.

Types of Show
There are six types of dog show held in the United Kingdom, and they all come under the jurisdiction of the Kennel Club. Exemption

shows and matches are permitted by the Kennel Club Committee;
sanction shows, as the name implies, are sanctioned by the Committee; whilst the other shows are licensed, these being limited,
open and championship shows. Exemption shows are not very
serious and they are often held at garden fêtes. They have only four
pedigree classes and the dogs do not have to be registered at the
Kennel Club. They include fun classes such as 'the dog with the
longest tail' or 'the dog most like his owner'. The show is intended
for amusement and perhaps for fund raising.

Matches are unbenched and are largely social affairs for members
of the organising club, but the dogs have to be pedigree dogs and
over six months old. Up to thirty-two dogs compete against each
other in couples. On arrival at the show each dog is given a number.
The numbers are drawn two at a time and the two dogs then compete
against each other. The winner of this heat must be prepared to
compete against another dog when his number is called. The first
round consists of sixteen pairs, the second round of eight pairs, the
third of four pairs, and so on until the last two dogs compete for best
in match. It is all great fun and excellent training for the dogs
because they compete with dogs of all shapes and sizes in other
breeds, gaining experience for the time when they may compete in
variety classes or even perhaps one day in the best-in-show ring.
Sanction shows may have up to twenty-five classes, but there is no
class above postgraduate (see page 163). The shows are unbenched,
dogs must be over the age of six months and no dog may be entered
if he has won a challenge certificate. Exhibitors must be members of
the club, and there is an entry fee. Rosettes, cards and trophies may
be won and sometimes there are commercial donations.

In limited shows the number of classes is limited by the Kennel
Club, the shows are unbenched, dogs must be over the age of six
months, and no dog may be entered if he has won a challenge
certificate. Exhibitors must be members of the club, and there is an
entry fee. Rosettes, cards and trophies may be won and sometimes
commercial donations are received. As the name implies, open
shows are open to all dogs, irrespective of whether or not they are
champions. The shows may be confined to one breed or they may be
open to many different breeds. The shows are usually benched, and
dogs must be over the age of six months. Junior warrant points may
be gained, one point per win. A junior warrant requires twenty-five
points before the age of eighteen months. Sometimes breed clubs
join together to award club trophies.

Championship shows may be confined to one breed or they may
include many breeds. Dogs must be over the age of six months and

Two superb collies, beautifully groomed, waiting to leave for a show

the shows are benched. There is an entry fee and some shows are for members only. Points towards junior warrant may be won, three points being awarded as opposed to the one point at open shows. Challenge certificates are awarded for most of the scheduled breeds, provided that more than 150 registrations in that breed have been made at the Kennel Club.

Show Awards
A challenge certificate is the highest award granted by the Kennel Club at a championship show. Challenge certificates (CCs) are

awarded to the best dog and the best bitch in each breed (when they have qualified by sufficient numbers of registrations in the breed). In order to become a champion a dog must win a challenge certificate under three different judges, including at least one challenge certificate after the age of twelve months (in dog parlance this is known as being 'made up'). Gundogs require a qualifying certificate at a field trial in order to be eligible for the title of full champion, which includes both field trial and show qualifications.

With the enormous increase in registrations, the Kennel Club decided to increase the number of challenge certificates awarded in a breed each year according to the number of dogs registered over a five-year period, the first period starting in 1972.

'International champion' is an unofficial title and is used for dogs which have been awarded the title of champion in two or more countries.

To gain a junior warrant a dog must win twenty-five points before the age of eighteen months in breed classes at open and champion ship shows. It is not essential for challenge certificates to be on offer at these shows. Only one point is won at an open show by the winner of each breed class, but at a championship show three points are gained by the winner of each breed class. Any dog that wins a junior warrant must be outstanding to win so many first prizes in one year since he cannot be exhibited before he is six months old. The owner of the dog must apply to the Kennel Club for this award and must send in full details of all the first prizes the dog has been awarded, including the name and date of each show and which judge awarded the prizes. In the fullness of time the Kennel Club, having checked the details, will award the dog a junior warrant certificate.

Prize Cards

At all shows other than matches, not less than three prize cards are awarded for each class. In the larger shows the maximum number of cards awarded is seven. All the cards have the name of the show printed on them and also the venue and the date. There are two spaces on the cards: one is for the number of the class, which is stamped on; the other is for the number of the exhibit, which is inserted by the exhibitor. In general, first prize cards are red, second prizes are blue and third prizes are yellow. The fourth prize, which is called 'reserve' (not to be confused with the much more exalted win of 'reserve best of breed' or 'reserve best in show'), is a green card. The remaining three prize cards are white. The white cards are for 'very highly commended' (which in dog parlance is known as 'VHC'), 'highly commended' and 'commended'. If a special prize is awarded it may be a gift, a donation or a trophy, and the card is pink.

Owners place the winning cards on the benches or pens of the successful dogs. Sometimes money prizes are attached to the back of the card so, before placing the card on the bench, make certain that you detach the envelope containing the prize money. If the prize money is not attached to the card you will see a detachable slip at the side of the card. This must be removed immediately and you must fill in the class number and the number of the exhibit. This slip must be signed by the handler or the exhibitor and taken at some stage to the secretary's or treasurer's office to claim the prize money.

The most prized cards are those for 'best in show' (BIS), 'best of breed' (BOB) and, at championship shows, 'challenge certificate' (CC) and 'reserve best of sex', the latter often being incorrectly referred to as 'reserve CC'. The two top honours are 'best in show' and 'reserve best in show'. These cards are red-and-white striped or green-and-white striped. Sanction and exemption shows are permitted to award white prize cards printed in black. They may have a coloured stripe across the top left-hand corner to signify a first, second or third prize.

The challenge certificate card is a large one, 220 × 190mm (8¾ × 7½in) in size. It is white with a green border and with green printing. The name of the show, the date, the breed and the sex of the dog are filled in at the top of the card, and the name of the dog and his owner must be written on the card. The judge signs the card to the effect that the dog 'is of such outstanding merit as to be worthy of the title of champion'. When the Kennel Club have confirmed the win the exhibitor will receive a much larger document, 300 × 175mm (12 × 7in) in size. This is a white certificate printed and decorated in black, with the words 'Challenge Certificate' printed in red. On the right there is a large red Kennel Club seal and a printed signature of the Kennel Club secretary.

The reserve best of sex card is green and white, 150×115mm (6×4½in) in size, and is awarded to the second best dog in the relevant sex. The best of breed card is red and white and measures 200×125mm (8×5in). It is awarded for the best of breed, which is judged between the best dog and the best bitch. The winning dog then goes forward to be judged, with all the other dogs that have won best of breed, for the awards in the group classes or for the final 'best in show' award.

Cups and Trophies

All canine show societies and clubs have a considerable number of cups and trophies which have been presented to the club over the years. These trophies are often presented by leading breeders, large firms or by other people interested in certain breeds for varying reasons. A cup may sometimes be donated by a widow in memory of her husband.

Each club must keep a trophy and cup register. After each cup or trophy has been presented the exhibitor must sign a declaration in the book that he or she has accepted the cup, and the name and address of the exhibitor must be entered. At the same time the exhibitor will have been told precisely when the cup must be returned to the club. More often than not this will be at the next club show. Occasionally cups may be kept by the exhibitor for a year. If the name of the winning dog is to be inscribed the secretary arranges this, but sometimes the exhibitor is expected to pay for this honour. If the trophy is a large one then the exhibitor is often presented with a small cup to keep. There are some trophies which become the property of the exhibitor at the time; sometimes they must have been won three years in succession. Some of the poorer clubs may expect the exhibitor to pay a small sum towards the insurance of the trophies.

If you win a cup or a large trophy, you are responsible for its safe keeping and its condition. It is also extremely important that you should return the trophy highly polished and in plenty of time for the next show. If you are not going to the show, then it must be packed most carefully, insured and sent by registered post to the secretary of the club. It is most disappointing to win an important cup only to find that it has not been returned by the previous holder. If it is your first cup, the gilt has certainly been taken off the gingerbread. If the cup is sent to you by post several months later you will have missed the applause and congratulations that normally go with winning a high award.

Even if you have been showing dogs for years and have accumulated many cups and trophies, always accept the cup and never return it to the club secretary after the show because you cannot be bothered to clean it. It could be most hurtful for the donor of the trophy to find that what had perhaps cost him a great deal of money was held in such low esteem.

Attractive and colourful rosettes are always popular with exhibitors and they are cheap for clubs to present. The rosettes are made of pleated nylon or satin ribbon surrounding a coloured cardboard disc, which has the name of the show and the date in gold lettering. Grander rosettes may support a second row of ribbon in perhaps a second colour. The whole rosette is finished off with flowing streamers. Rosettes for best of breed, best of group and best

162

in show are always presented at championship shows. Rosettes are often presented by kind donors at small or open shows, and breed clubs may give rosettes for all wins up to fifth place and for best puppy and best in show.

Sashes of honour are always an exciting presentation and are usually won outright, although some canine societies expect them to be returned by the exhibitors annually. A sash of honour is a highly decorative, wide, brightly coloured ribbon presented for best in show. It is worn by the dog, draped across his back and shoulders whilst he does the lap of honour.

Plaques and medallions may be presented for special classes, as are salvers, spoons and silver ornaments. Kind donors of such prizes give enormous pleasure, particularly to novices; exhibitors with excellent dogs that somehow always seem to get pipped at the post, either by a well known breeder or a famous dog, may sometimes find a special prize awarded perhaps to the best dog that has not won a first prize.

Show Classes

At open and championship shows there may be, up to and including the open class, as many as thirteen classes. At some shows there are extra classes, but these do not count towards challenge certificate awards. At a championship show, where variety classes are included, the same class classifications apply. Classes are: puppy, junior, maiden, novice, tyro, debutante, undergraduate, graduate, postgraduate, minor limit, mid-limit, limit, open, veteran, field trial, brace, team, and sweepstake.

Judges

There are two types of judge, specialist judges and all-rounders. The specialist judge is generally someone who has perhaps devoted many years to one breed, owned and bred a number of well known dogs, and probably over the years made up a number of champions. Some specialist judges may themselves have bred and exhibited only comparatively few dogs in their breed but they will have been involved with the breed for a long time. They will have given many hours of voluntary work on a breed committee, acted as treasurer for a breed club, edited a breed magazine, etc. After a few years in a breed a breeder may be asked to judge a small limited show. Later, if he has acquitted himself well, he may be promoted to judge an open show.

Many specialist judges start their judging career by stewarding at small shows, graduating to larger shows and then taking the respon-

163

Mr Stanley Dangerfield examining borzois in the Team class at Windsor Championship Show

sibility of judging a breed. After a few years of judging one breed a judge who has a good eye for a dog may learn to judge another breed, generally by owning and exhibiting a few dogs in this breed. After a judge has been on his breed club's judging list for five years he may be invited to judge at a championship show. Before a judge may award challenge certificates he must satisfy the Kennel Club on his five years' judging experience and on the dogs he has bred and their show accomplishments. Only when the Kennel Club are fully satisfied with all the answers is the judge elevated to be a championship show judge in one breed. Quite a number of kennel staff become excellent judges themselves, having gained much knowledge and experience through their employers' dogs.

The Kennel Clubs in some countries insist on their judges passing examinations, either oral, written or both, as well as a practical examination. Unfortunately, passing such examinations with very high marks by no means proves that a person will make a good judge. A good judge must have a good eye, the right temperament and an excellent memory. British judges do not have to pass any examinations and yet they become some of the best judges in the world. The reason for this is that they have at least a five year apprenticeship before being permitted by the Kennel Club to award challenge certificates. Judges in Britain gain much experience owing to the tremendous size of many classes.

When a specialist judge is judging his breed he will be looking for all the finer breed points. He may perhaps be mainly interested in the colour of the eyes, the shape of the tail, the tan markings, the trace, pencilling, etc. He may attach great importance to the set of the ears or to some other breed idiosyncrasy. A specialist judge particularly likes a good head and expression. He will often overlook a body fault but he will seldom tolerate or even make allowances for a less than good head.

The all-rounder judge is someone who is knowledgeable about many breeds. He will have graduated from giving challenge certificates in one breed to a group of breeds and then to several groups. He will have gained experience in variety classes and he has probably judged abroad many times. Unlike the specialist judge, the all-rounder goes first for soundness and the overall appearance of a dog. Balance and quality have a much higher priority than individual characteristics.

The all-rounder judge and the specialist judge are both equally important for breeds as a whole. Between them they keep the balance between the fetishes of the specialist judge and the general high qualities demanded by the all-rounder. The best dogs are those that can win top awards under both types of judge. It is interesting that in the USA there are more all-rounder judges than specialists, whilst in Britain there are more specialist judges than all-rounders. This may be the reason why British dogs keep their type so well. Many thousands of dogs are exported from Britain each year, all over the world, and yet the demand for British-bred dogs still continues. The expertise of breeders who are also judges has developed to a very high standard owing to their long apprenticeship before being allowed to judge at championship shows.

What the Judge is Looking for
Every judge has a mental image of the perfect dog as defined by his interpretation of the breed standard. He judges each dog according to this image. There is, of course, no such thing as the perfect dog, so

he must select the dog nearest to this mental picture. He then compares the other exhibits with the dog nearest to the standard and places them accordingly. A judge first looks at the dog as an entity and will judge on his good points. The judge assesses type first— does the dog look like a good specimen of his breed? Next in importance comes the dog's temperament. Temperament comprises a dog's natural tendencies as determined by his physical constitution, so that the dog's primary function is a most important consideration when he is being judged. Nervousness and aggressiveness are extremely undesirable traits in all breeds. Temperament also includes viciousness, alertness, docility and any other behavioural idiosyncrasies.

Each breed of dog has its own correct breed temperament and it is important that temperament should be rated highly. For instance, according to the breed standards, a bull terrier is 'the gladiator of the canine race, with a jaunty air'; an english setter is 'friendly and quiet'; a fox terrier 'on tip toe of expectation'; a maltese is 'sweet'; mastiffs, pyrenean mountain dogs and newfoundlands are 'docile'; norfolk terriers are 'demons'; pekingese 'have dignity'; pomeranians have 'buoyancy'; St Bernards are 'benevolent'; bloodhounds are 'reserved and sensitive'; german shepherds are 'incorruptible

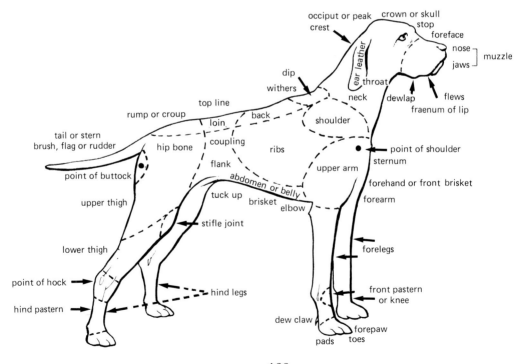

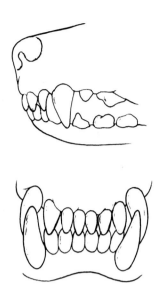

Scissor bite

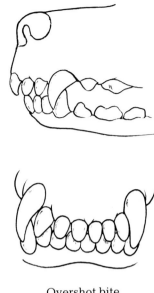

Overshot bite

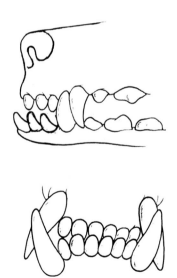

Undershot bite

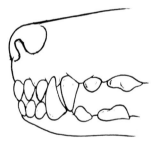

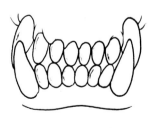

Edge-to-edge bite

and discerning'; afghans are 'aloof'; and so on. These epithets are apt and descriptive.

In making a general assessment of a dog and watching him move, the judge will have noted his balance, soundness, condition and general showmanship. The judge then proceeds to examine the dog's individual points. He will note his front and throat. He will go over the head carefully, looking at the set of the ear, the leathers, the skull, the stop, the expression, shape and colour of the eyes and their placement. He will note the muzzle, lips and chin. In some breeds he will have to look at wrinkles, thumbmarks, black moles, pencilling, lozenges and, in the chow chow, the black colour of the tongue.

The mouth is most important. The judge looks at the teeth and jaw and notes whether the dog has a scissor or edge-to-edge bite; whether the jaw is overshot or undershot; and if the teeth are clean, level and even. In some breeds the judge must ascertain whether the dog has the correct number of teeth (see page 167).

The judge looks at the dog's front, fore pasterns and forefeet, his nails and sometimes the pads and dewclaws. He will note the length of the neck and will place great importance on well laid-back shoulders. He will assess the rib cage and the depth of chest, the length of loin, the angle of the croup, and note whether the dog's back is level or roached. He will notice the depth of flank, the set of the dog's tail and any particular tail idiosyncrasies. He will feel the strength of the muscles of the hindquarters, and he must ascertain if the dog is entire. He will note the turn of stifle, the angulation and let-down (length) of hock, and whether the hind pasterns are vertical to the ground. In just these few minutes the judge will also have taken in the length of leg and bone structure and the hind feet. He will note the suppleness of his skin and the condition, colour, length and texture of the coat.

After looking at the dog in such detail and watching him perform

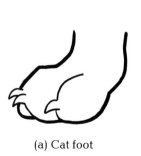 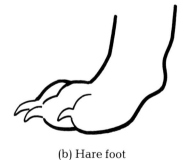

(a) Cat foot   (b) Hare foot

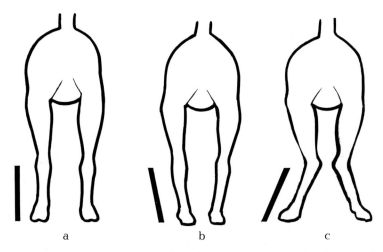

(a) Correct stance, pasterns parallel; (b) incorrect stance, hocks turned out, hind pasterns inclined inwards; (c) incorrect, cow hocks

his individual gaiting to see how sound he is, the judge compares this dog with his individual mental image of the perfect dog of the breed. The points he is looking for are: type, temperament and soundness; followed by balance, style, condition, harmony and beauty of the dog's entire conformation; and his showmanship.

With certain breeds and varieties the dogs have to be weighed or measured in some restricted classes. Scales and measuring hoops or sticks must be provided by the show committee and the weighing and measuring will be done by the judge. Sometimes a judge has mixed classes where dogs of both sexes are in the ring together. A judge may often prefer to separate the dogs from the bitches in the same line-up because it is important that male dogs should look masculine and bitches should be feminine. It is also easier for the judge to have the dogs together so that he remembers to check that the dog is entire.

In a variety class there is obviously no one standard by which the judge can judge all the breeds. He has to look at each breed of dog and compare each dog with his mental image of what he should look like in accordance with his interpretation of the breed standard. The judge does not in fact judge one dog against another. He judges against his standard and then decides whether the dog is a good representative of his breed. He chooses his winning dogs according to which appear to him to be nearest to his interpretation of the standard of that breed. In the United Kingdom the standard is really set by the breeders and type is controlled by the specialist judges. In the United States, however, the standard is controlled by points; the shows are dominated by professional handlers and type is kept (or lost) by the all-rounder judges.

16

Entering for a Show

All dog shows come under the jurisdiction of the Kennel Club and they are for pure-bred registered dogs only, except in obedience tests where spayed or castrated dogs may be shown as well. In England there are hundreds of licensed dog shows held all over the country during the year. There are six types of show, so that there is no difficulty in choosing one in your area where you can compete with dogs of a similar standard to your own.

Shows are held by individual dog clubs. You will find the lists of forthcoming shows published in the weekly dog magazines *Dog World* and *Our Dogs*. The Kennel Club also have an official magazine, *The Kennel Gazette*, and in this you will find the name and type of show and date or dates. Shows may last one, two or three days. The show secretary's name and address will also be given.

Once you have been bitten by the 'show bug' and intend to show your dog fairly frequently, you can write to the various show secretaries and ask to be put on their mailing list so that you will automatically receive the schedules for the shows. A show schedule will include all the information that you require to know: venue, date, judges, prizes, conformation classes and obedience classes if there are any, the time they will be judged and also the closing date of entries. Inside the schedule you will find an entry form. Entry forms come in various sizes but the layout is similar in all of them. It is important that you should read the entry form carefully and note the date by which the form must be received by the show secretary. This date is usually printed prominently both on the entry form itself and also on the schedule.

The Entry Form
It is essential that you fill in your entry correctly, legibly and in bold print with a ball-point pen or in ink. You will find that the first column is for the full, registered name of your dog. Only dogs that are registered at the Kennel Club may be entered at a show. The exhibitor must also be the sole owner of the dog at the time of entry, unless you own the dog in partnership with someone else.

If for any reason the transfer of ownership of your dog has not come through from the Kennel Club before you make your entry, you should write in capitals 'TAF' (Transfer Applied For) immediately after the full name of your dog. In the case of the registration of your puppy not having come through in time, you should write the capital letters 'NAF' (Name Applied For) after the name for which you have applied.

The second column is for the breed. If your dog is a variety of a breed, for example a long-haired dachshund, then under dachshund you should write the words 'long-haired'. The third column is for the date of birth of your dog, so you should fill in his full date of birth. The fourth column is for sex, and you simply fill in a capital 'D' for dog or capital 'B' for bitch. In some countries the word 'male' or 'female' is entered instead of the letters 'D' or 'B'. The fifth column is for the name of the breeder of your dog, that is the owner of the dam at the time of the birth of the puppies.

The sixth column is for the sire of the dog, and you must fill in his full name. If the sire is a champion you should prefix his name with 'Ch'. The seventh column is filled in if the dog is for sale. If this is the case then the price of your dog must be entered. Some clubs take 10 per cent on the sale price of a dog sold through a show catalogue, but the majority of clubs require no commission. The final column is headed 'To be entered in classes numbered'. So you should write the class numbers clearly, making certain that you have not confused dog classes with bitch classes or made an error with the number of a class.

It really is extremely important that you should read and understand the declaration that you, the exhibitor, must sign on the bottom of the entry form. If you co-own your dog with someone else then you and your partner must both sign the form. You are signing that you will abide by the rules and regulations of the Kennel Club. You may not exhibit a dog that is totally blind, defective in hearing, or prevented from breeding as a result of a surgical operation, except as provided for in Regulations for the Preparation of Dogs for Exhibition. This regulation does not apply to a bitch that has been spayed, provided that she has had a litter of puppies that have been registered at the Kennel Club. The Kennel Club altered the rule on cryptorchid dogs in December 1970. A dog may be exhibited if he is cryptorchid (not entire), the fault being considered in the same way as any other external fault.

You are also signing—and this is very important—that the dogs entered have not suffered from or been knowingly exposed to 'the risk of distemper or any contagious disease, including any reaction to immunisation, during the six weeks prior to exhibition, and that

171

A toy poodle having his mouth examined by the judge. The table has been covered with a cloth to prevent the dogs from slipping

you will not show them if they incur such risks between now and the day of the show or, if they have been immunised, within fourteen days prior to the show'. Finally, you must fill in your name and address in block capitals, not forgetting to add your postcode. It is advisable to put your telephone number in brackets at the bottom.

The entry fees will be stated in the schedule. The cost varies according to the show. You must calculate the total sum payable by you, which will include not only the fees for the classes in which you have entered your dog but may also include a benching fee for each dog and a car park fee. If you enter in a brace class your two dogs count as one entry. There could be a reduction in entry fees if you are a member of the club. It is certainly a wise precaution to ask someone to check your entry form before you make out your cheque or postal or money order.

Without fail you should send off your entry form and fees in good time, a few days prior to the closing date, which is generally three or four weeks before the show. In the USA entries have to be made seven to twelve days before the date of the show. For an important show it is advisable to enclose a stamped addressed post card with your entry so that the secretary can return it as confirmation of receipt of your entry. This will avoid the disappointment of preparing your dog and travelling a long distance to a show only to find that your entry was not received in time.

About a week before the show you will be sent an entry slip, which is your admission ticket. You will also receive your bench number(s), if it is a benched show, and your car park ticket, if you ordered one. If you have a caravan there will be a special area for these.

If your show entries do not arrive at the show secretary's office by the requisite date, so that your passes and removal cards are delayed in reaching you, you should inform the secretary by telephone. If you arrive at the show and find that your entries are not in the catalogue you will be permitted to exhibit your dog in the classes you entered by completing an entry form and paying the requisite fees. After the show the secretary will write to the Kennel Club submitting a full report. The Kennel Club will write to you asking you to provide proof of posting your entry. They will also want to know whether you sent your entry fee by postal order or by cheque. If the former, you must send the postal order counterfoil. If you wrote a cheque you will be required to send three cheque stubs: the one for the cheque you wrote before your entry-fee cheque; the entry fee stub itself; and the one for the next cheque written. The show regulation committee will then examine your proof of entry for the show and upon their decision will rest whether your entries will stand or be disqualified.

Which Classes to Enter

When entering your dog for a class it is essential to calculate all his previous wins at open and championship shows. Wins in variety classes do not count at breed shows, nor do the awards to junior warrant points. Your dog's wins are calculated from midnight preceding the closing date for entry as shown on the schedule. Your puppy is eligible for the puppy class provided that he is six calendar months old and not more than twelve calendar months old on the first day of the show. It is most important that you should remember these facts, particularly when you make your entries at a two- or three-day show. Your puppy may not be exhibited if his date of birth is six calendar months prior to the last day of the show. In this case he would be one or two days too young. It is easy to remember that the first day of the show is the official date and all your calculations must be made from that date.

Your dog is not eligible for variety classes unless he has been entered and exhibited in a breed class—that is, provided that there is one. You may, however, enter your puppy in a variety puppy class if there is no breed puppy class scheduled. Field trial and veterans (dogs above a certain age) are also exempt from this regulation. There is nothing so infuriating as entering your puppy in a class for which he is ineligible.

Having established your dog's eligibility, one of the difficult decisions to make is the correct choice of class in which to enter him. Many mistakes are made and prize money lost through insufficient thought being given to this problem. But, at the same time, the choice is a lottery as you do not know in which class other dogs will be entered. Most classes have qualifying conditions and these conditions act as handicaps, making the competition fairer. Puppy classes provide good experience, although maturer puppies generally do better. This applies even more in junior classes where the age span is from six months to eighteen months. A dog of nearly eighteen months of a small breed could be almost in his prime, so that, unless a young puppy were outstanding, he would have little chance of even being placed.

The class with the least competition is the maiden class because here no dog may have won a challenge certificate or a first prize at any show. The novice class is also a good class to enter because here no dog may have won a challenge certificate or three or more first prizes at open and championship shows (puppy and minor puppy excepted). There is also no age limit. However, owing to the handicapping, these classes usually have large entries.

The other classes that are well handicapped are classes for novices which are described as 'For owner, handler or dog never having won a prize', or 'For dogs or bitches shown by an exhibitor who has never won a first prize in the breed at a show'. Here it is the exhibitor that has to qualify, not the dog.

It is not wise to enter a dog in classes which are too advanced. It is better to work your way up, class by class. In this way both handler and dog gain experience. Some dogs mature much more slowly than others, and there are cases where it would be more sensible to keep the dog out of the ring for a few months and then enter him perhaps in a maiden or novice class or even in a higher class.

Most large shows have variety classes and it is extremely good experience for novice handlers to enter their dogs in these classes. Standing next to handlers with different breeds and watching the different ways in which the various breeds are handled is fascinating. You will get to know the characteristics in other breeds. You will also be showing your dog under all-rounder judges. These judges have tremendous experience of many breeds and they will be judging your dog from a different viewpoint from that of a specialist judge. In some breeds, where the competition is high, you may find that a few specialist judges do not judge uniformly, that they are prejudiced regarding certain breed points, and that they may even be under pressure from friends and enemies. A few breed classes become virtually 'closed shops', but even so a really good dog will get to the top eventually, although it could take quite a long time.

An all-rounder judge is under pressure from nobody. He will take a wider view of the dog game and he will be judging dogs on general impressions—he will prefer temperament and soundness to special points. The existence of the two types of judge is important for the breeds because it keeps a balance between fine points looked for by the specialist judges and general qualities demanded by the all-rounders.

If your dog is beautiful, well-bred and intelligent you will have tremendous fun taking him to obedience classes. Here you will meet a new set of people whose object is totally different from that of the dog show fraternity. Some owners attend obedience classes solely to have a well behaved dog at home. In this case they will only need to attend a short course. It takes much longer to train your dog in a class than teaching him on your own. The latter is much better, provided that you know what you are doing, but a class does have the advantage of allowing your dog to get used to being with many dogs of various sizes, some well behaved, many badly behaved. There will be much barking and noise from time to time. This is especially good for a shy dog since he will be distracted by all that is going on around him and will forget his shyness.

The basic purpose of obedience classes is to ascertain a dog's ability to work and to obey his handler with precision. They also demonstrate a dog's intelligence to some extent. Each exercise is designed with a particular purpose in mind so that it constitutes a step forward in the dog's training. To train a dog to a high standard of obedience is a tremendous achievement, provided that it is done with love and kindness, and a well trained dog is worth his weight in gold.

However, although dogs enjoy their training for the most part, I do not personally believe in or like the very high precision training required for top awards in obedience tests, as I feel that very few dogs really enjoy this extremely high achievement. They are not permitted to use their intelligence and become mere robots. There can be very few trainers who have sufficient rapport with their dogs to ensure that they truly enjoy this precision work. Most all-breed shows have obedience classes, so if you enjoy this type of training and have the expense of going to a show, you might just as well have the additional enjoyment of entering your dog in the obedience classes too.

If you intend to enter your dog for a number of shows and then start showing regularly, you should keep a record of all your dog's wins so that you know exactly how many first prizes he has won and how many challenge certificates. If you do not do this you could easily enter your dog in a class for which he is not eligible. It also saves time, when entering your dog for a show, if you keep an old entry form filled in which you can copy each time you enter for a new show. In this way you will immediately know the name of the breeder of your dog, the full name of his sire and the date of his birth.

If you have a number of dogs which you are showing, then it is much better if you keep a record book to include your dogs' pedigrees, their wins, and also their critiques from the various judges when they are printed in the dog papers.

17

The Laws of Dog Shows

Breed Standards
Some breed standards were compiled well over a century ago and many of these standards have had only minor alterations during this time. Breed standards are compiled by breed club committees and, once the Kennel Club have accepted a breed standard, they are not inclined to allow it to be altered. Unfortunately, you will find that not all standards are well worded nor are many of them written in good English. The headings of standards consist of: Characteristics, General Appearance, Head and Skull, Eyes, Mouth, Neck, Forequarters, Body, Hindquarters, Feet, Tail, Coat, Colour, Weight, Size, Faults. In the USA standards there are also: Disqualifications, Movement and Carriage, and a scale of points. Breed standards, unfortunately, have never been standardised, either in the USA or in England, and some of the descriptions are both vague and ambiguous. Some standards are exceedingly short, whilst others, like that of the boxer, are unnecessarily long and liable to misconstructions.

Judges and breeders use the standards as blueprints on which to base their interpretations of what constitutes the perfect dog. It is fascinating how the loose wording of these standards lends itself to varying interpretations. Typical examples are: '. . . neither too long nor too short'; '. . . medium size'; '. . . preferably dark' (at what stage are eyes no longer dark?). It is such ambiguities which lead to creations of fashions in breed type. Breeds do change, as can be seen from old photographs, yet the standards remain the same.

It is most important that you should know and understand the breed standard for your dog. Seek after the good points and make the most of them but, on the other hand, do not be blind to your dog's faults. There is, of course, no such thing as a perfect dog. No doubt in your eyes your dog is perfect, but if you refuse to open your eyes to his faults you will not have much success either in showing your dog or in breeding, should you decide to start.

Kennel Club Publications
The *Kennel Club Stud Book* was first published in 1874. Some of the pedigrees went back to 1859. All dogs exhibited at Kennel Club

shows have to be registered at the Kennel Club. This rule came into force on 31 July 1904 and has remained a strict regulation ever since. The *Stud Book* is the only record published in England of dog shows, field trials, obedience tests and working trials. It contains group registration figures, breed statistics, a summary of events, lists of championship shows and judges and of shows at which championship obedience tests have been held. There are sections for each group and for each breed, and details of breeds and pedigrees. There is also a list of breeders and owners of championship winning dogs who have been placed first, second or third in limit and open classes. It is both important and exciting when your dog gets into the *Stud Book*—it is a record for ever more. When this happens your dog will receive a new registration number which will include letters as well as figures. When you notice these letters in a pedigree you will know at once that the dog has had an important win. This also applies for obedience tests, field trials and working trials. There is also a list for junior warrants claimed and granted. The names and addresses of persons whose dogs are entered in a particular volume of the *Stud Book* are also included in that volume (a useful reference).

The *Kennel Club Gazette* is issued each month and with it comes the *Kennel Club Stud Book Breed Record Supplement.* This contains the details of all newly registered dogs: name; date of birth; breeder; names of sire and dam; and name of owner. The supplement also contains changes of name, transfers, export pedigrees, champion certificates, challenge certificates and junior warrants. It also has a list of hip dysplasia and progressive retinal atrophy (PRA) certificates for dogs that have passed veterinary tests clearing them of these breed problems. There are also lists for working trials, obedience tests and field trials. On the last page will be found the current list of Kennel Club fees from 'registration by breeder' down to 'cost of running field trials'.

Show Regulations

If your dog has been so fortunate as to be awarded best of breed he automatically goes forward to compete for that most coveted position of best in show, provided that he has not been beaten in a variety class. It is always most upsetting to have done so well in your breed, then to enter your dog in some variety classes in which perhaps he is not even placed, and then find that you have lost the chance of competing for the best-in-show award, with its splendid rosettes and perhaps a large cup with the winning dog's name engraved on the silver for ever. But it is the saga of the dog game—a glorious game of chance.

However, if your dog has been unbeaten he is eligible to go forward, as are all the other unbeaten dogs. Where there have been no scheduled breed classes, provided that he has won a variety class, your dog may be entered for best in show.

Once your dog has been admitted to a show he must be exhibited in all the classes for which he has been entered, otherwise he is liable to be disqualified by the Kennel Club Regulations Committee should he have been 'in the cards'. He would also be disqualified if a judge has requested his appearance and you then do not take him into the ring. There are, however, three exceptions to this Kennel Club regulation: if another judge is substituted for the scheduled one at the last moment you have the prerogative of withdrawing your dog, provided that you give notice to the show secretary in writing that you wish to withdraw your dog from competition; should your dog become ill at the show or suffer an injury the same applies, although you would probably have to allow your dog to have a veterinary examination, should there be a veterinary officer on duty; your dog may also be permitted to miss his class if the class is judged after the authorised time for the removal of exhibits.

I remember well my first best of breed win at which I was so thrilled and elated that I drove home on cloud nine. Unfortunately for me the show was running late, I had two or three hundred kilometres to drive home, a bitch due to whelp, young puppies to cope with, and all the usual problems when one leaves home for a full day. I decided that I could not possibly win best in show or reserve best in show, and that I would leave for home instead. I was well satisfied with my best of breed win. How enormously wrong I was! Little did I know the importance of having one's best of breed in the best-in-show ring for all to see. Knowing now what a game of chance dog showing can be, I realise that my dog might have won best in show at one of the largest championship shows in the world and she would have thus got to the top rather more quickly. But more important still, the dog would have been seen by many influential judges and breeders. The moral is never to be too easily satisfied and to make the most of your wins. Needless to say, on my return home all was well, no one had missed me, and my bitch did not whelp for a few more days.

You may not enter your dog if he has been bred by the judge, nor must you enter a dog that has been handled by the judge, boarded by the judge in his boarding kennels, or given any other attention by him within a period of twelve months. The judge, of course, would not be penalised but you would be.

All dogs may only be removed from a show at the specified time. This rule is made so that the general public, who have paid an entry fee to the show grounds in order to see all the dogs, should have the opportunity to do so. There is no point in your going to the show secretary and asking for dispensation, as it is not in his power to grant your request. If you do leave the show ground before the appointed time, however genuine the reason, you could be fined by the Kennel Club should a malicious exhibitor report your act to the Kennel Club in writing. However, a fine is all you would incur; your dogs' wins would still stand.

No one is permitted to attract an exhibit's attention from the ringside. It would obviously be most unfair to find a friend to handle a dog of yours that is perhaps not very well trained and for you then to encourage the dog to look alert or walk towards you whilst you stand outside the ring making discreet encouraging noises. Showing is a sport, so to behave in an unsporting manner would obviously be more than frowned upon. You may report any discreditable conduct to the show secretary, provided of course that you are absolutely sure of your facts. For example, you would be justified in doing so should a fellow exhibitor take the wrong black poodle into the ring, having shown his champion black poodle in a novice or junior class instead of the junior or novice dog he should have shown. Black poodles can look as alike as two peas in a pod, except to the people who know the dogs.

Anyone may make an objection against a dog, provided that he is not under suspension from the Kennel Club. However, should you wish to make an objection you must do so in writing, with all the relevant details. These must be handed personally to the show secretary with the requisite deposit. Provided that your objection is upheld by the Kennel Club Committee your deposit will be returned to you.

During the show all dogs are required to wear a secure collar, and they must be tethered by a strong chain to one or both rings on the bench, unless of course your breed is of the toy group and the dogs are securely caged in show pens. When you are handling your dog he may wear a slip lead or he may be handled with a leash and collar. Your dog must be on a lead of some kind throughout the show. The two exceptions are: if your dog is in the exercising area; or if he has been entered in obedience tests. Occasionally a judge may grant permission in the case of a toy breed for the dog to be gaited without a lead. This would probably only be done in the puppy class if the judge particularly liked an outstanding puppy that he felt was perhaps overawed at his first show by all the noise and strangeness around him so much so that he was refusing to walk on a lead.

When you sign your entry form you have to declare that your dog has not been exposed to the risk of distemper or any contagious disease. If your dog is the least off colour or has come into contact with dogs with infections, whatever you do you must *not* take your dog to a show where he could spread the infection to hundreds of other dogs. There are some people who do not believe in having their dogs immunised and for years they will go to shows and proudly announce that they do not believe in wasting money on inoculations that may not be effective. Take no notice of these cranks; always have your dogs inoculated. I have known several breeders who never had their dogs inoculated but who, when the crunch came, lost almost every dog in their kennels—everything they had spent years in achieving. So please, never take such a risk.

The Kennel Club may inflict fines upon exhibitors for any breaches of show regulations and even for errors made on entry forms. There are probably few exhibitors who have not at sometime or other made a genuine mistake on an entry form. It could be something silly like leaving out the date of a dog's birth, or perhaps a breeder, having imported a dog some years previously, might enter on the form in error that he himself was the breeder. This is very easily done when a breeder has a large kennel of dogs and automatically assumes that all the dogs that he is entering were bred by him, as most of them would have been. So just take care that you do not inadvertently make a mistake. It is not only costly but it wastes a tremendous amount of time explaining to the authorities what really happened.

The Unwritten Laws of Dogdom

There are some quite sensible unwritten laws regarding relations between exhibitors and judges. It is not advisable to travel to a show with a judge under whom you are going to exhibit. The judge may be your best friend or your neighbour, but if you are seen getting out of the car together in the show grounds tongues are more than likely to wag, especially should you win under the judge. By travelling with a judge you may be putting him under pressure, with the result that your dog might be put down when he should have been put up.

It is also unwise, however well you know the judge, to be seen in animated conversation with him in the show grounds or just before exhibiting under him. If you should encounter the judge before going into the ring do not of course cut him, but simply pass by with a pleasant 'Good morning, what a glorious day!' Whatever you do, do not prance round the judge with the dog you are going to show under him. Obviously, if an honest judge and exhibitor talk to each other it would make no difference to the results. If they are friends, the judge obviously knows all the dogs in his friend's kennels. But it looks bad to other exhibitors, and also to the public, if the judge happens to be well known. So be discreet if you know the judge well and keep out of his way.

Never be so stupid as to offer a judge a drink before judging, or to invite him to a party a couple of weeks before the show, or make any other pre-show contact with him. All judges can see through unnecessary telephone calls and invitations to dinner. If you have a good dog he will win, so do not fall for cheating. Showing your dog should be a pleasure and a sport. It is not usually done, particularly in some breeds, to show your dog under a judge who has already awarded him a challenge certificate. I feel that the exception to this should be Cruft's, where the public come to see the top dogs in the country, as do many foreigners and many breeders. Should your dog have previously won a challenge certificate under the Cruft's judge, he would not then be seen at Cruft's if the rule were observed. The dog would have met few of the dogs he would be competing against, and it would be a shame if he were denied the honour of being seen at Cruft's. The Kennel Club, moreover, have no objection to a dog being exhibited under a judge who has already awarded him a challenge certificate. Added to this, the dog has already had to qualify for Cruft's.

Many breeders also feel that champions should not be exhibited at open shows, but this really depends upon the breed. When you first start exhibiting, this will not be one of your problems. There is no specific rule against showing your bitch in season, but it is a most unfair thing to do, particularly in the top awards of best of breed and best in show, since it obviously affects all the male dogs coming into the ring after your bitch has been exhibited.

There is etiquette to observe as a spectator too. Always applaud the winning dogs, even if you do not agree with the judge's placings. It really is bad form to refrain from clapping the winning dog and to clap loudly for the second and third placings, or to make loud exclamations, or to show your disapproval by any method at all. Slow handclapping or complete silence can be even worse. Do not be unkind and mean. It is quite horrifying how slow handclapping catches on in a crowd, and the majority of the spectators do not even know why they are doing it. It would be better by far to sway the crowd with vigorous, generous handclaps.

If you have been fortunate enough to have won well under a judge, it is not really advisable to enter your dog under this judge in show after show, following him round the country and hoping to win many more awards for your dog. You may well find that if you do so your dog may not even be placed another time. Although the judge liked your dog at the first show, perhaps at the other shows there were better dogs competing which your dog had not met previously. By all means enter under the judge again at the next show, but perhaps enter another dog. Some judges really resent exhibitors following them from show to show, hoping for more awards.

As a novice you should also beware of the few judges who tout for entries. They may come up to you at a show and look at your dog, telling you how much they like him and that he should go far. The judge may be absolutely genuine; on the other hand he may only be touting for extra entries for his next show, and when you go to that show, having entered your dog in many classes with high hopes of success, you may come away completely cardless.

A judge who has perhaps done an exhibitor well with a good dog will always appreciate an entry under him with another dog—not necessarily a top winning one—expecting more awards. Good brood bitches are useful for such entries once you become a breeder, which of course is nearly always what dog showing leads to. Brood bitches are often not quite good enough to become champions, but they often produce better puppies than the champions, and knowledge-able breeders may well be interested in buying puppies from such well bred bitches when the time comes. These brood bitches are also useful when making an entry under a novice judge or a variety judge who is judging the breed for the first time. You can imagine that the well known breeders, who have been breeding for several decades, would not be too happy for a novice judge to practise judging on one of their famous champions and not placing it; or they might feel that by entering such a well known dog they might be pressurising the new judge. On the other hand you should never insult the judge by entering an appalling dog or one that is out of condition, hoping that such a novice might not recognise his glaring faults.

It is sometimes worth giving a judge, who you know prefers another breeder's dogs, a courtesy entry or two but then not actually going to the show itself. If you enter regularly under all the judges you and your dogs get known and you will eventually win with good dogs. If you want to reach the top, you will find the path uphill and thorny, but if you play your cards carefully and with tact, get on to show committees, put some work into your chosen breed, tread with care, and keep your eyes open and your mouth shut, you will certainly have a very good chance of becoming a top exhibitor.

Once a dog has been made a champion there is a tremendous temptation to enter him at every show, hoping perhaps to beat the breed record of fifteen challenge certificates or whatever the number might be. If a dog has won a number of challenge certificates from the top judges then it is generally found that lesser judges follow suit. The dog may have won very little before his first challenge certificate and then he has a tremendous run of luck. There may well be a dog equally as good following on behind with perhaps two challenge certificates and umpteen reserve challenge certificates to his credit. By the time the first dog has stopped being exhibited the number two dog may also be too old to win his third certificate in order to become a champion. I feel that if the dog is really good it would be sporting of the owner of the champion to stand down and allow the other dog to win his championship, and then to continue to compete against him. Breeders may mutter about cheap champions, but such a dog would probably be a worthy champion if he had been perhaps a year older when he started his show circuit. I remember years ago seeing the pedigree of a dog with two challenge certificates and fourteen reserve challenge certificates. I felt that this was very bad luck but I learned many years later that the dog was a monorchid, so that he did not really deserve his first two challenge certificates! Some kennel clubs do not allow monorchids to be exhibited, and from a breeding point of view I think that this is correct. But many people feel that a dog that is outstanding in every way except for that one serious fault, which cannot be seen, is a better specimen than one with slipping stifles, hip dysplasia or a bad mouth. Show dogs are exhibited for conformation, so that there will always be some exhibitors taking each point of view, particularly if they own an outstanding monorchid dog.

You may come across some malpractices at shows. There are a few cunning handlers who, when told by the judge to go and stand in second place, will calmly walk over to the line up and stand in top place, hoping perhaps that, by the time the judge has gone over all the dogs, he will have forgotten what he had said earlier. It is sometimes difficult for nervous novices to stand up to the tough old hands at the game. Such things do not happen often, but when they do, politely stand your ground. The steward or judge will soon notice something going on in the ring behind their backs and will quickly put the matter right. The judge may be so angry that he may even ask the offending handler to move to the bottom of the line. Sometimes handlers will let their dogs out on a long lead in order to bump a rival or put him off his stride. They may walk too closely behind you or walk too slowly in front of you. They may even step on your dog. Just beware of such unsporting behaviour and another time stand next to someone more congenial.

If for any reason you have not brought your dog to the show you must report to the ring steward and inform him that your dog will be absent from his class or classes. If you do not go to the show, you should ask a friend to inform the steward for you. It will save time if the steward knows if your dog is absent because a good steward will very often go round the benches to remind exhibitors that they are about to miss a class.

If you have entered dogs in different breeds in classes that overlap you should go to the ring steward of the later class and explain the situation. The steward will in turn inform the judge. The judge will nearly always continue judging the class and then permit the latecomer to handle the dog at the end of the class. It can be very disappointing, when the judge has placed all his dogs and you think that you have won the first prize, only to find a handler and dog come into the ring with a great flourish at the last second. The judge goes over the new arrival, watches him gait once, and, without seeing him move with the rest of the class, places him first, perhaps for the challenge certificate! You can never be absolutely sure that you have won until you are holding the place card firmly in your hand.

18
General Show Preparations

The majority of people become inveigled into dog showing either by the breeder of their dog or by a keen exhibitor or friend. Having once entered your dog for his first show you will undoubtedly find that, without knowing it, you will have joined the 'dog game' for life, and you will soon find yourself hooked on dog showing. Even if you give the game up for a period you will probably be back at some time or other, even though you may strongly resist the urge. However, here are some words of wisdom. You must always try to remember that dog showing is only a game, although like many games of the present day where money is involved, it is often spoilt by un-sportsmanlike behaviour. You will get the most fun out of showing your dog if you remember other exhibitors are as proud of their dogs as you are of yours. Never, therefore, make critical or disparaging remarks about other people's dogs. They would resent such remarks as much as you would. On the contrary, be generous with genuine praise of other exhibitors' dogs—you will find that they, naturally enough, lap up such praise with enormous pleasure.

There are times, of course, when you may feel that your dog should have done better, but never take your placings too seriously, how-ever much it may hurt at the time. As all dog people know only too well, there is always another judge and another show. You may even find that the same judge could put your dog up at another show. Such is the suspense and fun of showing dogs that you never know what is going to happen. Before a show, always set your mind on enjoying your day, have fun meeting old and new rivals, and most important of all have a winning attitude.

Having entered your dog for a show, first of all make certain that you know where the venue is. This is important since some shows are not held in the town named. For instance, the Richmond Championship Show is not held in Richmond but in London. You must also make certain that you know the day of the week and the date of the show and the time it is due to start. It is also important to be quite clear which dogs you are exhibiting and in which classes. Imagine how awful it would be to go to the wrong place, or, even worse, to go to the right place with the wrong dogs—it has happened! So do ensure that your pre-show preparations are meticulous; entry fees, petrol, not to mention your time, are costly, and unnecessary mistakes are extremely frustrating.

Travelling To and From the Show

Exhibitors may travel to a show by car, coach, train or plane, or even a combination of two or more of these methods. If you intend to travel by car, make quite certain that your car is roadworthy, that it has a full tank of petrol, has water in the radiator, and that the tyres (including the spare) are at the correct pressure. Pack as much as you can in the car the night before so that you can get away in the morning with a minimum of delay. If you have not been to the show ground before and do not know the town nor how to get there it is wise to apply to the Automobile Association to provide you with a route to the show. If you ask them they will also provide an alternative way home. Some of the most enjoyable experiences of dog showing, particularly in the months of summer, early spring and autumn, are the many, varied, cross-country drives in the early hours of the morning. You will feel very superior to all the sleeping inhabitants of the villages and towns through which you pass.

Finding the show ground is not always easy. It is astonishing how frequently it can take you half an hour or more to find the venue of a show, since everyone you ask is inevitably a stranger in the area. It is essential that you should arrive at a show in good time so that you and your dog are in a relaxed, happy state of mind rather than harassed and flustered. It is all too easy to transfer your feelings to your dog so that neither of you will be likely to have a relaxed and happy day. If you are going to travel a long way by car it is sensible to drive with another exhibitor so that you can share the driving and the cost of the petrol, and you can also help each other with your dogs. Long journeys pass very quickly when you have a congenial companion, not necessarily in the same breed. Do remember to make frequent stops, both for your own benefit so that you do not become over-tired driving, and for that of your dog so that he may relieve himself in suitable places, have a drink if the weather is hot, and take some exercise to keep him supple and alert.

It is always safer for a dog to travel in a box or a show case. He could strangle or break a leg if tethered in a car by a lead. There are far fewer serious injuries suffered by dogs in boxes than by dogs sitting on a car seat. Also, an unruly dog jumping about in a car could make the driver take his eyes off the road, or the dog could even escape and cause an accident. Bear in mind that you should take plenty of newspaper in case of 'accidents' in the car, some tissues for general mopping up, and disinfectant for car sickness. A first aid kit should always be carried in the boot of a car. A card should be placed in a conspicuous place with your name, address and blood group. It should also give the telephone-number of dependants in case of an accident.

Do ensure that you have enough petrol for your homeward journey, and that you have had sufficient to eat during the day and not too much to drink before you set off home. Always let your family know the latest time you are likely to be expected home. If you are going to be delayed, telephone home so that animals may be fed and supper eaten before your arrival.

Quite a number of keen exhibitors go to dog shows towing a caravan, or go by camper. At many outdoor shows there are special camping facilities in the show grounds. Camping and showing can be enormous fun, giving opportunities for socialising with fellow campers after the show. A caravan is particularly useful for large three day events when the exhibitor may be handling two or three breeds, one on each day. Instead of having to drive endless distances to and from home, the handler with a caravan can stay in one place for the whole period. Camping can also be convenient if you happen to win best of breed, when best in show is to be judged a couple of days later. You can take a couple of dog playpens which can be erected beside the caravan, where your dogs will be safe and out of the way. Such pens are convenient when you are entertaining friends because your dogs are not then jumping about all over the place, nor are they likely to make a dash into the unknown when someone opens the door inadvertently.

It is also tremendous fun going to a show by coach, particularly if it is a long journey. There is no quicker way to be initiated into the dog game than to travel in a coach full of people with the same hobby and love of dogs. You will meet all sorts of people from all walks of life and with every conceivable variety and breed of dog. If you travel regularly to shows you will make many good friends in other breeds and you will be surprised how wide your horizons will become. Coach parties are advertised in the dog papers, and each person is allotted a double seat, one for himself and one for his dog. An exhibitor with more than one dog may even be allotted a seat for each one, up to a maximum of five dogs. There are frequent stops in suitable places, both for the dogs and owners. Some people take their own picnics, whilst others prefer to have a hot meal at a restaurant stopover. Coaches generally start from large car parks where exhibitors can park their cars and get on the bus with little inconvenience to themselves or their dogs. There are generally other pick-up places along the route for travellers living nearer the show. Buses travelling long distances often go overnight.

The fun and excitement in the bus on the return journey is remarkable. There is generally someone who has had a wonderful day. It may be a novice with his or her very first prize card. Another exhibitor may have made up his first or fiftieth champion; someone else may have won best of breed or best in show. It is all tremendously exhilarating for those who have won. Even the despondent ones can join in the happiness of other people's successes, especially in other breeds. As the dog fraternity knows, there is always another judge and another show. One day it will be your day and everyone will be happy for you and your dog. Top honours may be years away for you or may perhaps never come, but that does not mean that you cannot enjoy showing your dog. But of course it is fun to win, especially if you are a sincere breeder with your breed at heart. While taking part in this great game you will hear endless show stories and dog gossip, but most of all you will learn to observe and listen and get to know about other breeds and breeders. A few years ago the owners (not even breeders) of a lovely pet dog won the most coveted prize in the dog world, the best in show at Cruft's. So you never know your luck.

In the old days a coach or two on the train used to be reserved for owners travelling with their dogs to a show; it was often as much fun as travelling by coach, and much faster. Sadly, those days are past. Dogs now have to travel in crates in the guard's van, so there is no need for the special coaches for dog fanciers.

In these days many dogs travel by plane in their crates or dog boxes, particularly in the United States where the distances are great. This applies equally in Australia. However, many dogs travel by air even in England and New Zealand. It is essential to get the air travel permits and tickets in good time and to know exactly where to go for loading your dog. Some air authorities require dogs to be sedated and to be at the airport earlier than other freight, so it is as well to find out all details well in advance. You must take into consideration travelling time to the airport, traffic jams, the time it could take to park your car and to find your way to the requisite places.

Before you set off home after the show, particularly if this is held at the opposite end of the country from where you live, you may wish to take the opportunity of calling on a well known breeder of your favoured breed or breeds. If you are tactful you may be permitted to visit the kennel. In such a kennel you may find a suitable stud dog for your brood bitch or perhaps a better dog for exhibiting. Even if you require neither of these, you can learn a great deal from a visit to the

189

kennel: how the dogs are kept; how they are fed; what kind of kennelling is used; and a myriad of other things. You must, however, be tactful, charming and obviously admiring. There is no need to gush; simply show that you are genuinely interested. Few experts can resist showing off their knowledge, especially when the enquiries come from an obviously keen dog lover, from a potential buyer, or from someone who may some day use their stud dogs.

What You Need for the Show
If your dog is travelling in a box, you must prepare it. Make certain that it is scrupulously clean, especially the corners, which should be free from hairs and dust. The box should be regularly disinfected. Line the bottom of the box with plastic sheeting and some flat layers of newspaper. Then take a large sheet of newspaper and tear it down from top to bottom in 8cm (3in) strips (newspaper will not tear across its pages). Place the strips of paper in the box. Should the dog have an 'accident' in the box, or drool excessively, the loose strips of paper will move over the wet areas and absorb any moisture. This prevents the dog's coat from becoming soiled.

You must decide what you are going to wear to exhibit your dog. The most important consideration is comfort, closely followed by adaptability. You should wear a sensible, suitable outfit that can be adjusted according to the changeable weather, including heat, cold, rain and even snow. For men it is extremely easy; neat country clothes, clean shoes and, in most countries, a tie or polo-necked sweater. It is not done for a man to wear a hat in the ring in England, but obviously in countries where the weather is hot and the sun dazzling it would be only natural for a man to wear a hat to avoid sunstroke.

The lady handler has a certain advantage over men as she may choose an outfit to go with her breed of dog or a colour to enhance the colour of her dog's coat. It is obvious that too tight a skirt would not be suitable for gaiting a german shepherd at a flying trot. On the other hand, too full a skirt could blow up embarrassingly. It is the dogs that are to be judged, so handlers should dress accordingly. Too low a neckline distracts from the dog, but a smart, simple outfit enhances the general appearance of both handler and dog. Materials should be chosen so that dog hairs do not show, and clothes should be fitted so that the handler can run, bend, stretch and walk with comfort. Shoes should be flat-heeled, well polished and comfortable. The soles should be made of something that does not clatter or make a noise on the floor of an indoor show. Trouser suits are sensible. Whatever you choose to wear, though, it is more than useful to have one or two pockets so that titbits can be stored and perhaps the odd brush or comb secreted for the long-haired breeds.

Many handlers prefer to wear white overall coats, especially those with white-coated breeds which require chalking. Show aprons are sold at most shows, and these can be both pretty and useful because they often have a number of good pockets. Certainly, in England a raincoat is a must, and a change of shoes or boots or even wellingtons is useful in slushy weather. Headscarves or small rain hats are excellent for windy days, as are wigs for those with unruly hair. Large, chunky jewellery and Ascot hats are not suitable for the show ring. Beautifully turned-out dogs require immaculately turned out handlers in order to present a pleasing team.

There are various essentials you should take with you to a show, but it is very important that you take only the things and equipment that are really necessary. There are always good catering facilities at shows, as well as bars, but like all public places they are inclined to be expensive. You will regret being overloaded with equipment when you trundle what is often a long way across a bumpy, wet field from the car park to your bench. You will find it quite exhausting, particularly if you have a breed which requires to be carried in order to keep it clean and dry. There will be many times when you wish that you had four pairs of hands. Leave your valuables at home, and never leave your handbag on your bench or dog cage unless your dog is a good guard dog. Always find a friend who will look after your possessions when you are in the ring.

Exhibitors' Requirements for a Show
Suitable clothes, flat heeled shoes.
Mackintosh, spare shoes or boots.
Camp chair or folding stool, table and umbrella.
Strong shoulder bag.
Show pass.
Tickets for car park, railway, plane or coach.
Cheque book and small amount of money (beware of pickpockets).
Small coins for telephone and parking meters.
Make-up (if appropriate), comb, sponge bag, soap and damp flannel.
Small hand towel.
Tissues.
Bottle of aspirin.
Good clothes brush.
Ring clip or safety pin (should be worn).
Diary or note book, two biros.

191

Stud cards and kennel cards.

Ring numbers when applicable. Write these numbers on an accessible piece of paper, or on the back of your hand.

Schedule, to check the classes entered.

Picnic bag with sandwiches, cake, biscuits, fruit, strong coffee or tea, a thirst quencher, bottle opener, knife, and spare plastic bags for rubbish. Coca Cola is very reviving on a hot day, as is hot soup on a cold day.

What the Dog Requires

Travelling box lined with newspaper and blanket, padlock and chain.

Collar and strong bench chain, spare leather leash.

Show leash.

Dog coat, mackintosh and boots for some breeds.

Bench rugs, newspaper and disinfectant.

Curtains for dog pens in the toy breeds.

Trolley, two- or four-wheeler.

Dog food and biscuits, diced liver for bait.

Water bowls and large plastic bottle of water.

Drool bibs for certain breeds.

Stud cards and advertisement pulls with photographs of dogs.

Permanent show grooming bag containing brush and comb, flea spray, hand glove or velvet pad, boracic powder for eye strains, small dog towel, scissors, thinning shears, band aids and small bandage, mink oil, Johnson's baby powder, water spray bottle, cotton wool for eyes, resin, block for pads, damp spontex for wiping feet, chalk block or starch, Betsolan eyedrops, ribbons, elastic bands, curling papers for certain breeds, TCP, nail file.

Keep all these things separately in their own bag so that they are ready for each show. This will save you endless time searching for important small items the day before the show. You will have plenty to do without doing unnecessary work.

The Day Before and the Day of the Show

If you have a family to look after, make all your plans well in advance so that your home will run smoothly while you are away. Meals should be left ready, and the care of any other dogs or animals should be arranged in case your journey home is delayed.

Most dogs will require a pre-show bath, depending on the breed. American cocker spaniels, for example, should have a five-day preparation before a show, with different parts of the coat being clipped each day. Whatever the breed, show dogs must be presented with: clean coats, free from fleas; short, trimmed nails; clean ears and eyes; and sparkling white teeth, the latter cleaned with bicarbonate of soda on a cotton cloth. Prepare all the show paraphernalia, both for yourself and your dog, the day before the show.

On the day of the show there are three important matters which should be attended to before you leave home. Firstly, you should fortify yourself with a good, cooked breakfast—something like bacon and eggs—as you will have a long, hard, exciting day in front of you. You will be amazed how tiring dog showing can be with all its excitements and unexpected happenings. The adrenalin is really flowing at times, and your heart may be thumping too. There is nothing dull about showing dogs, I can assure you. A good solid meal before you start the day will almost certainly prevent you having a nasty headache at the end of the day, and will stop your blood sugar from becoming low.

Besides fortifying yourself, you should give your dog his breakfast as soon as he wakes, and a glycerine suppository half an hour before you leave. If your dog is generally fed at midday you will find that he may stop concentrating in the show ring, because dogs know the exact time to the second. He will be thinking about his dinner and not concentrating on what you want him to do. Feeding your dog early will make him sleepy during the journey. He will enjoy his exercise when you arrive at the show and will remain contented all day.

Always give yourself at least half an hour's grace before your departure. You should have everything in hand to ensure that there is no last minute rush when things can so easily be left behind. If you are wise you will endeavour to arrive at the show at least an hour before the first judging commences. By doing so you will find a better parking place and you will not have so far to drag all your equipment. You will also have time to chat to old friends and rivals before showing starts. It is truly wonderful how friendly people are at the start of the day, old rivalries forgotten and each exhibitor hoping it is going to be his day. So, make the most of this enjoyable part of a showing day.

At the Show
Having parked your car carefully, disembarked, given your dogs a run and collected all your paraphernalia, you will make your way to the show entrance. There is the same procedure to follow, whether it is an indoor or an outdoor show. At the entrance to the show there will be a special exhibitors' entrance where entry passes must be shown. Always have your pass to hand in an outside pocket—it is far

easier than having to delve into a handbag. Queues at the entrance are often long and exhibitors who hold up the waiting handlers and dogs are not exactly popular. Extra tickets may be bought at the entrance for a kennelmaid or friend.

Catalogues are sold at the entrance to a show, and it is important to buy one of these in order to find out about details of the show, the benches and the classes in which you have entered (it is easy to forget in which classes you entered your dog three weeks previously). Unfortunately, catalogues are often stolen, particularly at championship shows because they are more important and expensive, so write your name in large letters across the top of the cover. It is also useful to tear the corners off the pages containing your breed and entries, because it can take quite a time to thumb through a large catalogue to find your breed. By tearing off a small area of the top right hand corner you will be able to find your place with the minimum of effort. You should then mark the classes in which you have entered your dog, and you can eventually mark the results.

It is exceedingly important, if you find that you have made a mistake in your show entry, to go immediately to the show secretary and point out your error, before the judging of the class or classes takes place. You might have entered your bitch in a dog class; or you might have miscalculated the age of your dog and entered him in the puppy class, when he should have been entered in another class; or you might have entered your dog for a class for which he is ineligible. The show secretary may then transfer your entry to the equivalent class for your dog's breed, colour, sex, weight or height. Should there be no equivalent class, your dog will have to compete in the open class.

Having found your way to the correct benching area, start to prepare the bench for your dog. Benches have to be disinfected according to Kennel Club regulations. Nevertheless, it is wise to cover the bench with thick newspaper and a heavy benching rug so that your dog can lie contentedly and comfortably for the many hours that he will be required to stay on his bench. Benching rules are most strict and a dog must remain on his bench except when he is in the ring, being exercised or being watered. Fifteen minutes is the time allowed off the bench. The reason for these restrictions is that many people visit shows to look at the dogs and, having paid an entrance fee, they are entitled to look at the dogs they have particularly come to see. So always play fair and keep your dog on display; one day it could pay dividends.

Small breeds are penned and not benched. All the toy breeds are

194

A dandy dinmont waiting patiently on the show bench. He has been secured correctly with a chain leash to the bench. His normal lead has not yet been removed. He is kept warm by a soft blanket to lie on and a cardigan of his owner's to keep him happy

penned in special cages provided at the show. These should be lined with newspaper and the floor covered with a pretty blanket and perhaps a small cushion. The pens are permitted to be decorated with curtains round three sides, obviously leaving the front free. The curtains are easily hung by small coloured clothes pegs, curtain hooks or elastic. The curtains are only decorative but they keep the small dogs free from draughts, as well as also preventing the more aggressive ones from barking and disturbing their immediate neighbours. Water bowls and toys may be kept in the pens if the owner wishes. All the grooming equipment and other paraphernalia must be kept neatly under the cages. Grooming tables and chairs must on no account block the gangway or prevent spectators from seeing the dogs.

Not all shows are benched. At unbenched shows, dogs in crates and boxes should be kept on level, dry ground out of draughts and not in the hot sun. In hot countries exhibitors usually come armed with colourful sun umbrellas which are staked round the ringside. Whether your dog is benched or penned, make quite certain that he is comfortable and has settled down for what can sometimes be a long wait until his class.

You will find at the back of each bench two strong metal rings, one on each side. It is a Kennel Club regulation that all dogs on benches should be securely fastened with a strong collar and a metal chain lead. The length of the chain is extremely important. It must be long enough for the dog to be able to lie down comfortably, but not so long that the dog can jump off his bench; nor should it be long enough for an aggressive dog to try to get at an unfriendly neighbour, and in the attempt possibly to fall off the bench and strangle himself.

There is an important Kennel Club regulation that only one dog, and that the correct dog as marked in the catalogue, may be on a bench. The rules seem to be not so strictly adhered to in the toy breeds since you will often see several small dogs in one pen, to keep each other company. Owners usually sit by their dogs all the time or find someone to guard their dogs in their absence, because, sadly, it is not unknown for jealous exhibitors to poison winning or rival dogs. It does seem absolutely unbelievable but, unfortunately, it has happened. Should you suspect that your dog has been poisoned— perhaps he is sleepy or lethargic or frothing at the mouth—call for the show veterinary surgeon immediately. Always be on the alert, keep all food sealed and only pour out fresh water from a bottle as your dog needs it. It is a very wise precaution to teach your dog not to take food from strangers, although this in itself can have obvious repercussions.

Two well trained standard poodles, standing and sitting correctly, beautifully clipped and ready for the show ring

Only regulation-size bench cards may be displayed on benches and pens, and these cards may only have the prescribed wording printed on them. When applicable, a card 'Not for Competition' may also be hung on the bench or pen. Many breeders have their advertisement 'pulls' on the benches, advertising their kennel successes. Prize cards are always proudly displayed on benches and pens, and it is important to fill in your dog's name in case the cards get stolen.

There are strict Kennel Club regulations regarding exercising dogs. Most male dogs will use a scenting post. If there isn't one, screw up a newspaper and he will probably use that. There is generally no problem with dogs urinating, but with bitches it is another matter. Some will not relieve themselves at a show all day, whilst others may even wait until they are on home ground once again, which is exceedingly bad for them.

Finding Your Judging Ring

Once you have settled your dog comfortably on his bench and all your equipment is neatly stowed away, find a kindly neighbour who will keep an eye on your dog whilst you make a preliminary survey of the ring where your dog is to be judged. If you are early enough there is no reason why your dog should not accompany you. Note where the entrance to the ring is because it may be difficult to find once judging has started. Not only should you know exactly where your ring is but you must also know the expected time of judging. As soon as you have ascertained this you may make your plans for the day.

There is often a large crowd of spectators and sprawling children round the rings of popular breeds, not to mention people with their dogs at the ringside, watching the judging or waiting for their classes. There are handlers leaving a class with their dogs and new handlers endeavouring to enter the ring. You can imagine the confusion that can be caused where there are perhaps as many as fifty dogs in a class. If you do take your large dog to the ringside, ensure that you do not let him sprawl and encroach on the ring. Exhibitors with toy dogs often sit at the ringside with their dog boxes and they also are liable to encroach. If you are early enough at the show, you and a friend may reserve a chair for the day so that you can watch the judging and become familiar with the handling procedures.

It is very wise to observe the judge in the early classes if you possibly can. You will be able to watch his particular methods—no two judges judge in the same manner. Note where everyone stands and the general procedures. If it is your first time in the ring you may well feel very nervous and imagine that all eyes are upon you, but this is seldom the case. The spectators are far more interested in the dogs. Find a kind old hand in the game (probably a lady) and ask if you might perhaps stand next to her. Explain that it is your first show and I am sure you will find that she will give you all the help and advice you will need. Keep your ears open and try to remember any advice given. Before judging commences you might care to ask your mentor what she thinks of your new dog. Do not be hurt if she is direct and rather too honest about your dog for your liking; she probably has a very high standard. You will soon know whether she is right or not, according to what the judge thinks about your dog at this particular show.

19

Handling Your Dog in the Ring

Inspection of the Ring

If you are going to exhibit your dog, whether at an indoor or an outdoor show, it will be well worth your while to study the ring carefully. The show ring is always oblong in shape; its size, however, may vary considerably, depending on whether the show is an indoor or an outdoor one. The dimensions of the ring will often depend not only on the size of the breed being exhibited but also on the number of exhibits. The ring is enclosed by ropes and poles. Across one corner of it (or sometimes in the middle of one short side) is generally a trestle table, behind which are two chairs, one for the judge and the other for the steward. On the front of the table facing the ring will be attached one or two posters. These are provided by one or both of the two dog papers, *Dog World* and *Our Dogs*. Emblazoned on the poster or posters will be the name of the officiating judge. The number of posters depends on whether the judge is reporting for one dog paper or for both.

On one corner of the table there is usually a bowl of disinfected water and a towel and soap, provided for the use of the judge to wash his hands between exhibits, or to be used only at his discretion should he have a mangey dog presented to him or one about whose health he does not feel happy. Also on the table are the judge's judging book, a ballpoint pen, the prize cards and rosettes, and challenge certificates if it is a championship show. Behind the table there is generally a blackboard set slightly to one side. The senior steward will chalk up on the board the class and the awards. The steward will also attach to it the judge's initialled award slips. If you have not had time to mark up your catalogue, you will be able to find all the winning dogs marked up on the judge's slips.

Look carefully at the surface of the ring and notice where there are any irregularities such as bumps or depressions where you will be expected to gait your dog. If your breed is large and strong such problems may hardly affect him, but should you have a toy breed your dog could well almost disappear from the judge's view should there be a deep depression in the ground.

Many indoor shows are held in halls which are used for indoor games such as badminton. In these halls the rings may often be covered in matting to protect the polished floors. Inspect the matting and have a good look for any holes that should be avoided or rucks that might upset your dog.

Stewards
The smooth running of all shows depends upon the efficiency of the stewards. There are two kinds of steward, ring stewards and judge's stewards. These may be separate officials, but at smaller shows, where there is only one steward, he or she will have to fulfil both roles. Ring stewards may have to go round the benches to find and organise handlers and hurry them into the ring, although by Kennel Club rules they are no longer required to do this—it is the responsibility of the handlers to know when their classes are scheduled. When the new handlers enter the ring the stewards have to hand out ring numbers. They shepherd the novice handlers and answer innumerable questions. If the exhibitors are in other classes with their dogs, the stewards may have to go off and find them so that they do not miss their classes.

Stewards also have to announce the winners in each class in a loud clear voice for the spectators to hear. They also help the judge with the paper work involved, and some efficient ones, who have been stewarding for many more years than the judge has been judging, may offer to fill in the judge's judging book for him (in some countries this is not permitted). If this is done—and it certainly saves time—the judge is, nevertheless, absolutely responsible for everything written in the judging book and he must sign each entry slip personally. There are other duties which stewards are expected to do such as clearing away any dog excreta and mopping up puddles. Stewards do all this hard work for no reward except for the love of the dog game. Stewarding is wonderful experience before endeavouring to become a judge. A good steward is worth his weight in gold to a hard-worked judge, who can relax in the knowledge that he can rely on his steward to keep the handlers well organised and standing in their correct places.

Gaiting Your Dog in the Ring
No two judges adopt exactly the same methods of judging dogs. Much will depend on the size of the ring and also the breed being judged. Obviously, if the ring is large and the dogs being judged are german shepherds, which are gaited at a fast, flying trot, then the whole ring will be utilised. If the next breed in the ring happens to be

201

a dainty little pomeranian, with perhaps only four dogs in the class (instead of perhaps forty), the judge may ask the handlers to move their dogs up only half the length of the ring. The size of the class is also an important factor when time is at a premium.

There are nine methods listed below by which a judge may ask you to move your dog in the ring. Study the diagrams carefully in order to familiarise yourself with the various possible procedures, and also to learn how to manipulate your feet and the leash so that your dog is always between you and the judge.

1 The judge most usually asks the handlers to move their dogs round the ring in an anticlockwise direction.
2 You may be asked to move your dog straight up and down the centre of the ring.
3 The judge may ask you to gait your dog in a triangle. You will then move your dog to the top right-hand corner of the ring, across the top to the left-hand corner and down to the centre of the bottom of the ring where the judge will be standing.
4 The judge may stand at the bottom right-hand corner of the ring and ask you to move in a triangle in this position. In this case you move your dog up the right-hand side of the ring, across to the top left-hand corner and straight back to the judge.
5 Some judges prefer to have the dogs gaited across the ring, corner to corner.
6 Another method, not often used, is for the judge to stand in the bottom right-hand corner and to have the dogs move in an upside-down 'L' formation. You move your dog up the right-hand side of the ring and across the top of the ring to the left-hand corner, then about-turn back to the right-hand corner and return down the side of the ring from which you started.
7 The 'T' method is occasionally asked for by judges and is a little complicated, since you must manipulate your feet, your dog and your leash so as to keep your dog between you and the judge the whole time. The judge stands at the centre of the bottom of the ring. You will move your dog up the centre of the ring and turn sharply to the top left-hand corner; here you must change the leash to the other hand so that your dog is now on your right side and between you and the judge. Continue to the far right-hand corner of the ring, about-turn, changing the leash to your other hand, so that once again your dog is on your left side. When you reach the centre of the top of the ring once more you make a sharp turn left and continue down the centre of the ring towards the judge.

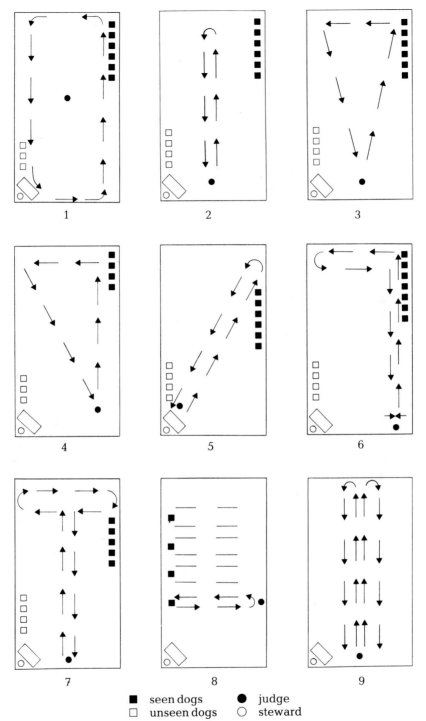

1   2   3

4   5   6

7   8   9

■ seen dogs   ● judge
□ unseen dogs   ○ steward

Methods of moving your dog round the ring (see page 202)

203

8 Some judges prefer to line up their dogs down the left-hand side of the ring and each dog is then moved across the ring and back individually. This formation is often asked for when the judge is assessing his dogs for the next stage, leading up to his final placings. The number of dogs in the final line-up will be the same as the number of place cards that are to be awarded.

9 The judge may like the two last competitors to move up and down the centre of the ring together, especially if there is very little to choose between them. He will then ask the handlers to gait their dogs for the last lap round the ring before he brings the winning dog into the centre, to be followed by his reserve dog. Sometimes the line-up is kept to the side of the ring and the dogs stand in front of small boards marked first, second and third.

Conversations With the Judge

The Kennel Club lays down a clear rule that handlers must not speak to the judge in the ring, and this rule must be adhered to. However, the judge may perhaps enter into a short conversation with a nervous handler in order to relieve the tension or he may pass an amusing remark to demonstrate that showing dogs is an enjoyable pastime and not something too serious. However, should the judge enter into a harmless conversation with you, do not take advantage of him and continue chattering to him. Keep all conversations to a minimum, even when the judge is one of your best friends. Chatting to the judge looks bad from the ringside, however harmless the conversation may be.

Many judges like to ask the age of the dog they are going over. In case the judge should ask you this, make certain that you know your dog's age. If he is a puppy give the age in months (use months up to the age of eighteen months). After that it would be sufficient to tell the judge that your dog is nearly two or just three, or whatever he is. The judge may be asking your dog's age merely to break the ice. On the other hand he may be interested in the teeth, or perhaps he requires to know the dog's age when he is assessing the dog's coat or furnishings or his general development. The judge may ask you about the length of your dog's nails and he might suggest that you keep them shorter so that the dog does not slip so easily on a polished floor at an indoor show.

The judge might also notice from the coat of your dog, that he looks as if he has been bitten by fleas or, if your dog happens to be a black dachshund and his skin shows through the coat, he might ask you about mange. If you are showing an overweight bitch the judge might ask you if your bitch is in whelp. Should she be in whelp, you could tell him when she is due to whelp.

Occasionally, a stud dog that has had a great deal of stud work or has been over-used at stud will become very thin. You may find that a judge will ask why the dog is so thin. The reason could equally well be that the bitches in his kennel are all in season and he has not been used, with the result that he is frustrated and is not eating well. Sometimes the judge might even drop a hint of advice. If a dog has not been trained properly, a judge might help a novice to make his dog stand correctly on a table. He might also give some advice as to how the novice handler should hold the leash. At the end of the class, if you are in the winning line, the judge will come up to each of the first two or three dogs and write a few notes about them for his show report. You might then be asked to describe the colour of your dog should it be an unusual one.

No handler should give the judge information such as that his dog only requires one more challenge certificate to make him up to champion, or that a certain very well known judge gave his dog his last challenge certificate or that, if he wins the class this time, he will have the trophy for keeps. These underhand methods, intended to influence the judge, seldom work because most judges resent being pressurised, and any attempt to do so may result in the judge putting your dog down (this refers to the judge's placing of the dog and not to a death sentence!).

In the Ring for Your First Class
When the time for your first class is approaching (note that the dog classes are always judged before the bitch classes) you must make your final preparations. Having exercised your dog to warm him up and allowed him to relieve himself, collect up any combs, brushes and titbits that you feel you may require in the ring, change your dog's collar and put on his slip lead or leash, pin on your ring number if you have one, finish your last-minute grooming and reach your ring in plenty of time. You are now ready to exhibit your dog. It is for this that you have been preparing for so long. Think too of the money you have spent in order to show your dog. So, make sure that you do not 'fluff' it. Give yourself a few moments to collect yourself, take a few deep, long, slow breaths, and enter the ring calmly and slowly and with a winning attitude.

First you must look for the ring steward who will have your ring number with his catalogue. Sometimes ring numbers are sent to the exhibitors prior to the show, or occasionally in lieu of entry passes, but they are more generally handed to the handler by the ring steward. It is therefore important that you should know the number of your exhibit so that you can ask the steward for the appropriate number without delaying matters by having to ask him to look up the number of your dog in the catalogue.

Your ring number must be displayed so that the judge can see it easily and also so that the spectators at the ringside can see it too. The wise exhibitor will buy a special card clip. These can be bought at the stalls at most dog shows. Some handlers prefer to wear their number on a button of their coat or dress, but this is not advisable because the card may blow off the button and it may be difficult to see from the ringside. Judges find it much easier if all exhibitors wear their cards in the same place, easily visible to him and to the spectators. Some ring numbers are issued to be worn on an armband on the left arm, while many terrier handlers like to sport their ring number in the band of their hat (in all other breeds it is not normally done for men to wear hats at an indoor show). Ring numbers of winning dogs must be kept carefully because they will be required to be worn once again by the handler in the best-of-breed judging, the best-in-show ring or in the variety classes.

Once you have collected your ring number, look at the other handlers, who have no doubt started to line up round the edge of the ring. Choose a pleasant looking handler to stand next to, one who you feel would be kind to you and be helpful; also choose someone who does not have an aggressive dog that might put your dog off. You will notice that the judge is probably sitting quietly at the ringside table. From time to time he may well look up and survey some of the dogs already in the ring. The moment you enter the ring your dog is on show.

As soon as the steward is sure that all the dogs are present he will announce to the judge that the dogs are ready. The judge will then go to the centre of the ring, where he will stand and survey his class. You will find that all the dogs have been lined up at the edge of the ring, facing in an anticlockwise direction. Each handler will be endeavouring to make his exhibit four-square, with an alert expression, or in whatever stance is the fashion for the breed.

The judge will indicate that the dogs are to start moving, either by saying something like 'Take them round, please', or by waving his arm at the first two handlers. All the dogs should move smartly round the ring. The handlers must make certain not to cut corners or to touch or upset the dog in front of them. After one of two circuits of the ring the judge will stop a particular handler, usually at the corner of the ring by the judging table. The handlers then stand their dogs correctly for their breed on a loose lead or stack them by placing their dogs manually, or, if they happen to be yorkshire terriers, they will

206

stack them on their boxes. The judge will generally have a quick look at this line-up and then he will go over the first dog in the line. Most judges will watch the dogs gait round the ring, examine them individually and then watch the class once again. If there is a marshalling ring, as in Australia and New Zealand, the dogs are often put straight on to the judging table without first gaiting round the ring. This is a pity because the dogs do not then get a warm-up before being examined and the judge does not get a preliminary view of all the dogs together.

The procedure for the individual examination of the dogs remains the same whether with the small breeds, which are examined on the table, or with the larger breeds, which are examined on the ground. If your breed is to be examined on the table the first handler will immediately stand his dog at the far narrow end of the table. The judge will stand back a little and will look at the dog from the side, the top and the front. He will allow the handler to stack his dog correctly and will then move forward and start going over the dog, gently and carefully, looking for all the good breed points starting with the head.

As soon as the judge has been over the first dog he will ask the handler to gait the dog for him. While the handler moves down the ring with his dog, the next person in line should start setting his dog up on the table so that as soon as the judge has finished watching the other dog he can turn round without wasting time and go over the new dog. Handlers may stand on either side of the judging table, but on the whole it is probably better for them to stand on the outside of the table facing the ring. It is then far easier to keep out of the judge's way—especially if the handler and judge happen to be stout. The handler must keep his hands and leash well out of the way of the judge when his dog is being examined.

If you decide to stand behind the judging table you will have to change the slip lead to your right hand. You will then have your left hand free to support your dog's tail or to alter the position of a hindleg should it be necessary. There is another advantage in standing behind the table; when you come to place your dog on the ground after the judge has asked you to move him he will be on your correct side, which is your left-hand side, and you then just change the lead to your left hand. Allow your dog a few seconds to become accustomed to the ground again; he may perhaps sneeze and shake himself but, as soon as he is settled, move off smartly and do exactly as the judge has requested you.

When you place your dog on the table, always lift him up slowly and gently and place his forefeet as close to the edge of the table as

207

convenient, perhaps 15cm (6in) from the edge, to make it easy for the judge to go over the dog from the front. Remember to keep the slip lead well under the angle of your dog's jaw and the end of the lead wound round your fingers or neatly folded in the palm of your hand. Never drop the lead on the table or leave the stray end dangling over the dog's head. If the lead is dropped on the table the handler loses control of his dog and the lead may get in the way of the dog's feet. It also looks most unprofessional and untidy.

Whilst your dog is on the table, keep a keen eye on the judge and at the right moment set up (pose) your dog in the correct way for his breed. If you stack your dog make certain you drop his forelegs into position first and then drop his hindlegs into the correct position. Be very careful of the use of your slip lead; do not pull on the lead but just hold it sufficiently taut for you to make your dog keep his head facing directly forward. At the same time, have enough control to prevent him from jumping off the table.

The big moment for which you have gone to so much trouble has

---

A bloodhound being trained to stand on a low platform. His handler has the dog's legs well placed and is supporting his stern with her hand

really arrived. The experienced handler realises exactly how much handling a judge will tolerate and he will endeavour not to overstep the mark, as this will surely be penalised. It is never wise to groom your dog with a brush whilst the judge is assessing him, nor should there be a display of titbits or squeaky toys. Set about handling your dog in a brisk professional manner.

The judge will always give you sufficient time to set up your dog. He will look at your dog from a distance and will then move forward slowly, extend the back of his closed hand for your dog to sniff and will then proceed to look at your dog from the front. He will then take your dog's head between both his hands and study every detail. He may or may not ask you the age of your dog. He will certainly want to look at your dog's mouth. Some judges prefer to open the mouth themselves, lifting the side lip and counting the teeth, whilst others, in the interests of not spreading infections, may prefer to ask the handler to open the dog's mouth for inspection.

The judge will proceed to go over your dog thoroughly and, when he has finished, he will ask you to gait him. An experienced handler knows only too well how to make the most of a dog when he is standing; many serious faults can be covered up by clever handling. It is only when the dog is gaiting that the faults can no longer be concealed.

If your dog is of a breed that is examined on the ground the entire procedure is similar to that for a dog examined on a table. Some breeds do not need to be stacked. The handler simply guides the dog into position by bringing him forward slowly and stopping at the exact spot required, so that the dog is standing with his four feet in the correct position. If one leg is not quite correct the dog is moved round again slowly and brought back into the same position (see page 210).

When the judge is going over your dog, it is important that you have complete control over him, but at the same time you must keep well out of the way of the judge. When your dog's head is being examined, particularly in the case of a large breed, the handler should stand at the rear of the dog. When the judge goes over the dog's hindquarters and tail you should move to the front of your dog. In the case of a male dog, whether he is examined on the table or on the ground, the judge has to ascertain whether he is entire, ie that he has two testicles fully descended in the scrotum.

After the judge has gone over your dog you will be asked to move him. The judge will either tell you in detail what he requires, or simply say 'Straight up and down, please', or 'A triangle, please'. If you watch all the other handlers moving their dogs you will know

An american cocker spaniel puppy being trained to stand in a show stance

exactly what will be expected of you. Concentrate hard on what you are to do and set forth confidently with your dog, giving him encouragement very quietly or, if he is inclined to be obstreperous, correct him by the use of your voice and your leash. Do not over-handle your dog and do not string him up. The leash is there to guide your dog and it should be held straight above the top of his neck. The judge will like to see your dog on a loose lead at least once so, having completed your dog's individual gaiting, bring him to a smart standstill a short distance in front of the judge.

You will find that many judges like to attract a dog's attention in order to see his true expression, how alert he is and how he uses his ears. To do this some judges drop an object, such as a bunch of keys or a match box, on the ground in front of the dog. Make your dog look as alert as possible—you may even be able to get more response from him than the judge by crackling a piece of cellophane paper in your hand or even showing your dog a piece of his favourite titbit.

As soon as the judge has seen all he requires, he will dismiss you with a 'Thank you'. If you happen to be the first handler he will probably indicate with his hand where he wishes you to stand. This will probably be in the opposite corner from the judging table, and you will be starting the line-up of the 'seen' dogs. As each dog finishes his gaiting, his handler moves across the ring and joins the line of examined dogs. Each handler must stand in the same position in the line-up as previously. The second handler in the line will be on the left-hand side of the first handler and so on.

If the class is a large one and the judge is likely to be fully occupied for a considerable time, you should take the opportunity of allowing your dog to relax, particularly if it is a hot day. You should, however, keep a wary eye on the judge and be ready for his occasional glance round the ring. The handlers of some of the toy breeds like to hold their dogs in their arms, and there is nothing against this except that the spectators at the ringside are unable to see the dogs. If the judging is taking a long time exhibitors often stand and chat to each other. However, particularly if you are a novice, you would do better to concentrate on the dog the judge is examining and to watch each rival's conformation and movement and all the other show points. If you are observant you can learn a great deal.

As soon as the judge starts to go over his last dog, collect your dog up and be ready for the moment when you should have him looking alert and at his best. You must keep your eye on both the judge and your dog. When the judge has seen all the dogs in the class individually he will spend a little time looking at them together and making his decisions. He will then start placing the number of dogs for which there are cards. He may ask one handler to move his dog up two places or make another handler change places with someone further down the line. Some judges finish their decisions at this stage, leaving the dogs where they are in front of the winning numbers (though not all shows provide numbers for exhibits to stand by). Usually the judge prefers to ask the handlers to gait their dogs once or twice more round the ring, stopping his winning dog when he reaches the top of the line. The handlers once again make their dogs stand as perfectly as possible and the judge then 'pulls out' his selected dogs to the centre of the ring. This means that when the judge points to your dog you must move promptly to the centre of the ring and stand where the judge has indicated. If you are not told to stand in a particular position you should stand next to the handler who was called before you, who will be on your right.

The judge will pull out five or seven dogs, according to how many cards are provided. Do not become too excited at this stage, as judges often make last-minute decisions. The judge may not remember a particular dog's mouth or the colour of his eyes and he may want to have another look. In toy breeds like the chihuahua the judge may ask to see 'heads' and compare one or two at close range. If some handlers happen to be pretty girls, spectators often joke about whose heads the judge is really looking at. Often there is little to choose between the top dogs, so that the one that looks the most alert and intelligent and is handled the best will win by a hair's breadth. Handlers must be alert themselves and ready for any unforeseen demands from the judge. He may, for instance, wish to see the last two dogs move together down the centre of the ring before he makes his final decision.

The judge has his selected dogs standing in order of merit going from right to left. The dog placed first will be at the top of the line-up, with all the other dogs below him in order on his left. The judge then tells his ring steward that this is his final line-up. The steward hands the judge his judging book and a ballpoint pen and announces the numbers of all the prize winners, handing out to each handler his card and rosette. The judge will now move down the line, making notes on the first three dogs for his show report which will be printed in one or both of the dog papers. In some countries judges are not expected to write a report. Many judges prefer to use a dictaphone; this is sensible since important points are recorded immediately before there is time to forget them. If your dog is one of the first three make him look his best while the judge writes his report. When this is going on all the other dogs may leave the ring, making room for the next class. As soon as the judge has finished making notes on his winning dogs he will dismiss the class by saying 'Thank you'. The second handler must congratulate the winner.

If your dog is not in the next class, take him back to his bench or cage and see that he is comfortably settled and has had a drink. If possible leave your dog under the eye of someone he knows, whilst you return to the ring to watch the rest of the judging. You will be able to learn a great deal by watching the other dogs and handlers. You should try to sit next to a breeder of long standing and listen to all the conversations going on around you. You will hear many dogs being criticised and many others being admired. You will overhear learned conversations mentioning 'slipping stifles', 'lovely reach of neck', 'good turn of stifle', 'fearful cow-hocks', and so on. Slowly, you will learn what all these dog expressions mean and how important they are. From time to time try to ask a few intelligent questions. Show language is not difficult to learn. It comes almost by instinct after a few shows and you will soon find yourself talking the same jargon.

Subsequent Breed Classes

There is always a short interval between classes whilst the dogs that have been judged and their handlers leave the ring and the new ones come in. The procedure for ring numbers and absentees is always the same and, when all is ready, the steward informs the judge that his next class is waiting. If you have entered your dog for this new class the judge does not have to go over him individually a second time. The 'seen' dogs and their handlers stand diagonally opposite the judge's table and opposite the area where the new 'unseen' dogs will be lining up.

All the seen dogs will line up in the same order, with the winning dogs in order of merit, and any other dogs from previous classes will line up next to them. It is important that the handlers of the seen dogs should stand well back so that they do not intrude into the ring when the judge is looking at his new class. As the dogs of the new class are seen they may be required to join the line of the previous class or they may stand in front of it.

When the judge has made his decisions on the new class the dogs he has selected will be required to line up with the previous class. From this line-up the judge will compare the new senior class with the previous one, and he will then decide on his new order of winning dogs. Some judges will place the dogs in order of merit, or perhaps only the top ten or so, dismissing the others if it is a large class. The judge will call out his winning dogs in order of merit and the procedure of handing out the prize cards and taking notes will be the same as for the previous class and for all subsequent classes.

The most senior class for dogs is the open dog class. Here the procedure for handling remains the same. When the judge has made up his mind which dog is to be placed first he will call that dog into the centre of the ring and the runner-up will remain standing at the side of the ring. Most judges will then ask for all the unbeaten dogs to be brought into the ring. So, if your dog has not been beaten in any of his classes, you should be ready standing at the side of the ring for the final competition for best dog. The stewards consult their catalogues and make certain that all unbeaten dogs are present. The judge then asks the handlers to take the dogs round with the winner of the open dog in the lead. If the judge decides that his original open dog winner is the best dog, the second dog in the open class will then compete against all the previously unbeaten dogs, and whichever the judge selects out of this line-up becomes the reserve best of sex. If there are challenge certificates to be awarded the first dog receives the challenge certificate and the second dog the reserve challenge certificate.

This may all sound rather complicated to the novice, but to the ring steward it is quite straightforward since all winning dogs are marked up in the judging book. It is the responsibility of the steward to see that all the dogs and handlers for each class are in the ring at the right moment.

The bitch classes follow the same procedure as the dog classes before them. The bitch classes are generally larger than the dog classes because breeders keep more bitches than dogs, but many good bitches may be absent from the ring owing to maternal duties.

It is entirely up to the judge when the best puppy class is to be judged, but usually the best puppy is chosen after the judge has finished the puppy bitch class. It is less tiring for the puppies to be judged as early as possible. The judge has already gone over the two puppies, so the handlers will be asked to take them round the ring. The judge may want to see one or both of the puppies on the table again, just to refresh his memory, or he may ask the handlers to move the puppies up and down the centre of the ring to compare them. The judge will take one last look at the two puppies and he will then pull out his winning puppy.

Provided that the puppy has not been beaten in any subsequent class, he or she goes forward with all unbeaten dogs to compete for best of breed, although most puppies are generally too immature for such top awards unless they are almost a year old. Puppies in the large breeds mature slowly, so that they would be unlikely to win best of breed at such an early age.

The excitement mounts as owners, handlers, breeders and spectators at the ringside speculate about which dog the judge is going to decide is his best of breed. If your dog is the best dog then he will probably have been lying on his bench or in his cage for many hours. You should allow about half an hour before your dog will be required to enter the ring for this exciting moment, and take him to the exercise ring; give him a last minute grooming and make him realise that you are expecting the very best from him. Talk to him and tell him what a fantastic dog he is. If you happen to be the handler of the winning bitch you will have had her in the ring in the previous class so she will already be warmed up and in her stride.

Enter the ring at the right moment and make certain that you are wearing the correct ring number. Have a titbit in your pocket for your dog. As handler of the best dog you will stand at the top of the line with the best bitch's handler on your left. This is a tremendous moment for both handlers, each trying to get the most out of his dog. Get your dog to stand in the correct position for the breed. The judge spends some time comparing the two dogs. He will then signal to the

214

handler of the dog to move round the ring and the handler of the bitch will follow on behind. After one or two circuits of the ring the judge will stop the dogs in their original positions. He may like to examine some particular point, such as the mouth, colour of the eyes, the trace, etc. The judge may then like to see both dogs move together down the centre of the ring away from him so that he can compare the movement of the two dogs together.

The adrenalin is probably really flowing, but try to keep calm. The judge may well have a very difficult decision before him, particularly if there is not much to choose between the two dogs. The ringside spectators will undoubtedly be airing their knowledge and will be trying to do the judge's work for him. They will probably be judging the two remaining dogs on their faults. But only the judge will have seen the finer points at close quarters and he will be judging on the good points and balancing the result with the faults. There is no such thing as the perfect dog, nor for that matter the perfect judge.

However, the final decision is made and the judge will point to one of the dogs. If it is the bitch, her handler will move above the dog's handler. The judge will then shake hands with the handler of the best of breed. The handler of the other dog must shake hands with the handler of the winner and congratulate him. There is generally a splendid rosette for best of breed which is presented to the winner by the judge. Sometimes the winning dog does a lap of honour round the ring on his own, but often the best-of-opposite-sex handler moves his dog round with the winning dog too.

At a few shows the best of breed is presented with a sash of honour. This may be draped over the shoulders of the dog so that he moves round the ring wearing his sash of honour.

If the show is a championship show and there are challenge certificates to be awarded, the judge's steward will give the judge the prepared challenge certificates to sign and these will then be handed to the winners by the judge from the ring table.

In the case of an important breed show or a large championship show there will probably be several photographers waiting to take some good photographs of the winning dogs. These photographs may appear in the dog papers and the photographers will take your orders or send you proofs.

If your dog has won a top award in his breed, try not to appear too triumphant. Of course you are thrilled and delighted, but not all the exhibitors will feel that your dog really deserved his win. There are always jealous exhibitors, but there are far more generous ones who will be happy for your win. If you are the loser, do not be too despondent—your day will come. And whatever you do, do not show your disappointment in any way. Be sincere and congratulate the winner as if you mean it. Accept all the congratulations graciously when you receive them and give full credit to your dog.

It is worth noting that it is more difficult to win with a good dog than with a bitch of equal quality. A top winning stud dog can serve a great many bitches over the years, whilst a top winning bitch will have only five or six litters during her lifetime, with perhaps twenty-five to thirty puppies all told. The stud dog, on the other hand, may sire as many puppies in a month as a bitch has in her entire life. Thus, on the whole a stud dog is more important to the quality of a breed than one bitch. For this reason, if the dogs and bitches are equally good, judges will often 'put up' the stud dog belonging to an old hand in return for many entries in the past. However, when an outstanding new star arrives on the scene he will get to the top whoever his owner. It is this that makes the dog game so fascinating.

Group and Best-in-Show Judging
If your dog has become best of breed he will go forward to the second series of judging, the group judging. There are six groups, comprising hounds, gundogs, terriers, utility dogs, working dogs and toys. The winners of each of these groups will then go on to the third round of judging, which is for best in show. The group judges also choose the second dog as reserve best of group. These reserve dogs should be prepared to go into the final best-in-show ring should they be required.

There are usually two judges to choose the best dog in an all-breeds championship show. A referee is also appointed in case the judges are unable to agree in their choice. The referee's decision is, of course, final. Group judges and best-in-show judges normally only give a cursory examination of each dog, without examining mouths. It is felt that previous breed judges will have examined the dogs thoroughly before sending them forward as their best of breed.

The senior best-in-show steward is responsible for lining up the winners of the six groups and their handlers in the enlarged best-in-show ring. The other steward is responsible for having all the reserve best-of-group dogs near the entrance to the ring in readiness to send in the dog which will compete for the reserve-best-in-show title with the remaining group winners.

The handlers in the best-of-group rings wear their best-of-breed rosettes, and the handlers in the best-in-show ring wear both their best-of-breed and best-of-group rosettes.

The best-in-show judges now proceed to make their selection. The dogs will be gaited round the ring together for one or two laps, with the large breeds in front. Each dog will then be examined and gaited individually and then the whole class will be gaited together again. The excitement mounts, the judges confer, and finally the best in show is selected.

As soon as the judges have selected the best in show they must decide on the reserve best in show. The competition for this has now narrowed down to the five remaining group winners plus the reserve best of the group from which the best in show has been chosen. When the judges decided on their best in show they would also have selected the second best dog in the line-up as the probable reserve best in show. The reserve best of group, which has just been brought into the ring, could be awarded reserve best in show, although it is more likely that the judges would nominate their second choice from the remaining best-of-group winners.

These two final dogs will parade round the ring in a lap of honour. Trophies will be presented by a VIP amidst tremendous applause, then photographs will be taken of the judges, the presenter of the trophies and both handlers and their dogs, and finally the best in show will be photographed alone in all his glory.

Some of the larger championship shows last two or three days. Breed winners at these shows will be required to be present on the final day to compete in the group and best-in-show judging. A large show may have as many as 12,000 entries. There are up to eleven eliminating classes before the best dog is chosen, and the same number leading up to the choice of the best bitch.

Quick Guide to the Do's and Don'ts in Dog Showing

Do's
Keep a permanent list of all your showing requirements.
Check your list the morning of the show.
Allow plenty of travelling time.
Have a good cooked breakfast yourself.
Feed your dog before you leave.
Give your dog a suppository.
Spray insecticide on your dog's coat.
Arrive in good time at the show.
Exercise your dog before benching him.
Make your dog's bench chain short enough.
Hang your bench cards correctly.
Make your dog comfortable.
Stow all your paraphernalia under the bench.

Keep an eye on your dog all day.

Find the show ring and check the time of judging.

Make certain that you and your dog are immaculately turned out.

Exercise your dog before entering the ring.

Get to the ringside in good time.

Go to the ring promptly once your class is called.

Take as little as possible into the ring.

Wear the correct ring number for the dog you are handling.

Do what the steward asks you to do.

Know your ring number and the age of your dog.

Stand quietly in line at the side of the ring.

Give yourself sufficient room.

Concentrate on your dog once you are in the ring.

Make certain that your slip lead is tight enough and under the angle of the jaw, unless your breed is shown on a loose leash.

Keep the surplus lead in the palm of your hand or round your fingers.

When gaiting, do not cut corners.

Always keep your dog between you and the judge.

Keep your eye on the judge.

Set your dog up at the far edge of the judging table.

Keep your dog alert and attentive at the appropriate times.

Allow your dog to relax when the judge is fully occupied.

Collect your dog up in good time.

Hold the bait at the correct height and distance.

Get the sparkle out of your dog at the right moment.

Always do what the judge asks you to do promptly.

Keep your concentration at all times.

Learn to be a good loser and a gracious winner.

Accept your dog's placings in a sportsmanlike manner.

Remember that the reserve best-of-sex handler shakes hands with the winner.

Always try to hide your feelings if you are upset.

Showing dogs is a sport, so keep everything in perspective.

Remember there is always another show and another judge.

Don'ts

Never take your dog to a show if he is ill or off colour.

Never take your dog to a show if there is an infection in your area.

Never block the gangway.

Never enter the ring in a flurry when judging is nearly over.

Never allow your lead to trail on the table.

Never mask another dog in the ring.

Never let your dog look like a puppet on a string.

Never move forward and crowd the judge whilst he is judging.

Never step on another dog.

Never permit your dog to touch another dog.

Never allow your leash to dangle in front of your dog's head when gaiting.

Never call a famous dog by name.

Never shout commands at your dog.

Never chatter ceaselessly to your neighbours.

Never show off your dog at another dog's expense.

Never speak to the judge unless spoken to by him.

Never try to influence the judge in any way.

Never enter the ring armed with lots of brushes and squeaky toys.

Never enter the ring wearing winning rosettes, except in the group and best-in-show rings.

Never move to a placing higher than the judge has ordered.

Never move to the centre of the ring before the judge has called you.

Never look too triumphant or too dejected.

Never hand back your winning card to the judge or steward if you are angry.

Never tear up a prize card in pique.

Never make disparaging remarks about a judge.

Never boast.

Never criticise other exhibitors' dogs unkindly.

Never take criticisms of your dog to heart.

Never slap your dog in the ring; it is unnecessary and gives a bad impression.

Never take previous trophies to the secretary's table when the judge is sitting there and announce 'One more win and the cup is mine!'

Never be despondent if you have had a bad day.

Never follow a judge you have just won under from show to show with the same dog. Give him a different entry.

Never forget that a judge cannot choose the exhibitors, but exhibitors can choose their judges.

Never be unkind to other exhibitors.

Glossary of Canine Terms

Abdomen   The portion of the body that lies between the chest and the pelvis.
Achilles tendon   The tendon and muscle that extends along the lower thigh between the femur and the hock joint.
Action   The way a dog moves.
Affix   A kennel name attached to the registered name of a dog. It may be placed before (prefix) or after (suffix) the dog's name.
AKC   American Kennel Club.
Albinism   Hereditary deficiency of colour pigment.
All-rounder   A person qualified to judge all recognised breeds.
Almond eyes   Oval eyes slanted at the corners.
Amble   An easy gait with both legs on the same side moving almost as a pair, often seen as a transitional movement between the walk and a faster gait.
Angulation   The inclination of bones to each other; at shoulder and upper arm and at stifle and hock.
Anticipating   Acting before the command in obedience training.
Anus   Opening at end of rectum.
Apple-domed   Rounded or domed skull.
Apron   The long hair on the throat and front which forms a frill.
ASCOB   'Any solid colour other than black.' Pertains to american cocker spaniels.

B (or b)   Abbreviation for bitch.
Babbler   A hound that barks when not on the trail.
Back   The five vertebrae between the withers and the loin. Not to be confused with the top-line or with length of body. There is variation in meaning in some standards.
Back line   The top-line from neck to base of tail, including withers, back, loin and croup.
Bad mouth   Crooked or misaligned teeth, overshot, undershot or edge to edge.
Balanced   Well proportioned, referring to the whole.
Bandy legs   Legs bent outwards (bowed).
Barrel hocks   Hocks that turn out and toes that turn in; spread or divergent hocks.
Barrel ribs   Rounded ribs.
Basewide   Paddling front movement causing the body to rock from side to side.
Bat ears   Ears which are erect with a wide base and rounded tips and pointing outwards.
Bay   The sound a hound makes when on a trail.
Beard   Bushy whiskers.
Beauty spot   Small coloured spot on a white blaze on the top of the skull.
Beefy   Over-heavy development of hindquarters.
Bell-ears   Ears in the shape of a bell.
Belton   A finely mottled colour combination in the coat seen in english setters; lemon- or blue-flecked, orange or liver on white.
Benched show   A dog show where there are benches to which dogs must be leashed, and cages for the toy breeds.
Best in show   The dog judged to be best of all breeds at a show, or the best of breed if there is only one breed.
Best of breed   A dog which is unbeaten in its breed at a particular show.

Bilateral cryptorchid   A dog with two undescended testicles.
Bird dog   A breed of dog used in shooting birds. Pointer or setter.
BIS   Best in show.
Bitch   A female dog.
Bitchy   A male with a bitch's characteristics.
Bite   Refers to the set of the teeth when the mouth is closed.
Blade   Shoulder.
Blanket   Coat colour on the sides between the neck and tail.
Blaze   A white mark running up the face between the eyes.
Blinker   A gundog that points a bird and then leaves it.
Blocky   Head with rather square formation.
Blooded   Of good breeding.
Bloom   Glossiness of coat denoting good condition.
Blue merle   A grey-blue colour flecked with black; marbled. Associated with a recessive gene.
Blueprint   Preconception of finished article.
Blues   Portion of coat with bluish tinge, associated with light or blue eyes and liver or grey pigment in nose, lips and eye rims, eg pembroke welsh corgi.
Board   The care of a dog for a fee.
BOB   Best of breed. A dog which is unbeaten in its breed at a particular show.
Bob-tail   A dog born with a stump of a tail. Another name for the old english sheepdog.
Bodied up   Well developed.
Body, length of   Tip of brisket to point of sacrum.
Bolt   Drive an animal out of its earth or burrow.
Bone   The conformation and girth of a dog's forelegs.
Bossy   When the muscles of the shoulder and upper arm are too heavy.
Bow-legged   Bandy-legged of fore- or hindlegs.
Br   Breeder.
Braccoid   Refers to the hound group.
Brace   Two dogs of a kind exhibited together.
Bracelets   Long hair left on legs of poodle after clipping, originally to keep the joints warm.
Breastbone   Sternum to which all ribs other than the floating ribs are attached.
Breeches   Feathers on hindlegs.
Breeching   The tan markings on the inside and back of thighs, eg manchester terrier.
Breed   A variety of pure-bred pedigree dog.
Breeder   The owner of a dog's dam at the time of whelping, someone who breeds animals.
Breeding particulars   Kennel Club registration details; sire, dam, sex, colour, date of birth.
Bridge of nose   Bones between nostrils and stop.
Brindle   A mixture of black hairs with light hairs, which are often in even stripes on a tawny or brown background.
Brisket   The lower part of the body below the chest and between the forelegs; includes the breastbone (sternum).
Broken colour   The main colour of a dog's coat broken up by another colour.
Broken-haired   Wire coat roughed up.
Broken-up face   Deep stop, wrinkle, receding nose, undershot jaw.
Brood bitch   A bitch which is kept for breeding.
Brush   A tail like a fox, with thick bushy hair.
Brushing   A gaiting fault when the pasterns brush each other in passing.
Bull neck   Heavy, over-developed neck.
Burr   The visible irregular formation of the ear.
Butterfly nose   Mottled nose of two colours, usually dark brown or black spotted with flesh colour.
Buttocks   Fleshy part of hindquarters.

222

Button ear   The tip of the ear leather folding forwards as in the fox terrier.

By   Refers to the offspring of a stud dog.

Bye   Odd dog left after pairing of braces at field trials.

CACIB   Le Certificat d'Aptitude au Championnat International de Beaute. The European equivalent to a challenge certificate.

Camel back   Roach or arched back, the opposite of sway back.

Candle-flame ears   The shape of the ears of an english toy terrier.

Canine   Referring to an animal group including dogs, foxes, wolves, jackals, coyotes, etc.

Canines   The two upper and two lower long, sharp, pointed teeth next to the incisors; fangs.

Canter   Gait between trot and gallop in speed; a three-beat stride, two legs moving as a diagonal pair and two moving separately.

Carinated   Keel-shaped with central line like the bottom of a ship.

Carpals   The small bones forming the pastern joint.

Carp back   An arched back.

Cartilage   Firm elastic tissue.

Castrate   To remove the testicles of the male dog by surgery.

Cat foot   A short, compact, round foot with short third digits.

CC   Challenge certificate. It is awarded by the Kennel Club and signed by the judge. It is given for the best dog and the best bitch in a breed at a championship show.

CD   Companion dog, AKC obedience trials award under three different judges.

CDX   Companion dog excellent. AKC award in three open classes at obedience trials.

Cephalic index   The ratio of breadth of head to distance from occiput to root of nose.

Ch   Champion.

Chamois ear   Ear that is soft and thin.

Champion   In the UK a dog that has won three challenge certificates under three different judges. In the USA the winner of fifteen points won under three or more judges, which must include two or more wins of three or more points.

Character   Disposition of a dog in accordance with its essential breed characteristics.

Check-chain collar   A chain or leather collar which tightens or loosens. Sometimes called a choke-chain.

Cheek   Side of face below the eye.

Cheeky   Heavy and pronounced cheek development as in the bulldog.

Chest   The part of the body between the brisket and the belly, excluding the front part of the body, and enclosed by the ribs.

Chicken-breasted   Having a short, protruding breastbone.

China eye   A light blue eye.

Chippendale front   Forelegs out at elbow, pasterns close and feet turned out (fiddle front).

Chiselled   A well defined moulding beneath the eyes or muzzle.

Chops   The heavy pendulous lips which hang down below the lower jaw.

Chorea   A nervous jerking of the muscles, generally affecting the face or legs.

Clip   Trim with clippers, eg poodles, american cocker spaniels.

Clipping   Hindfeet striking the forefeet when the dog gaits. To avoid this the dog 'crabs' or moves with his body at an angle to the line of progress.

Cloddy   Low, thickset, heavy build.

Close-coupled   Short in loin.

Coarse   Lacking refinement.

Coat   The hair covering the dog.

Cobby   Short-bodied, stocky, compactly made, well ribbed up and muscled.

Collar   A marking round the dog's neck, usually white. A chain or leather band as an ornament or means of restraint.

Common   Coarse, not typy.

Companion dog   Obedience title (see CD).

Condition Denoting health, shown by eyes, coat, weight and general appearance.
Conformation Structure of the dog.
Corky Compact, nimble body, and spirited in character.
Corny feet Horny pads.
Couple A brace of hounds.
Coupling The part of the body joining the forehand with the hindquarters; the loin, the flank. Not to be confused with length of body.
Couplings A ring between the collar and lead on a brace of dogs.
Coursing Hunting hare with greyhounds or whippets.
Covering ground The stretch of a dog's stride.
Cow-hocked The hocks turn inwards, with hindlegs like those of a cow. This is a serious fault in most breeds; the hocks are out of straight line from hip to pad.
Crabbing Moving at an angle to the line of travel like a crab; also known as side-winding, side-wheeling or yawing.
Crank tail A short tail which curves down and away from the body like a crank, caused by mutation.
Crest The arched part of the top of the neck.
Cropping The cutting off of a portion of a dog's ear in order to make it stand erect. Legal in some countries but illegal in the UK.
Cross-bred The progeny of dogs of two different pure breeds.
Crossing over Weaving and purling. An unsound action. Forelegs crossing and toes turning out.
Croup The part of the spinal column between the loin and the tail. It consists of three fused vertebrae, usually set at an angle of 30°.
Crown The top part of the skull.
Cry The baying of hounds on a trail.
Cryptorchid A dog with undescended testicles. Both sides undescended is 'bilateral cryptorchid', one side is 'unilateral cryptorchid'.
Cull Destroy sub-standard or weak puppies. In some breeds mismarked and pure white puppies are destroyed, eg boxers.
Culotte Long, thick hair on the back of the thighs.
Cur A mongrel.
Cushion The pad of muscle over the foreface.
Cynology The study of canines.

D (or d) Dog.
Dam A female parent of puppies.
Dappled A mottled colour, usually silver and tan or black, or black and tan, in patches.
Daylight The distance from the brisket to the ground between the forelegs.
Dead grass Dull tan or straw colour.
Dentition The number, arrangement and type of teeth in a dog's mouth.
Depigmentation Loss of pigment colour.
Derby A US field trial competition for novice sporting dogs.
Dewclaws The extra rudimentary claws found on the inside of the lower portion of a dog's forelegs and sometimes on the hindlegs, usually removed. Those on the hindlegs are required on briards and pyrenean mountain dogs (great pyrenees).
Dewlap Loose skin under the throat.
Diagonals At the trot, diagonal legs move together, ie right fore and left hind, and left fore and right hind.
Diehard Nickname for scottish terrier.
Dimples The depressions on either side of the breastbone.
Dish-face The description given when the tip of the nose is above the level of the stop, as in pointers.
Disqualification A condition rendering a dog ineligible for winning or competing at a show.
Distemper teeth Discoloured and/or pitted teeth caused by a high temperature

during distemper, and by certain drugs. Only the portion of the tooth that is seen is affected.

Divergent hocks Hocks that turn out, causing the toes to turn in; also known as barrel hocks.

Docked The cut or shortened dog's tail.

Dog A male dog of the species *Canis familiaris*.

Dog show An exhibition of dogs judged according to Kennel Club standards.

Dome The rounded part of the skull.

Double coat Consisting of an undercoat of soft woolly hair and an outer coat of coarse hair, to keep out dampness and cold.

Down-face Having a muzzle which is tilted downwards from stop to muzzle.

Down in pastern Weak or faulty pastern with excessive slope.

Down-stay! Command for dog to lie down and stay down.

Drag A trail made by dragging a scented bag.

Drawing Selection of pairs of dogs in a field trial stake.

Drive Strong hind movement.

Drop ears Soft, floppy ears hanging close and flat to the cheek.

Dropper A bird-dog cross.

Dry neck A tight-skinned, steep neck (clean throat).

Dual champion A dog who has won championships in show and field trials.

Dudley nose Flesh or liver-coloured nose.

Ear Organ for hearing; term often used for leather.

Ear fringes Long hair on the edges of ears.

Earrings Hair on ears left unclipped.

Elbow Joint between upper arm and forearm.

Elbow, out at Elbows not close to the body.

Endurance Staying power.

Entropion The eyelids turn inwards and the lashes irritate the eyeball.

Erect pasterns With little angle at the knee joint.

Euthanasia An induced, gentle and easy death.

Even bite Incisor teeth meeting without overlap. Incorrect in most breeds.

Ewe neck A thin, sheep-like neck, concave at the top.

Ex Refers to a puppy out of a bitch.

Expression An aspect of the face typical of the breed.

Eye teeth The upper canines.

Face Front of head.

Faking A common but dishonest practice performed on a dog to make it appear better than it is.

Fall Long hair falling over the eyes.

Fallow Pale yellow colour.

False ribs Ribs which are not connected with sternum or cartilage of other ribs; also called 'floating ribs'.

Fancier A person active in breeding, showing and/or judging purebred animals.

Fangs Canines.

Faults Inconsistencies with breed standards.

Fawn Cream colour.

FCI Fédération Cynologique Internationale.

Feathering The long, fine fringe of hair on the ears, legs, body and tail, eg in setters.

Feet Toes, nails and pads.

Feet east and west Feet turned out.

Felted A matted coat.

Femur Bone between hip and stifle joint.

Fetch Retrieve. May be used as a command.

Fiddle face An elongated, pinched-in foreface.

Fiddle front Crooked, bandy, forelegs; out at elbow, pasterns close together and turned out feet. Forearm usually curved.

Field trial   A competition for hounds and sporting breeds in retrieving and trailing.

Field trial champion   A top winner at field trials.

Fill-in   Bony structure below the eyes.

Flag   The long, fine, silky hair under the tail, longer in the middle and shorter at the root and the tip. In setters this is the correct word for the tail.

Flank   The fleshy part of the side between the ribs and the hip.

Flare   Blaze which grows wider towards the top.

Flat bone   Bones of the legs, elliptical rather than round.

Flat croup   Having insufficient downward slope, probably of less than 30°.

Flat-sided   Lacking in roundness of the rib, particularly from the fifth rib backwards.

Flat withers   A fault caused by a short upright shoulder blade.

Flecked   Lightly speckled in spots of another colour, neither roan nor spotted, eg english setter.

Flesh nose   Light nose, pink or tan.

Flews   Pendulous inner corners of the upper lips.

Flicking pasterns   Loose movement of the fore pasterns.

Floating ribs   The last, unattached ribs (see False ribs).

Fluffies   Extreme length of coat with exaggerated feathering.

Flush   To drive birds from cover; to spring.

Fly ears   Pendulous ears that do not lie close to the cheek.

Flying lips   Incorrect lip position, not close to the teeth.

Flying trot   A suspension trot. A fast gait in which all four feet are off the ground for a fraction of a second during each half stride.

Forearm   The part of the foreleg between the elbow and the pastern.

Foreface   The front part of the head from the eyes to the nose; muzzle.

Forehand   The front assembly of a dog.

Foreleg   A front leg.

Fore pastern   The group of bones between the pastern joint and the foot.

Forequarters   The misnomer frequently given to the forehand of a dog.

Foster mother   A bitch who nurses young other than her own.

Foul colour   An uncharacteristic colour or marking.

Foxy   Having a pointed muzzle.

Fraenum of lip   The fold of mucous membrane which attaches lip to gum.

French front   The front of a dog with crooked or bandy legs.

Frill   The long hair on the front of the neck and chest.

Fringes   The general feathering on the ears, ruff, legs and tail of long-coated breeds.

Frog face   An excessive undershot jaw.

Front   All that can be seen from the front other than the head. It includes the brisket, forelegs and shoulders.

Frontal bone   Skull bone above the eyes.

Full eye   Eye which is round and slightly protruding.

Furnished   A term applied to dogs which have reached full growth of coat.

Furnishings   The long hair on the foreface of certain breeds.

Furrow   A groove running down the centre of the skull. Also called median line.

Futurity stakes   A class at dog shows or field trials.

Gait   The manner in which a dog moves.

Gallop   The fastest of dog gaits. A four-beat rhythm with an extra split second of suspension when all four feet are off the ground.

Game   Hunted animals or birds.

Gay tail   One that is carried up. The term usually implies a fault.

Gaze hound   A sight hound, that uses the eyes more than the nose when hunting game.

Geld   To castrate.

Genealogy   Recorded family descent.

Giving tongue   Baying when on a trail.
Good doer   A dog that eats well and thrives without trouble.
Goose rump   A sharply sloping rump.
Graioid   Belonging to the greyhound family.
Grizzle   Grey or steel colour.
Groom   To brush and comb the coat.
Group   A number of breeds grouped for judging.
Guard hairs   Long, smooth, stiff hairs that cover the undercoat.
Gundog   A dog specially bred and trained for shooting.
Guns   Those with the shooting party at a drive of game (not beaters).
Gun-shy   Frightened by gun fire.

Hackles   Hair on the neck and back which is involuntarily raised when the dog is frightened.
Hackney gait   A high-stepping gait; padding to avoid pounding; generally a fault caused by a 60° shoulder blade combined with too strong a rear action.
Ham   Well developed hindleg muscles.
Handler   A person handling a dog in a ring at a dog show, field trial or obedience test.
Hard mouth   Biting hard on retrieved game.
Hare feet   Long and narrow feet with well separated toes. The third digital bone is longer than the others.
Harlequin   A combination of colours, usually in patches on a white ground.
Harness   A leather strap round shoulders and chest with a ring at the top over the withers. Used for bloodhound trailing and guide dogs for the blind, but not good for other breeds.
Haunches   The rear part of the thighs on which a dog sits.
Haw   A third eyelid; a membrane of the inside corner of the eye.
Head   From occiput to nose.
Heat   The period during which a bitch is said to be in season (called the oestrum), usually every six months.
Heel!   A command for a dog to walk close to his handler with his shoulder in line with the handler's knee. Not a correction.
Heel free!   A command for a dog to heel without a lead.
Height   The measurement from the top of the withers to the ground.
Hie on!   A command in field trials.
High-standing   Upstanding with plenty of leg.
Hind pasterns   The group of bones between the hock joint and the foot.
Hindquarters   Rear assembly; pelvis, thighs, hocks, pasterns and feet.
Hip dysplasia   Malformation of the hip joint.
Hocking out   Hocks that turn out and feet that turn in.
Hocks   The joints between the pasterns and the upper part of the hindlegs. These are equivalent to the ankle joints in man and are the dog's heels.
Hocks well let down   Having the point of the hocks close to the ground.
Hold!   A command to a dog to retain an object in his mouth.
Honourable scars   Injuries incurred whilst working.
Hound   A dog which hunts by scent or sight.
Hound colours   White, tan and black.
Hound jog   Normal pace of a hound.
Hound-marked   Of fox terriers with hound markings.
Huckle-bone   The top of the hip bones, only seen in thin dogs.
Hup!   A command to jump.
Hurry up!   A command to make a dog defaecate or urinate.

Inbreeding   The mating of close relations.
Incisors   The upper and lower front teeth between the canines.
In coat   Having a full coat.

227

In season   During the oestrum.
In shoulder   Shoulder blade too far forward on chest.
Int Ch   International champion; a dog which has become a champion in more than one country. An unofficial title.
Interbreeding   The breeding between varieties of the same breed.
Isabella   A light bay colour seen in dobermanns.

Jabot   A white stripe down the chest.
Jewel eye   Phosphorescent eyes, ruby red, emerald, or amethyst in colour.
Jowls   Flesh of lips and jaws.
Judge   A person appointed to estimate the merits of the dogs at a show.

KC   The English Kennel Club.
Keel   The breastbone of a dachshund.
Kennel   A structure to house dogs.
Kinetic balance   Balance when in motion.
Kink tail   A short, bent tail.
Kissing spots   The tan markings on the cheek and over the eyes often found in toy breeds; also known as kiss marks.
Kiss marks   Kissing spots.
Knee   Manus; wrist or pastern joint.
Knuckle over   Weak pastern joint; double-jointed.

Lack of type   Deficiency in breed traits.
Landseer   A white and black newfoundland.
Layback   The angle of the shoulder blade with the vertical.
Lead   A strap, cord or chain attached to collar or harness; leash.
Leash   Lead.
Leather   The skin and muscles of the ear flap.
Leave!   A command not to touch.
Leggy   Too high on the leg.
Level back   Often misused for a level top-line.
Level bite   When the upper and lower front teeth meet edge to edge (pincer bite).
Level gait   Even movement without a rise or fall of the withers.
Liam   A lead.
Licence   Form of permission from kennel clubs to hold dog shows or field trials.
Lie down!   A command for a dog to lie down in a place of its choice, as opposed to the command 'Down!', which means to drop instantly wherever the dog is.
Light eyes   Yellow eyes or pale-coloured eyes not favoured by judges.
Line breeding   The mating of related dogs.
Lion colour   Tawny.
Lippy   Thick hanging lips.
Litter   The puppies born to a bitch at one whelping.
Liver   A red-brown colour.
LKA   Ladies Kennel Association.
Loaded shoulders   Thick, heavy, muscular shoulders.
Locomotion   Movement.
Loins   The part of the body between the last rib and the croup.
Long-coupled   Long in loin between the forehand and hindquarters.
Low centre of gravity   Short in leg.
Lower thigh   The bones between the stifle and the hock; second thigh.
Lumber   Superfluous flesh, bone and bunchy muscles.
Lumbering   An awkward gait.
Lupoid   Belonging to the wolf family.
Lurcher   A coursing dog, such as a greyhound, whippet, deerhound or saluki, cross-bred with a working dog, like a labrador, border collie, german shepherd, foxhound or terrier. It is not recognised by the Kennel Club, but is not simply a

mongrel as it is a planned cross. The best combination is possibly the cross between a greyhound for speed and a border collie for intelligence. It was first recorded in 1668.

Lymer   A hound of ancient times, led on a liam (lead).

Mad dog   A rabid dog.
Maiden   An unmated bitch. In showing, it is a dog or bitch which has not won a first prize of more than a fixed sum.
Mane   A profusion of long hair on throat and neck.
Mantle   Dark, shaded portion of coat on shoulders, back and sides.
Mask   A dark muzzle.
Mastitis   Inflammation of the teats.
Match   A competition arranged more or less privately.
Mate   To breed a dog and a bitch.
Matron   A proved brood bitch.
Mealy   Covered or flecked with spots.
Measurement   The height from withers to ground.
Median line   Furrow down the centre of the skull.
Merle   A blue-grey colour, flecked with black, associated with a recessive gene, eg in shetland sheepdogs and collies.
Milk teeth   First teeth, which are lost between the ages of four and six months.
Miscellaneous class   Any variety class not classified; usually called AV.
Mismarked   A dog with white markings on self colour or black and white markings with no tan; or a larger white area than permitted.
Mixed pack   A pack of hound dogs and bitches.
Molars   Large back teeth used for tearing and chewing.
Molera   An American misspelling of the Spanish word *mollera*, used in chihuahuas for an open fontanel. It is an abnormal ossification of the skull.
Molossoid   Belonging to the mastiff family.
Mongrel   A dog whose parents are of mixed breeding.
Monorchid   A unilateral cryptorchid. A dog with only one testicle descended in the scrotum.
Moulting   Seasonal loss of coat.
Moving close   When the hocks turn in and the pasterns move too closely to each other.
Moving straight   Balanced gaiting, but not necessarily with legs vertical.
Music   Baying of hounds.
Mute   Silent on the trail.
Muzzle   The part of the head between the stop and the tip of the nose; also a device to prevent biting, worn over the muzzle.
Muzzle band   A white marking round the muzzle.

NAF   Name applied for.
Near side   The left side.
Neck well set on   Good neck line, sloping with strong shoulders, forming a pleasing top-line.
NFC   Not for competition.
Nick   An old-fashioned term for a mating that produces top quality puppies, ie click.
Nictitating membrane   Third eyelid, ie haw.
No!   A word of command to correct a dog.
No! Shame!   A term of scolding.
Non-slip retriever   A dog that walks at heel, marks a fall and retrieves on command, but does not find or flush.
Nose   An organ of smell; ability to scent.

Oblique shoulders   Well laid-back shoulders, at right angles to upper arm and at 45° to the ground.

Occiput   The prominent bone at the peak of the skull.

Oestrum   The period of ovulation, the season of heat.

Off colour   Not well.

Off side   The right-hand side.

Open class   A class open to all dogs of a breed or variety.

Other end of the lead   Refers to the handler or owner of a dog in the show ring; a derogatory phrase insinuating that the judge has put up the handler rather than the dog.

Otter tail   A tail which is extra thick at the root, round and tapering; the hair is parted or divided on the underside, eg in labradors.

Out at elbow   Having the elbow joints turned away from the body, as opposed to being held close.

Out at shoulder   Having shoulder blades loosely attached to the body, thus increasing the breadth of the front.

Out at walk   A hound puppy leased or lent to someone to raise.

Out-crossing   The mating of unrelated dogs of the same breed.

Out of coat   In moult.

Out of season   Not in oestrum.

Oval chest   A chest that is deeper than it is wide.

Overbuilt   A dog whose hindquarters are higher than its forehand.

Overhang   A heavy or pronounced brow.

Over-nose wrinkle   A fold of blue skin on the bridge of the nose, eg in pugs.

Over reaching   A fault at the trot caused by more angulation and drive from the rear than in front. The rear feet step to the side of the forefeet to avoid clipping.

Overshot   The front teeth of the upper jaw projecting over those of the lower jaw; sometimes called pig jaw.

Pace   A gait when both legs on one side move together; it creates a rolling motion.

Pack   Several hounds or dogs kept and hunted together.

Pad   The cushioned sole of the foot.

Padding   A hackney gait in which a dog with a 60° shoulder blade lifts its forelegs unnecessarily high to avoid pounding.

Paddling   The forelegs swinging forward on a stiff outward arc caused by tight elbows. A gaiting fault.

Paper foot   Flat foot with thin pads.

Parti-colour   Term used for a coat of two colours such as black and white, red and white or blue roan.

Pastern   The part of the leg below the knee or hock.

Patella luxation   When the stifle slips or dislocates.

Peak   A prominent occiput.

Pedigree   A genealogical tree. In dogs, a record of four generations or more.

Pencilling   Thin black lines on the toes, eg in manchester terriers.

Pepper and salt   Even mixture of black and grey hair, eg in schnauzers.

Pied   Two colours of unequal proportions, generally unequal in shape.

Pigeon breast   A prominent breastbone.

Pigeon toed   Toes pointing inwards.

Pig jaw   Overshot mouth.

Pile   Dense undercoat.

Pily   Having a coat of soft and coarse hair.

Pincer bite   Edge-to-edge bite.

Pitching   Hindlegs swinging forward in wide arc, instead of bending normally at the stifle and hock. This causes the haunches to rock excessively.

Plume   A long fringe of hair growing from the tail.

Point   The rigid stance a dog adopts naturally, indicating the presence of game.

Points   The colour on the face, ears, legs and tail, generally white, black or tan; also the parts of a dog.

Poke   To carry the neck abnormally forward and low when moving.

Police dog A dog trained for police work, generally german shepherds and dobermanns.

Pompon The hair left on the end of a poodle's tail.

Pounding A gaiting fault in which the stride is shorter in front than in the rear. The pad hits the ground too early, causing unnecessary shock. It is the result of a 60° shoulder blade.

Prefix A kennel name which identifies dogs belonging to a particular owner or owners.

Prick ear Erect, pointed ears.

Professional handler A person who is paid a fee to show dogs.

Progressive retinal atrophy (PRA) A hereditary defect causing early loss of sight.

Pump handle A long tail carried high.

Puppy A young dog up to the age of six months by law. At shows, however, it is a dog between the age of six months and one year.

Pure-bred A dog whose sire, dam and forebears belong to the same breed.

Purling (pearling) Twisting elbows and toeing out; also know as weaving.

Put down To put a dog to sleep. In the USA, to prepare a dog for the show ring. When a judge 'puts down' a dog it means he is not giving it a prize.

Quality Refinement.

Racy Slight in build, lean and long in leg, eg greyhound, whippet.

Ragged Muscles that are not smooth.

Ram's nose A slightly convex muzzle.

Rangy Long-bodied, usually lacking in depth of chest.

Rat tail A long, round, thin, pointed tail with short, flat, thin hair.

Reach of front Length of the forward stride.

Red A rich brown colour.

Register To record a dog's particulars with the Kennel Club.

Reserve Fourth place in a class, or runner-up as in reserve best in show.

Retrieve To bring back shot game; to fetch an article.

Ribbed up A dog is said to be 'well ribbed up' when the ribs are neither too long nor too wide apart, making the dog appear compact.

Ringer A substitute in a show for another dog.

Ring tail A tail curled over in a circle.

Roach back A back arched convexly along the spine, especially towards the hindquarters. It is an ugly, hereditary fault.

Roan White hair mixed equally with red or blue hair.

Rocking horse A stance when the forelegs and hindlegs extend forwards and backwards respectively from the body.

Rolling gait A swaying, ambling action of the hindquarters.

Roll over! A command for a useful trick for tense dogs.

Roman nose A slightly convex muzzle from stop to tip of nose; ram's nose.

Root of tail Where the tail joins the back.

Rose ear A backward folding ear showing the inner ear, as in the bulldog.

Rounding Cutting or trimming the end of an ear leather. Illegal in the UK.

Rubber hocks Weak or twisting hocks.

Rudder Uncommon word for the tail.

Ruff The thick long hair round the neck.

Running on The keeping of a puppy, hoping that it will turn out well.

Russian wolfhound Borzoi.

Sable Black hair incorporated in a coat of another colour.

Sabre tail Tail carried in a semi-circle.

Saddle A solid area of colour extending over the shoulder and back.

Saddleback A long back with a dip behind the withers.

Scapula Shoulder blade.

231

Scent   The odour left by an animal on the trail or wafted through the air.

Scissor bite   A bite where the lower incisors touch the inside of the upper incisors. Correct for most breeds.

Screw tail   A short, twisted tail, tapering to a point.

Scrotum   The sac containing the two testicles.

Season   Another term for oestrum or heat in the bitch.

Second mouth   A dog's mouth when the second-or permanent teeth have replaced the first or milk teeth.

Second thigh   The bones between the stifle and the hock; lower thigh.

Seeing-eye dog   A guide for the blind in the USA.

Self-coloured   A single colour with or without shadings.

Self-mark   A whole- or solid-coloured dog with white or cream brisket, feet and tip of tail.

Semi-prick ears   Straight, erect ears with the tip of the leathers bent forward, as in the collie.

Septum   The division between the nostrils.

Service   A mating.

Set-on   Where the root of the tail is set on the hindquarters, also placement of the ears.

Set up   Posed by the handler ready for the judge.

Shake hands!   A command to make the dog give his right paw. Useful for shy dogs with strangers.

Shame!   A reprimand.

Shelly   Having a weedy, narrow body, lacking in correct amount of bone.

Shoulder height   The height of a dog measured from the top of the withers to the ground.

Sickle hocks   Hocks sloping backwards so that the dog is unable to straighten the hock. A serious fault in all breeds.

Sickle tail   Tail that curves upwards in a semi-circle above the level of the back.

Side-wheeling   Crabbing; moving at an angle to the line of travel.

Side-winding   Side-wheeling, crabbing.

Sight hound   A hound which hunts by eyesight in preference to scent.

Single-tracking   To achieve balance the legs angle inwards towards a central line beneath the body. The faster the speed, the closer the feet come to track on a single line.

Sire   The male parent.

Sit!   The command to make a dog sit straight up on his haunches.

Sit up!   The command to make a dog sit on his haunches with his forepaws up, ie Beg!

Skully   Having a coarse skull.

Slab-sided   Flat ribs with too little spring.

Sled dogs   Teams of dogs for pulling sleds.

Slew feet   Turned out feet.

Slipping stifle   Patella luxation; dislocation of the joint.

Sloping shoulder   A shoulder blade laid well back on the body.

Smoothcoat   A dog with short, sleek, close hair.

Smudge   The dark thumb marking on the head of a pug.

Snatching hocks   A gaiting fault. Rocking of the hindquarters; the hind pasterns are twisted far in beneath the body.

Snipy   Having a long, narrow muzzle.

Soft-eared   Tipped ear leathers in dogs whose ears should be erect.

Soft-mouthed   A dog which can retrieve game without damaging it.

Sound   Moving and standing correctly on all four legs with static and kinetic balance, and free from disease and defects; of good quality throughout.

Spay   To remove womb and ovaries to prevent a bitch from having puppies.

Speak   Bark. Also used as a command to bark.

Spectacles   Marking round the eyes.

Spike tail   A straight, short, rapidly tapering tail.
Spitz   A group of northern breeds.
Splashed   A solid colour with irregular patches of another colour.
Splay foot   A foot with the toes turned out.
Spread   Width between the forelegs, eg in a bulldog.
Spread hocks   Barrel hocks.
Spring   Flush. To drive birds from cover.
Spring of rib   The extent to which the ribs are well rounded.
Squirrel tail   A tail curving over the back like a squirrel's.
Stack   To set your dog up for a judge.
Stake   A competition at a field trial.
Stance   Manner of standing.
Standard   A description of an ideal dog of a breed as a pattern for judges and breeders.
Stand-off coat   A harsh coat which stands up, as in the spitz breeds.
Stand-stay!   A command essential in the show ring to enable a judge to see and go over a dog.
Staring coat   A coat which stands up when a dog is out of condition.
Static balance   Balance when standing.
Station   The height of a dog from the ground.
Stay!   A command for a dog to remain in the same position.
Stern   Tail of a sporting dog or hound.
Sternum   Breastbone.
Stifle   The joint in a dog's hindleg between the upper and lower thigh. It is equivalent to the knee in man and is often weak in some breeds.
Stilted   The uneven movement of a straight-hocked dog.
Stool   Faeces.
Stop   The depression at the junction of the nose and skull.
Straight-hocked   Lacking in angulation of the hock joint.
Straight in pastern   With little or no bend between the pastern joint and the foot.
Straight shoulders   Lacking in angulation so that the shoulder blades are straight instead of lying well back.
Strain   A family which are all related and throw offspring of correct type.
Stud Book   A book issued by the Kennel Club once a year, relating to championship-show winners and their breeding.
Stud dog   A male dog used for breeding purposes.
Substance   Refers to strength of bone.
Suffix   A breeder's kennel name attached to a dog's name to identify it as belonging to a certain kennel.
Suspension trot   Flying trot; the fastest speed at a trot.
Sway back   Sagging back.
Symmetry   A well balanced outline.

TAF   Transfer applied for.
Tail set   The set of the tail on the rump.
Tawny   Creamy brown colour.
Terrier   A group of dogs originally used for hunting vermin.
Terrier front   A straight front, eg fox terrier.
That will do!   Reprimand.
Thigh   The hindquarter from hip to stifle.
Throaty   Having too much loose skin under the throat.
Thumbmarks   Round blackish marks on the pasterns.
Ticked   The small dark flecks of colour on a white-coloured dog.
Tie   The locking together of a dog and a bitch during mating, caused by the dog's penis swelling inside the bitch.
Timber   Generally refers to the bones of the legs.
Toe in/out   The feet turning in/out.

Tongue   The sound that hounds make when trailing.

Top-knot   The long hair on the top of the head, usually tied together with an elastic band or ribbon.

Top line   The outline from behind the withers to the root of the tail, not necessarily parallel with the ground.

Toy dog   One of a group of very small dogs.

Trace   A dark line running down the centre of the back as in a pug.

Trail   Hunt by following a ground or air scent.

Transfer   Change of ownership registered at the Kennel Club.

Triangular eye   Eye set within triangular-shaped tissue.

Tricolour   A coat of three different colours, usually black, tan and white, blue, roan and tan, or liver, white and tan, the tan being at the eyebrows, cheeks, under tail and sometimes on feet.

Trim   To groom a dog by clipping, plucking or cutting its coat.

Trot   Rhythmic, two-beat diagonal gait, with the left foreleg and right hindleg moving forward together.

Trousers   The long hair on the hindquarters.

Trumpet   A slight hollow on either side of the skull, just behind the eye socket.

Truncated   Cut off, eg jaw of old english sheepdog.

Tucked up   A dog not looking well; also when the loin is lifted up and the chest is deep, eg greyhound, whippet, borzoi, etc.

Tulip ears   Ears which are carried forward, slightly open but erect.

Turn up   An up-tilted foreface.

Twist   The twist of a pug's tail.

Twisting hocks   A gaiting fault with the hock joints twisting both ways; rubber hocks.

Type   The quality of conforming to the breed standard.

Typy   An adjective denoting conformation to the breed standard.

Undercoat   Soft woolly hair beneath the longer outer hair. It is often a different colour from the latter.

Undershot   The lower incisor teeth projecting beyond the upper teeth.

Underslung   Low to the ground, with short legs.

Unilateral cryptorchid   A dog with only one testicle descended in the scrotum.

Unsound   Unable to move and stand correctly on all four legs; suffering from a disease or defect; not of good quality throughout.

Up-faced   With the foreface slanting upwards, eg in bulldog.

Upper arm   The bone between the shoulder blade and the forearm.

Uterus   The womb.

Vagina   The female genital passage.

Varminity   A bright, alert expression, particularly in terriers.

Vent   The rectum and area of lighter markings round the anus.

Vulva   The external portion of the vagina.

Walk   Gaiting pattern in which three legs support the body at all times; each foot is lifted from the ground in regular sequence.

Wall-eyed   Having eyes which have a white and blue iris.

Wean   To induce a puppy, when old enough, to feed otherwise than from its dam.

Weaving   Crossing over of the forelegs with the toes turning out.

Weedy   Lacking in substance.

WELKS   West of England Ladies Kennel Society.

Well boned   Good strong bones of the foreleg.

Well let down   Short distance from point of hock to ground.

Well sprung   Well rounded ribs.

Wet neck   Superfluous skin with dewlap.

Wheaten   Refers to a creamy fawn colour as in a wheaten terrier.

Wheel back   A roach back.

Whelping   Giving birth to puppies.

Whelps   This term is not often used. It refers to the unborn puppy and to the puppy up to the time when it is weaned.

Whip tail   A stiff, straight tail as in the pointer when pointing.

Whiskers   The long hairs on the muzzle and the jaws; beard of the schnauzer.

Whitelies   White with red or dark markings, eg in pembroke welsh corgi. A serious fault.

Wind   Scent game.

Winging   A gaiting fault in which the forefeet twist outwards as the leg swings forwards.

Winners   An AKC award: best dog (winners dog): best bitch (winners bitch).

Wire-haired   A dense harsh coat.

Withers   The eight vertebrae between the neck and the back between the shoulder blades. The top of the withers is the highest point of the shoulder blades.

Wolf sable   The black, brown and grey hair distributed evenly over the coat, giving a wolf-coloured appearance.

Wrinkle   The loose fold of skin on the head, particularly abundant in bloodhounds.

Wry mouth   The lower jaw set to one side, a very serious hereditary fault.

Xiphoid   The shape of a sword (referring to bone).

Xoloitzcuintli   A Mexican hairless dog.

Yawing   Moving at an angle to the line of travel like a crab.

You're free!   Release command at end of lesson.

235

Index

237